Tarot
Spirit
Healing

Tarot Spirit Healing

A Shamanic Path to Clear Your Astrological Challenges

BY REID HART

BIRCHGROVE HEARTH, LLC
Eugene, Oregon, USA

Tarot Spirit Healing:
A Shamanic Path to Clear Your Astrological Challenges

BY REID HART

Published by:
BirchGrove Hearth, LLC
Eugene, Oregon

First Edition, October 2024

Library of Congress Control Number: 2024907633
Print paperback ISBN: 979-8-9903789-2-6
eBook ISBN: 979-8-9903789-1-9

Permissions and credits are included in the **Permissions and Image Credits** section of the Bibliography and are a continuation of this copyright page.

BIRCHGROVE HEARTH, LLC
Eugene, Oregon, USA
www.reidhart.com/bgh-books
BirchGroveHearth@gmail.com

Critical Praise for Tarot Spirit Healing:

A brilliant and engaging synthesis of shamanism, tarot, and astrology into a practical guide for calling upon the spirits for healing and the restoration of harmony. This book introduces the basic principles of astrology to identify the discordant energies indicated in your birth chart and entreat these kindly spirits to help you restore balance and harmony in your life. Step-by-step guided meditations and bonus sections on the history of tarot and astrology make this a must-have book.

— **Demetra George**, author of *Ancient Astrology in Theory and Practice*

Westerners have multiple mystery traditions to enrich spiritual growth and development: tarot, astrology, pathworkings, shamanism, and more. *Tarot Spirit Healing* masterfully demonstrates how tarot and astrology can partner up with shamanism to address many of life's challenges. Reid Hart brings years of metaphysical study and practice, along with an engineer's keen perspective, to provide engaging step-by-step programs that are safe and effective. No matter how difficult your life might seem, Tarot Spirit Healing will offer new approaches for happier and healthier living.

— **Tom Cowan**, author of *Fire in the Head: Shamanism and the Celtic Spirit*

Reid Hart's *Tarot Spirit Healing* guides the reader to a place where the Western Mystery practices of tarot and astrology dynamically intersect with humankind's oldest spiritual methods. This intersection provides the opportunity to work with the powerful entities of the tarot and planetary influences not as dry archetypes, but rather as compassionate guides who can support healing, provide guidance, and support continued spiritual advancement on your life journey.

— **Evelyn C. Rysdyk**, author of *Spirit Walking: A Course in Shamanic Power & The Norse Shaman*

Get your free resource material!

Check out the online resources that support the book *Tarot Spirit Healing*. They include:

- Shamanic journey drumming tracks for 10, 20, and 30 minute journeys.
- Blank forms for tracking pathwork and *AstroTarot mapping*.
- High resolution color graphics in pdf format.
- Video lessons: *Tarot Spirits: Who's on Deck?* and a *Tour of the Major Arcana*.
- Video lesson: *Shamanic Crossing*.
- Join the mailing list for updates on Tarot Spirit books and courses.
- Discounted offers for related online courses.

Check out these book resources at
www.reidhart.com/tsh-resources

Dedication

This book is dedicated to all the spiritual teachers I have learned from in my life, either in person or through their writings. Especially notable are **Edwin Steinbrecher** and **Michael Harner**, without whom this book and development of the teaching process behind it would not have happened. Others that contributed greatly to this work are the participants in my Tarot Spirit workshops and online courses. They helped refine the teaching so the method could be effective.

Book Description

Tarot Spirit Healing:
A Shamanic Path to Clear Your Astrological Challenges

Are you ready to make positive changes in your life? In *Tarot Spirit Healing* you create a direct spiritual connection for practical and spiritual growth!

Hidden in your astrological chart are tensions and conflicts that impact your life path. In *Tarot Spirit Healing*, you will learn a shamanic method to access Tarot Spirits in the Otherworld so you can receive compassionate healing and advice. Then, with the support of a loving guide, the Tarot Spirits are called on to reconcile those astrological challenges. Step-by-step instructions lead you through the process no matter what prior experience you have with shamanism, tarot, or astrology. You are invited to engage the Tarot Spirits to create the life you love!

The book unfolds in four parts:

Part 1 of this book leads you through the basic steps needed to engage each of the 22 Tarot Spirits that you choose to work with. You learn the Shamanic journey, meet a tarot guide, and then get to know the Tarot Spirits.

In Part 2, you find your special Tarot Spirits, and you take the steps needed to receive advice or healing from the Tarot Spirits. This begins your journey on the cycle of becoming: Healing, transformation, and initiation.

In Part 3, you can do the specific AstroTarot work needed for your birth chart. Find out where the challenges are, identify the Tarot Spirits who can help, and actively clear challenges in your birth chart.

In Part 4, discover what your personalized Tarot Spirit circles are and work with them to maintain the positive changes in your life over time. You also meet Spirit Constructs—combinations of multiple Tarot Spirits—and learn deeper meanings of the Western Mysteries from them.

Along the way, you hear from others who have taken this path, follow the story of Rachel and Isabel as they move through the process, and get access to online resources, including shamanic drumming tracks, tracking and mapping forms and other background material.

Table of Contents

An index of headings with all heading levels is near the end of the book.

Introduction

I invite you to take a journey into the Otherworld that can change your life. Engaging with the Tarot Spirits connects you with profound wisdom of the ages. Both your spiritual experience and practical life are enhanced. Here are instructions for pathwork exercises that engage with the compassionate and loving Tarot Spirits. Once you connect with the Tarot Spirits, they reconcile challenges in your natal astrological chart, producing positive effects in your life.

Why did I write this book? After seeking spiritual growth for half my life, I settled into a shamanic approach three decades ago. In shamanism, I work with Spirits from the Otherworld. Just over a decade ago, I found an intersection of spiritual work between the tarot, astrology, and Qabalah. This approach let me clear conflict and disharmony. I overcame challenges around authority and settled ghosts from the past. I realized I needed to share the method. So, I taught this technique to others, first in person and then through online workshops. After a decade of teaching others, I've written this book to share this profound approach with a wider audience.

Work with the Tarot Spirits is based on shamanic methods that are 100,000 years old. Shamanism is a healing heritage of human beings. Using these methods, you can progress through multiple levels of spiritual work with the Tarot Spirits as outlined in Appendix B. The first four parts are covered in this first book of the Tarot Spirit series:

1. **Do you want your tarot deck to come alive for you by meeting the powerful and loving Tarot Spirit of each card?** Your initial engagement involves meeting some or all of the 22 characters of the tarot Major Arcana. The Tarot Spirits are living spiritual entities in the Otherworld. You start by learning the shamanic journey. Then you meet a tarot guide. Finally, you engage with the living Tarot Spirits.

2. **Are you ready to receive healing and advice from a spiritual source?** You create reciprocity through partnership with these

compassionate and loving spirits. In exchange, you receive healing and advice from the Tarot Spirits.

3. **Do you want to clear the impact of challenging aspects in your natal chart?** You explore the planets and zodiacal signs of your natal chart to learn where challenges lie. Then you work with Tarot Spirits as representatives of the planets and signs to resolve challenges and open the way for a smoother and happier life.

4. **Are you ready to explore deeper spiritual mysteries?** You find personalized Tarot Spirit circles and meet regularly to maintain your improved life situation. Then, you work with Spirit Constructs as teachers of the Western Mysteries.

In this book, you learn a shamanic approach to access Tarot Spirits in the Otherworld. This connection gives you compassionate healing and advice. Work with Tarot Spirits resolves challenges in your natal chart. You receive both spiritual and practical benefits. This method works for everyone willing to engage. It does not matter if you know little or a lot about shamanism, the Western Mysteries, tarot, or astrology. If you encounter unfamiliar terms, check the Glossary.

At first, the overall process may look complicated. Yes there are multiple steps. Each step is straightforward. Just work through the instructions in the book chapter by chapter and you will arrive at the goal of clearing challenges from your astrological chart. Take it one step at a time.

The chapters lead you through the process of meeting and engaging the Tarot Spirits. You discover your special Tarot Spirits and receive advice and healing. You find challenges in your astrological birth chart. Then you work with the Tarot Spirits to remediate those challenges. You can also make a deeper connection to the mysteries. Additional material is included in the appendices for those who want more background. Those who have some experience with either shamanism, tarot, or astrology can skim over parts of the book they are already familiar with.

Enjoy your growing connection with the Tarot Spirits!

-Reid Hart
Eugene, Oregon, USA   October 2024

Part 1: Connect with Powerful and Loving Tarot Spirits

Figure 1. The Fool is an unnumbered card (zero) in the Tarot Major Arcana. The Fool carries the archetype of the exploring initiate, going through the life lessons of the Tarot. In this exploration, you follow the path of The Fool. *Credit: DruidCraft Tarot.*

Part 1 of this book leads you through the basic steps needed to engage each of the 22 Tarot Spirits that you choose to work with:

- Learn how to undertake the shamanic journey to access spirits in the Otherworld.
- Understand the basics of Tarot and an overview of the AstroTarot methods in Chapter 1.
- Connect with sacred space and learn the shamanic journey in Chapter 2.
- Find a sacred bridge as your personal launching place in the Otherworld and receive messages from each Tarot Spirit using Pathwork A in Chapter 3.
- Connect with your personal tarot guide in Chapter 4.
- Meet the Tarot Spirits and receive a gift from each one in Chapter 5 using Pathwork B.
- Get to know the Tarot Spirits at a deeper level in Chapter 6 using Pathwork C.

The main section of this book is designed to provide you with all the information you need to proceed with meeting the Tarot Spirits, receiving healing and advice, and resolving your astrological challenges. There is additional background for Part 1 in these appendices:

- Appendix A has resources and recommended books with descriptions of each book's contents.
- Appendix B discusses the overall scope of Tarot Spirit work available, includes a plan for working with them over time, and has worksheets to track your progress.
- Appendix C has a history of the Tarot and discusses the different Tarot decks available to you.
- Appendix D outlines different approaches to creating sacred space for your shamanic journeys and Tarot Spirit pathworking.

1: The Promise of Tarot Spirit Healing

Let us begin with a message I recently received from the Empress Tarot Spirit during a shamanic journey. Then we can overview the scope of working with the Tarot Spirits.

The Empress Speaks

I emerged from the tunnel, crossed the bridge with my tarot guide, and stood before the Empress in her realm. She held and suckled two babies, a girl and a boy, and emitted an aura of holding everything in her hands. She hands the infants to her handmaidens, and stares into my eyes.

I look up and ask, "Where do I go from here?"

The waterfall behind her burbles and the wind moves the luxuriant green fabric of her gown. As her mouth opens, her words are revealed as a rainbow mist that moves directly into my heart. "You have walked our paths for more than a decade and shared us with several hundred fellow seekers. You know the why and the how. Now look to those others who want to meet us. Share the hidden paths with them."

I sense a strength rising within me. The gift of a gold harp she planted in my jaw a decade ago vibrates with my breath. There is a song to share, and I let the music rise up to lead those who seek the path to wisdom, beauty, abundance, and peace.

For those who wish to meet these twenty-two holders of wisdom, welcome!

Welcome!

Count yourself among the few who delve deeply into the mysteries of life. By stepping into this work with the Tarot Spirits, you will join hundreds of others who have gone down this path. Time and effort are needed to make this spirit connection. The rewards are worth it. Make a positive spirit connection. Get healing and advice. Clear your astrological challenges. Manifest what you want in your life.

Figure 2. The Empress is key 3 (III) in the tarot Major Arcana. She is called "The Lady" in the DruidCraft Tarot. She represents the planet Venus and carries the archetype of the abundance of mother nature. *Credit: DruidCraft Tarot.*

On this journey, you will hear from Isabel and Rachel, two fictional characters who have engaged in the process you are starting. You will also hear about the experiences of others who have engaged in this process over the last decade. These reports are from actual participants in workshops and trainings on the Tarot Spirit process. In some cases, the names have been changed on request, but the reports are all based on actual experience.

In the 1970s, Edwin Steinbrecher wrote *The Inner Guide Meditation: A Spiritual Technology for the 21st Century*. It showed a method of working with Tarot archetypes using a meditation process. We rely on Steinbrecher for helping us identify the Tarot guide and basic natal aspects that may need resolution. The method in this book departs from Steinbrecher in several ways:

- We approach the Tarot Major Arcana as living Otherworld Spirits rather than as inner Jungian archetypes.

- We use shamanic methods rather than meditation to access these Spirits.
- Our process in AstroTarot is shamanic rather than psychological.
- We expand the Tarot Spirit circles to work more directly with your life goals.
- We explore the astrological houses in a later book in the series. The houses represent different areas of your life.
- We include some Hellenistic astrological concepts, especially for the potential challenging aspects to clear in your chart.

The Western Mysteries

To be clear, the "Western Mysteries" are not cowboy detective stories. The Mysteries have methods to achieve direct personal revelation of spiritual truth—methods that bypass learning religious doctrine. Also called Western Esotericism, the mysteries allow those willing to explore deeper meanings behind the obvious appearance of things. In the normal view, a stone has dimensional, density, color and hardness attributes. In a hidden way, it can reveal stories, vibrational qualities, and even a level of consciousness not apparent to the normal senses. However, one must go beyond the ordinary to find these esoteric qualities. The same ordinary vs. esoteric qualities applies to plants, animals, humans, minerals, planets, zodiac signs, tarot cards, symbols, seas, winds, and mountains.

Western Mystery methods engage us more fully in our daily world, unlike Eastern esoteric methods focused on detachment from the world. The Western approach is more suitable for spiritual seekers raised in Western cultures. There is a focus on practical changes in their lives and their communities.

I'm a long-term student of the Western Mysteries with more than five decades of study. I was amazed when the Tarot Spirits came to life for me. It happened in 2012 when I explored Edwin Steinbrecher's approach from the 1970s.[1] Using a shamanic method, I have made a strong connection with the Tarot Spirits. I delved deeper into the Western Mysteries with them, including the deep meaning of astrology and Qabalah.

---

[1] Steinbrecher, E. *The Inner Guide Meditation.*

The Tarot Spirits brought me gifts that enhanced my intuition and shamanic insight. I cleared challenging aspects in my astrological chart. Many areas of my life lightened up. I balanced the mystic work with emotional work by engaging shadow elements through Otherworld psychodrama. This is a method to resolve psychological conflicts using the tarot court cards. The resulting spiritual inspiration and emotional release opened me to the next round of opportunities in life.

A Different Kind of Spirit Connection

Normally we view tarot or astrology as interpretative or informative. There is a reader or astrologer—we will refer to them both as "readers"—who works with tarot cards or an astrological chart to deliver insight to the client. Sometimes, you are both client and reader, gleaning information for yourself. This process is informative and interpretative, by either drawing and reading the cards, or reading an astrological chart.

The AstroTarot process takes things to a different level. Instead of a reader consulting the cards or a chart, you consult the Tarot Spirits directly for advice, information, healing, or initiation. Rather than just getting information, the Tarot Spirits actually intervene. They make peace between planets and improve the astrological influence. The quality of your life gets better. All this happens with a shamanic journey that connects you to the Tarot Spirits. So, rather than information about fate, you have an opportunity to engage with future possibilities and create a successful outcome.

Why Do the Pathworking in this Book?

The exercises or pathworking in this book give you a powerful system for working with Tarot Spirits. You can resolve blocks in your life to live a life you love. Imagine a life free of the barriers that prevent you from reaching your goals in relationships, work, and play. Here is your opportunity to get into that magical flow of manifestation and move toward your chosen destiny. Perhaps you are unsure how to effectively and completely clear conflict and disharmony—within yourself and your relationships. Maybe you have worked with Tarot cards or astrology, but not found the support to make permanent positive changes in your life. Within your reach you have these "flashcards of the Western Mysteries."

But you may feel lost in heady interpretations that leave you without a concrete method to solve your problems.

The Spirits inhabiting the tarot are powerful teachers and mentors, available to everyone who learns how to access them. If you are unclear on how to put their skills of these Tarot Spirits to work in your life, you are not alone. Our modern Western culture has not taught us how to access divine support to create the life we want. Astrologers typically tell us about the challenges in our natal chart, but rarely give us tools to resolve them.

Imagine what life would be like if you had 22 spiritual advisers you could access for wisdom, healing, or advice? What if you could connect with these wise and compassionate spirits using the methods shamans have used for eons? What would happen if you could bring spiritual gifts into your everyday life using a simple pack of cards? You would find that opportunities appear and blockages resolve, transforming your life.

And the good news is that you don't need to make enormous shifts in your work, home, or relationships to access these special spiritual allies. Just learn how to connect for timely assistance. That's why I teach you how to connect to the Tarot Spirits: to help you clear challenges, receive the gifts you deserve, and make positive changes in your life. My unique approach to working directly with the tarot and your natal astrological chart is appropriate for both the novice and the experienced tarot reader or astrologer.

When you learn how to work effectively and deeply with the Tarot Spirits, you release the shackles of the past, receive empowering gifts, and walk powerfully on a path to the life you have always wanted. This book guides you in partnering effectively with the Tarot Spirits to grow beyond the limits of the past so you can move forward with the positive life you deserve.

My Own Experience

I have been seeking a strong spiritual connection since my teenage years. In high school I studied astrology and the Qabalah, with little result. But still, I sought further and studied widely in both Eastern and Western spiritual traditions. Carlos Castaneda's stories about teachings from a Mexican shaman were intriguing, but I had a family to raise and did not see myself wandering in the desert to become a shaman's apprentice.

After a decade spent with meditation and Tibetan Buddhism, I was still searching for a direct connection to the spiritual world. I was looking for a path that would help me resolve my issues and enhance my innate gifts—a path that satisfied my spiritual yearning and allowed me to make headway on things that mattered most to me. I did not know how to bring spiritual power directly into my life.

In the early 1990s I trained in core shamanism, two decades after my initial interest. This was followed by a deep dive into Celtic and Nordic shamanism, connecting me with my ancestral roots. Despite this powerful introduction to helping spirits and profound healing work, something was still missing.

Then I had a flash of insight, the beginning of a whole new approach. After an inspirational shamanic journey, I developed an approach that brings the methods of core shamanism to the Western Mysteries. Melding all I had learned from both human and spirit teachers over four decades, I found that I was able to clear conflict and disharmony from my own life, opening up new layers of possibility.

I began to flow with a strong and ancient spirit connection. I had access to a new level of gifts from the Spirits. Before this insight, the Western Mysteries were intellectual and stuck in my head. Now, I had a connection to powerful Tarot Spirits, a more direct way to access the issues in my astrological natal chart, and an experiential access to the Qabalah. As a result, I was able to reap clear personal benefits and deepen my spiritual connection.

For several years, I focused on deep exploration of the Tarot Spirits. They brought together the three legs of the stool that forms the Western Mystery school: astrology, spirit connection, and the Qabalistic Tree of Life. Using shamanic methods with the Tarot Spirits became the seat that linked all three legs together. A deeper sense of spiritual connection came into my life, enhancing my relationship with my partner, the land, and my community.

Then I realized that others would benefit from this work! I had the opportunity to work in circle with hundreds of participants over the past fifteen years, deepening and expanding the Tarot Spirit path. It is now time, with folks in need, to bring these methods forward in a book form so it is broadly accessible.

I now realize the Tarot Spirit system is not meant for me alone but needs to be shared widely, especially at this critical time. Welcome to this valuable spiritual path.

What is Your Goal?

Stop for a minute and think about what you want to get out of working with the Tarot Spirits. What areas of your life do you want to improve? What advice are you seeking? What healing would be beneficial? Get your journal or a pen and paper. Take a few minutes and write your goals and wishes down. As you move through the AstroTarot process, it takes time to get the foundation in place. It is good to have a goal to motivate you to put in the effort. We will clarify the goals and intentions later. For now, just get something written down that is important to you.

Tarot Basics

Here is a quick background on tarot, in case it is new to you. A tarot deck needs to have 78 cards (sometimes with a few extra cards). A tarot deck also has a set structure, with the Major Arcana distinct from the Minor Arcana that includes the numbered cards and court cards. There are many oracle decks that don't fit these requirements, so you want a tarot deck with 78 cards, or close to that number, with the organization listed below. The tarot cards are organized into certain groups:

- The 22 Major Arcana cards are also called "keys" or "trumps." Arcana means mystery, and the keys represent the major mystery of the tarot. Sometimes they are referred to as the "greater keys." These are the cards listed in the table later in this chapter. These cards have the images you can work with as the living Tarot Spirits. They are traditionally numbered from 0 for the Fool to 21 for the World.
- The 56 Minor Arcana cards include the 16 court or royalty cards and the 40 numbered or "pip" cards. These cards represent a lesser mystery of the tarot and are also called the "lesser keys." The lineup is similar to a modern playing card deck, although playing cards have only three court cards in each suit.
- In the Minor Arcana, there are 16 court or royalty cards, four in each suit. Some say they are a bridge between the Major Arcana

and the pips, representing different personalities active in the world, but without the archetypal quality of the Major Arcana. Different decks have different names for these:

- King, Queen, Knight, Page
- Mother, Father, Sister, Brother
- King, Queen, Princess, Prince
- Some have only three: (Maiden, Mother, Crone) resulting in a 74-card deck
- Other variations or names for the court cards exist

- There are 40 numbered or "pip" cards. There are 10 in each of the 4 suits, with numbers from 1 to 10. It's like a standard deck of playing cards, with the 1 card also called the Ace. The numerological impact of the 10 cards relates to the 10 spheres on the Qabalah Tree of Life.

Appendix C provides a concise history of Tarot for interested readers.

The Tarot Spirits by Key Order

The 22 Tarot Spirits are listed below in key number order. The names are based on the *Waite-Smith Tarot Deck* in the English magical tradition.

These Tarot Spirits are based on the 22 Major Arcana in the tarot deck. Typical archetypical qualities are also listed. For alternative names for some of the Major Arcana from several other decks, see Appendix C.

While there are 22 cards in the Major Arcana, 21 are numbered and the Fool is unnumbered. The Fool, an unnumbered card—often labeled "0"—is included between keys 20 and 21. This follows Waite's approach that he adopted from Lévi, both of which relate to a mapping of the 22 Major Arcana to the 22 Hebrew letters. Most modern authors place the Fool either at the beginning or end of the Major Arcana. Waite emphasizes that the Fool is actually an unnumbered card, although there is a 0 on the top of the card. In many interpretations, the fool represents the initiate, going on the Fool's journey through the rest of the Major Arcana archetypes.

Key #	Key Name	Key Archetypical Qualities
1	The Magician	Communication, timing, vision, empowerment, willpower, action, magic, focus
2	The High Priestess	Intuition, clarity, depth, wisdom, soul, depth, dreams, mystical teachings, balance, harmony
3	The Empress	Nurturance, abundance, sensuality, mothering, creativity, passion
4	The Emperor	Order, leadership, builder, stability, protection, competence
5	The Hierophant	Teacher, manager, tradition, conscience, education, conformity, initiation
6	The Lovers	Attraction, union, surrender, trust, win-win, passion, love, duality
7	The Chariot	Motivation, triumph, will applied, bravery, overcome obstacles, fame, unstoppable
8*	Strength	Courage, power, fortitude, faith, unconditional love, discipline, wildness
9	The Hermit	Seeker, introspection, meditation, studious, alone, retreat, guidance
10	The Wheel of Fortune	Reap rewards, cycles, prosperity, karma, synchronicity, progress
11*	Justice	Balance, discerning, fair, honest, precise, clarity, decision, truth
12	The Hanged Man	Patience, sacrifice, reversal, deepening, humble, surrender, initiation
13	Death	Clear out old, dissolution, transition, pre-transforming, divesting, transformation
14	Temperance	Synergy, harmony, alchemy, transformation, mix opposites, magic
15	The Devil	Master life-force, obsession, vitality, fear, shame, addiction, shadow, desire
16	The Tower	Revelation, upheaval, release, shaken, purification, fall from security
17	The Star	Optimism, openness, cooperative, healing, ideal, forgiveness, confidence
18	The Moon	Dreams, psychic awakening, imagination, withdrawal, passage, unconscious motivations, subconscious
19	The Sun	Happiness, radiant, wonder, freedom, expression, clarity, cooperation
20	Judgement	Rebirth, renewal, decision, follow a calling, new direction, origins
(0)	The Fool	Transcendence, courage, innocence, trust, play, journey, path of initiation
21	The World	Completion, wholeness, fulfillment, euphoric, top of the world, structure, the all, creation

* In the *Thoth Tarot* and derivative decks, Justice becomes "Adjustment" at position 8 and Strength becomes "Lust" at position 11.

Images of the Major Arcana

There are literally thousands of tarot decks. Throughout the book are several Major Arcana images from the *DruidCraft Tarot*. The symbolism of the *DruidCraft Tarot* Major Arcana cards is quite similar to the *Waite-Smith Tarot*. Spend some time looking at the images and noticing the details. Better yet, get your own deck(s) and spread them out, spending time to absorb the amazing imagery.

The *Waite-Smith Tarot* was originally published in 1909 and is also known as the *Rider-Waite® Tarot* where the name derives from the publisher, Rider, and the symbologist, A. E. Waite. The artist, Pamela Coleman Smith, is left out of this naming convention. Here, we will refer to it as the *Waite-Smith Tarot* to emphasize the creators of the deck. The *Waite-Smith Tarot* from 1909 is considered the source of the English magic symbolism used in many contemporary decks.

Which Tarot Deck Should I Use?

You'll need tarot cards as a companion for this journey. What tarot deck do you need to do the pathwork journeys in this book? Numerous tarot decks are available. At least 2000 are cataloged at Aeclectic Tarot (aeclectic.net/tarot/cards/list.shtml). How do you select one that makes sense to use in this engagement with the Tarot Spirits?

The short answer is that you can use any 78-card tarot deck you like. Oracle decks with a different structure are not suitable. The *Waite-Smith Tarot Deck* is recommended for those new to tarot. The *DruidCraft Tarot Deck* is also a good starting deck, as it shares much of the *Waite-Smith Tarot Deck* symbolism.

A more extended discussion of different tarot decks can be found near the end of Appendix C. Any deck that fits the 78-card format discussed in the previous section works. A video lesson about different tarot decks and several videos touring the major arcana are available for you. Check them out at www.reidhart.com/tsh-resources.

There has been criticism of the *Waite-Smith Tarot* as patriarchal. In the early 1980s several feminist decks or books with more feminine interpretations of the *Waite-Smith Tarot* appeared. Round feminist decks include the *Daughters of the Moon* and *Motherpeace Tarot*. If you search Aeclectic Tarot for "feminine tarot," 31 tarot decks are listed. Less patriarchal interpretations of the *Waite-Smith Tarot* can be found in the book *A Feminist Tarot*.[2] Any of the feminist-oriented decks will work for AstroTarot.

Tarot, Shamanism, and Astrology Intersect

This book focuses on the intersection of shamanism, tarot, and astrology. First, you learn shamanic methods to journey from ordinary reality into the Otherworld. There you will meet and engage with the 22 Tarot Spirits of the Major Arcana in the tarot deck. You can work with them directly for advice, healing, and learning. Then you discover where the challenges lie in your astrological birth chart, working with specific Tarot Spirits to resolve those challenges. Then you use the Tarot Spirit connection to begin exploring the Western Mysteries.

You may be familiar with either shamanism, tarot, or astrology. The integrated AstroTarot approach is different from each individual discipline. This active personal engagement with spirits allows you to resolve both practical and spiritual issues. You can also take better advantage of opportunities in your life. Once practical life issues are resolved, you can explore deeper learning about spirituality through the Western Mystery tradition.

The Tarot as a Map to the Stars

How can you experientially access the mystery of the tarot? What I know is that tarot is not just a quaint form of fortune telling or a card game. It offers us a powerful doorway for accessing keys to the Western Mysteries. There are multiple Western Mystery schools that emerged in the 17th through 19th centuries that used the tarot. Each of the tarot keys is assigned both a Hebrew letter and either a planet or sign of the zodiac. The Major Arcana are divided into three groups:

- Three represent the newer planets (Uranus, Neptune, and Pluto), although they originally represented the elements: fire, air, and water (water and earth were originally combined as one element).
- Seven represent the traditional planets and luminaries.
- Twelve represent the signs of the zodiac.

---

[2] Gearhart & Rennie. *A Feminist Tarot.*

These groups (3, 7, and 12 cards each) total 22, the number of tarot cards in the Major Arcana and the number of letters in the Hebrew alphabet. Tarot mapping to astrological signs and planets is further discussed in Chapter 12 and Appendix H.

Pathwork of the Tarot

The tarot has been called "a pictorial textbook of ageless wisdom."[3] The Tarot Spirits offer an opportunity to do deep spiritual work using ancient shamanic and Western Mystery techniques. These spirit connections can also be used shamanically to create practical changes for the betterment of your life and community. Working with the Tarot Spirits combines the best of both worlds. You use a readily accessible visionary technique—the shamanic journey—to connect with the cornerstones of the Western Mysteries. To explore spirit realms, the shamanic journey is more effective for most people than guided visualizations, meditation, or ritual. This first Tarot Spirit book focuses on engaging the Tarot Spirits, receiving healing and advice, resolving astrological challenges, and learning about the mysteries. This work has four parts:

1. Learn how to take a shamanic journey and engage with the 22 powerful and loving Tarot Spirits of the Major Arcana.
2. Discover your personal Tarot Spirits and your shadow-self. Work with the Tarot Spirits for advice and healing.
3. Understand the basics of your astrological chart. Clear your astrological challenges shamanically. Your goal is a smoother and happier life.
4. Regularly connect with personalized circles of Tarot Spirits. Engage in deeper mystical learning from Spirit Constructs.

Later you can go beyond the steps listed above that are covered in this book. The full range of additional work with the Tarot Spirits is listed briefly below. More detailed descriptions are in Appendix B. Specific instructions will be included in future books of the Tarot Spirit series.

• Accept your shadow and resolve real-world conflicts with the Tarot Spirits, creating positive changes in your life.

---

[3] Case, P.F. *The Tarot: A Key to the Wisdom of the Ages.*

- Expand your AstroTarot work with houses and their rulers to take advantage of the opportunities in your natal chart.
- Use astrological timing techniques with the Tarot Spirits to focus your current efforts for the greatest personal benefit.
- Engage in shamanic healing for others using AstroTarot methods.
- Explore the Qabalistic Tree of Life with the Tarot Spirits as a practical tool for manifestation of practical and spiritual results.
- Work magically with Tarot Spirits using shamanic methods to manifest your intentions.
- Engage in shamanic-based tarot readings.

There are additional resources for those who want to explore the work more deeply at: www.reidhart.com/tsh-resources.

Experiential Tarot Exploration

How do you access the mystery of the tarot experientially? Not just a quaint form of fortune telling, the tarot offers us a powerful doorway to access the Western Mysteries. The earliest surviving cards date from Italy in the mid-15th century. Yet, earlier references to many tarot symbols are found in the *Vita Merlini* (the life of Merlin), a 12th-century Celtic-sourced manuscript. [4] Even earlier sources exist in possible Egyptian [5] and Mithraic[6] symbols. In the 19th and 20th centuries, the symbolism of the tarot expanded. The connection with ancient Western Mysteries was documented. The tarot also connects with astrology and the Qabalah, two other cornerstones of the Western Mysteries. Carl Jung[7] commented that the tarot was an archetypal window into individual and group unconscious. A more expanded history of tarot is found in Appendix C.

Your Personal Experience through Pathwork is the Key

The healing power of the Tarot Spirits can provide incremental or miraculous life improvements. For spirituality, the tarot has both major and minor mysteries. Your experience and growth can be spiritually satisfying, and life changing. You will not get the results or embrace the

---

[4] en.wikipedia.org/wiki/Vita_Merlini
[5] Keizer, L and C. Payne-Towler.1999. *The Underground Stream.*
[6] Flowers, Stephen. 2019. *The Magian Taork*
[7] marykgreer.com/2008/03/31/carl-jung-and-Tarot/

mysteries by just reading this or any other book. Understanding tarot and astrological concepts is just a thinking exercise, although a helpful one. For helpful life results you must engage with the pathworking instructions and have a personal experience. The results come from shamanic journeys with clear intentions. The experience and spiritual connection makes the process work. The mystical initiations happen through personal experience. Spiritual connection results from an Otherworld journey experience.

The term "pathwork" refers to a Western Mystery tradition. You connect with the Otherworld to build your understanding, connection, and power. The term usually refers to working the paths of the Tree of Life in Qabalah. We expand it here to include other interactions with living spirits. Pathwork can be performed in a meditation, guided visualization, trance, or shamanic journey. The shamanic journey method with drumming or rattling makes the pathwork experience lucid and impactful. Other meditative approaches can also be effective. The important thing is to have a personal experience rather than just an intellectual understanding.

Many pathwork experiences are available to you. To keep track of the various pathworks, each one is referenced with a letter designator as outlined in Appendix C. These pathwork designations are not always introduced in order, but are held consistent across multiple learning paths. These paths include books, live classes, and video lessons.

The pathwork instructions may seem dry or distant from your personal needs. Descriptions of others' experiences give you some view into the different responses to the pathwork. The profound truth is personal. It comes from your personal engagement with the Otherworld pathworking exercises presented. Do commit to following the instructions and getting the personal experiential data about the Otherworld. Experience how compassionate Spirits can help you directly. Personal experience is where the value lies.

Shamanic Practice: Beyond Archetypes

When you move beyond the archetypal and symbolic meanings of the tarot cards, you use shamanic techniques to have a direct personal relationship with Tarot Spirits. They embody the wisdom of the cards. You use a combination of shamanic and traditional Western Mystery methods.

You contact these compassionate spirits for advice, healing, or intervention. This fits in with the shamanic tradition of accessing other realities to make a practical difference in this world.

Beyond Barriers

There are barriers to approaching the Western Mysteries. They include centuries of negative propaganda, a belief that intricate rote learning is required, and modern reliance on a scientific approach. Western Mysteries are put down by the Church, similar to the Church's repression of shamanism and the occult in general. The Western Mysteries are often related to ritual magic, seen to involve complex references to obscure spiritual practices. Modern attitudes emphasizing the scientific method eschew any spiritual existence beyond what we can see, measure, and touch.

Moving beyond these barriers using shamanic techniques gets to your direct experience. It allows you to reach your own conclusions based on your direct Otherworld experience and direct revelation by the Tarot Spirits. By entering the world of the Tarot Spirits with shamanic methods, a safe connection to primal spiritual forces can be made for either self-development or practical goals. The direct connection allows the true meaning of the symbols to be explored naturally and meaningfully, rather than memorized through book learning.

A Shamanic Process

This carefully designed process lets you connect with a personal tarot guide. The guide is a special Spirit who helps you connect with the Tarot Spirits of the Major Arcana. You use traditional shamanic methods. Your goal is to meet and work with the Tarot Spirits in a positive, loving way to clear obstacles in your life or gain personal insight into both spiritual and practical matters. In this work, you begin by adapting ancient magical lodge techniques to access divine knowledge through bridge-building.[8]

You experience your body connecting with the three Suns in the universe: our Sun at the center of our solar system, the sun or star at the core of the earth,[9] and the suns that are stars all around us. A further

---

[8] Stewart, R. J. *The Miracle Tree: Demystifying the Qabalah.*
[9] The Sun at the core of the earth is described further in Appendix D.

connection is made to the Moon, the reflection of our Sun. Through a basic practice that can be used daily, you connect with earth power and star power in the context of the Tree of Life, embodying the meaning of "as below, so above."

Engaging the Tarot Spirits

The tarot guide will escort you on a trek to encounter the Tarot Spirits. Each Tarot Spirit is connected to one of the 22 keys or Major Arcana cards in the tarot deck. You access the living Tarot Spirits via the shamanic journey in areas of the Otherworld or non-ordinary reality. Each of the Tarot Spirits has insight into part of your psyche, and can provide unique advice, healing, and gifts. They can also help resolve conflicts in your life, resolve astrological challenges, connect you positively to your shadow-self, and open your heart to the wisdom of the ages.

AstroTarot

Astrology is one of the cornerstones of the Western Mysteries. Astrology was sourced from Babylonia, Egypt, and Greece. Hellenistic astrology[10] formed around the 1st century BCE. It informed later Arabic, Indian, and Medieval astrology. Medieval astrology transformed into modern astrology by adding psychological considerations.

In AstroTarot, you work with your natal chart to find potentially challenging aspects. These aspects limit your life and can create disruption. Unlike typical astrological practice, rather than just interpreting your chart, you work shamanically to clear limitations in your life. You work with the proper Tarot Spirits to clear those blocks related to challenging planetary relationships. The next phase of AstroTarot work is with circles of Tarot Spirits that share a common theme based on your natal astrology. These Tarot Spirits can provide advice, healing, and learning.

It does not matter that you are new to astrology, or a student of modern, Hellenistic, or other astrological traditions. You can apply the AstroTarot process to the conditions that impact your natal chart and your life experience. For those new to astrology, the distinction between

---

[10] Hellenistic astrology is discussed further in Appendix F.

modern and Hellenistic astrology may introduce some confusion. While I apologize for the complexity, there is a Hellenistic revival in progress. Many readers desire these distinctions. For astrology newcomers, focus on one type and ignore the other. Those familiar with astrology may consider both modern and Hellenistic approaches. The AstroTarot method remains consistent for both, with distinctions in interpreting aspects when selecting Tarot Spirits in Chapter 12.

I invite you to join in the quest for personal and community growth through engaging with the Tarot Spirits as part of your spiritual and life path.

Chapter 1 Recap

In Chapter 1 you have learned about the basic structure of the tarot. You have also heard about some of the benefits of AstroTarot work, and the broad overview of this pathwork. Working with the Tarot Spirits step by step, you will first connect with them and a tarot guide. You will then work with them to receive healing and advice. Finally they can help reduce the conflicts in your natal astrology.

If you have not already, now is a good time to think about what you want to accomplish. How do you want to transform your life. Write some ideas down about how things could change for you. Hold these in front of you as you go through the process step by step.

2: The Shamanic Journey: the Path of Direct Revelation

Conversation 1: Learning About the Shamanic Journey

Enjoy this first conversation between Isabel and Rachel, two fictional characters who have engaged in the venture you are starting.

The Sun shone brightly on this crisp fall day as Isabel hurried along the sidewalk to lunch with her good friend, Rachel. The two had met in high school and continued their friendship with weekly meetings over good food and drink.

Isabel had experienced a shamanic journey for the first time last night. She couldn't wait to tell Rachel all about it. She arrived at Café Yumm, a local lunch spot, a few minutes late.

Rachel already had a table and was engrossed in some office paperwork, her long dark hair streamed over her face. Rachel gave her a quick smile, put the paperwork in her briefcase, as she said, "Let's get our order in. I've got a quick lunch today."

Isabel sat down. The pair ordered their meals and drank herb tea while they waited for their rice bowls. Isabel pushed a wayward curl behind her ear and said, "Well, listen to this! I tried something new last night."

With a raised eyebrow, Rachel asked, "What was that?"

Isabel needed no more prompting and launched into her story. "I was reading this book about tarot, astrology, and shamanism. So, I tried out the shamanic journey and met my very own power animal, just like that!" She snapped her fingers. "Really, it was . . ." She searched for a word . . . "amazing!" She grinned.

Rachel maintained a straight face while thinking: well, here we go again, more woo-woo . . . Isabel was always the impulsive and gullible one. "So, what was that like?" she asked.

"Well, it was different from anything I've ever tried before. I used a drumming audio track and ended up experiencing a completely different reality. With my eyes closed, I went to a place with caves and a beautiful green landscape, and—this was the best part—I met a wolf who actually talked to me. I mean, I could literally hear his words! There was a special feeling when connecting with the wolf. I felt entirely altered in a good way, uplifted."

"Is this a guided fantasy, a guided visualization?"

"No, it's very different. I just listened to the steady drumming and then followed the instructions I received before the drumming started. I saw unusual things, like crystals on the cave walls." Briefly silent, Isabel lifted her gaze to her friend. "Anyway, enough about me. What's up for you?"

"Oh, just the usual work pressure. The firm wants me to work extra hours, but there's never any extra pay. So, I'm dealing with the same money issues all the time. I thought I could afford that lovely apartment by the river I found, but every month I come up short. I need a raise!"

"That sounds awful. What do you think you can do about it?"

"I don't know. I could always move to a cheaper neighborhood, but the lower price tag goes with lots of sketchiness and I don't feel safe there."

"Shouldn't you be due for a promotion? You got a paralegal certificate a year ago, but they still pay you like clerical staff."

Rachel gave a quick nod. "I bring that up and it's like, 'blah, blah, blah . . . the firm is just not doing that well right now.' It's pretty frustrating."

"You know, I've just started with this shamanic journey thing, but part of the reason to do it is to make positive personal changes in my life. At least according to this book: *Tarot Spirit Healing*. Maybe you could look at it." Isabel looked at Rachel uncertainly, realizing it was probably beyond Rachel's comfort zone.

And, predictably, Rachel responded, "I'm pretty busy with all these extra hours . . ." Rachel paused. "But aren't you just making up what you experience in these journeys?"

"No, and that is the surprising thing. For example, when I asked the wolf, my power animal, some questions about my budget difficulties, his answer startled me. He said to look at my credit card for unexpected charges. I did and lo-and-behold, I had not realized that I had eight monthly streaming payments left over from when my last boyfriend put all those channels on my credit card. I got rid of half of them pretty easily, then I called him up and asked him point blank to reimburse me and he sent me the money!" Rachel looked surprised. But then both women laughed out loud and clinked together their teacups in victory.

"Congratulations! Score one for Isabel! And the wolf!" After a few seconds' thought, Rachel said, "I need some financial advice, too. Maybe I should check it out. Do you think I could borrow that wolf?" She laughed. "Well, I've gotta run. They can't keep the work going out the door without me." She rolled her eyes and grimaced.

"OK, see you next week."

The Power of the Shamanic Journey

The Otherworld is the preferred realm to work with Tarot Spirits. You can get there using a shamanic journey, which is relatively easy to learn. If you have trouble with that or prefer not to follow that practice, you can work in a meditative state with your eyes closed. Either will work, although the shamanic journey usually provides a more profound experience.

I will never forget my first shamanic journey almost 30 years ago. I was intrigued by attendance at a friend's soul retrieval—a shamanic healing practice. I bought Michael Harner's book, *The Way of the Shaman*, and followed the instructions there. I had the amazing experience of entering an Otherworld landscape. I met my first power animal. This place in the lower world seemed like an actual location, even though it was outside normal reality. I had been waiting for the clarity of the shamanic journey for twenty years, ever since reading Carlos Castaneda's book *Journey to Ixtlan*. Once I learned how to take the shamanic journey, my connection to the spirits was much stronger than through meditation or guided visualization.

There are many opportunities to learn the shamanic journey. They range from weekend workshops to online classes to introductory books. I encourage you to learn how to journey. I offer you this brief set of instructions. Try it. Pursue more in-depth learning opportunities if needed.

What does the shamanic journey entail? It is a trip into non-ordinary reality, also called the Otherworld. You enter a shamanic state of consciousness. While some indigenous peoples use drugs to enter this reality, most shamans use percussion as a path to the Otherworld. A steady beat of drumming or rattling changes human brainwaves. They go from normal consciousness or Beta wave state, into a deeper state called Alpha/Theta wave state. There, consciousness can expand so you perceive non-ordinary reality. You may enter similar states through meditation or guided visualization. The shamanic journey is distinguished by the use of percussion to reinforce and maintain a shamanic state of consciousness. You become open to connection to the spirit world without a visualization narrative.

Drumming or rattling (sonic drive) in the shamanic journey provides safety when you enter the Otherworld, also called non-ordinary reality. The sonic drive keeps you connected to your body. It creates a clear path to return to your physical body in ordinary reality. Drug-based journey methods do not have this safety connection and may produce challenges.

In many cultures, shamans use percussion to enter this state. There, they can ask the spirits to perform healing or gather practical information for the community. This practice is accessible to most humans and can be used to receive advice or healing, spur on creativity, or make a spiritual connection.

You can enter a shamanic journey intending to meet a power animal or spiritual teacher to gain information. Shamanism is not a religion, yet allows for a direct and deep connection to helping spirits. You connect directly to spirit helpers in non-ordinary reality. You can receive healing, messages, advice, or inspiration.

The Three Worlds

Non-ordinary reality is divided into three worlds: the lower world, the upper world, and the middle world. In the beginning, most shamanic journeys go to the lower world. It is the land of power animals, teachers, and plant spirits. More advanced journeys go to the upper world. It is the realm of the mysteries, teachers, and other spirits. Journeying into the middle world can be more challenging. The middle world is the non-ordinary counterpart to our physical world. Some middle world spirits may be lost souls that need healing work or entities that do not have good intent. The spirits and beings encountered in the upper and lower worlds are compassionate and loving spirits. They have your best interests at heart, although you need to ask a spirit "are you willing to help me." More background on shamanism can be found in Appendix A.

How to Enter the Shamanic Journey

Here are a few steps that you can use to create your first shamanic journey:

- Clarify your intention.
- Make an offering in sacred space.
- Relax, imagine, and become aware of all your senses.
- Go into another reality using percussion as a vehicle.
- Engage in the shamanic work for your intention.
- Thank the spirits and return to this reality.

Let's get to your first journey.

Before you proceed, address a few ordinary reality matters.

- Find a comfortable place to lie down.
- Have a drumming track ready to play: a 20-minute drumming track is recommended for your first journey.[11] Alternatively, you can rattle or drum for yourself, but that is more advanced.
- Turn off your phone ringer, put your pets in the other room, and ask anyone else around not to disturb you.
- I recommend you cover your eyes with a scarf, bandana, or cloth napkin. This encourages a deeper journey.
- Read through the following directions, then take your time to complete them.

Your first shamanic journey:

- Set your intention. For this first journey your intention will be "to go to the lower world of non-ordinary reality and explore."
- Create an offering to the spirits. Light a candle in a safe location and offer the flame to the spirits. Alternatively, jog in place for

---

[11] You can download shamanic drumming tracks at: www.reidhart.com/tsh-resources

about 30 seconds, offering your exertion to the spirits as a form of "raising power."

- Turn on the drumming audio track, lie down, and close your eyes. First, just relax and let your breathing slow, listening to the drumbeat. After about a minute, imagine yourself in a wonderful place in nature you have actually been to in ordinary reality—a place you love. Now tune into all your senses: what do you feel, see, hear, smell, taste? Perhaps you see the Sun through the trees, hear the birds singing, feel the wind on your skin. In the beginning, it is important to take your time with this step as you enter into non-ordinary reality. It can take between one and ten minutes to complete this step the first few times.

- Once you have a strong sense of being in your place in nature, and you have opened all of your senses, continue.

- Search for an opening into the earth—any kind will do. Some common openings people have used are a tree root that goes down, a hole made by an animal, a cave, or a pond. Know that in the journey you can change shape and size, so even an ant hole will do. Enter the opening and find yourself in a tunnel that is headed in a downward direction. Continue to move yourself downward through the tunnel until you come to the end. Emerging from the tunnel, you find yourself in the lower world.

- Explore what you see and sense around you. Again, use all your senses. Notice plants, animals, rivers, glyphs, messages, etc. Enjoy yourself and explore as much as possible. You are safe here. If an animal appears, ask it: "are you my power animal?" See the section titled Meet a Power Animal later in this chapter.

- When you hear the change in the drumming (the steady beat stops and there are four sets of drumbeats), send out a message of gratitude to the spirits for showing you their world and as the fast drumming happens, retrace your steps back to your place in nature. It is important to retrace your steps and not pop out of the journey. Bring nothing back with you. Then as you hear the last four sets of drumbeats, return completely into your body in ordinary reality and slowly open your eyes.

- Take time to readjust to ordinary reality. If you feel spacey you can eat a small snack, connect with the floor or earth, drink some tea, or hug a tree.
- Take some notes in your journal about what you experienced. Did you see animals or plants? What did you hear? What did you feel? If you did not have strong visuals, focus on what other senses you used to experience your surroundings. You may have heard messages or had kinesthetic feelings. Honor all your senses.

Questions about the Shamanic Journey

Is Shamanism a religion? The short answer is "No!" Core shamanism as taught here is a method to access Otherworld information. While shamanism is not a religion, its methods can provide spiritual experiences or a deeper experience of any religion. For example, you can explore Christianity with shamanism by meeting Jesus as a spirit teacher. As a Buddhist, you can meet the dakas and dakinis in the Otherworld. You can work without a religion, meeting power animals and spirit teachers. You can seek healing and guidance from Otherworld beings. You can work with a pantheon of deities, like those from Celtic, Greek, or Egyptian culture.

The point is that religion has an element of faith or belief, while shamanism does not have that requirement. Shamanism is just about a method you use to contact spirit helpers. It is not about what spirits you contact. It is not about belief. Belief in the Otherworld is unnecessary. Just create an intention, use shamanic drumming methods, and observe the results. Experiment with shamanic techniques and observe your personal experience.

I am not getting strong visualizations on my journeys. How do I? One solution is to look ahead to pathwork A in Chapter 6. There we introduce a card scanning technique. Scanning an image just before journeying increases visuals inside the Otherworld. Another important approach is to use all your senses in the journey. In her *Co-Creation Handbook,* Alida Birch has this to say:

> As you ask your questions, open up to all your senses so you can receive the answer. This may be something you can hear or see or taste or feel. Sometimes you will simply be infused with the answer you are seeking.

Sometimes the answers will come during the pauses, but answers can also come to you later during the day or even in a dream. The answer may appear synchronistically to you within something someone says or an experience that you have.[12]

Am I just making this up? Imagination is a vital resource that we were perhaps more in contact with as a child. In the education process we were often told to stop fantasizing. As a result, our imagination was downgraded. Alida Birch puts it this way:

> You will most likely struggle with the thought that you are imagining the answers and could not possibly be interacting with anyone other than yourself. This is a very common dilemma most westerners face when beginning shamanic journey training . . . There are many indigenous cultures that do not have a word for imagination . . . They interpret [imagination] as being inspired and this is a critical difference. To be inspired means to be in-spirited, to be filled with the Spirits. The inference here is that all creative thought comes from the Spirit, not from our imagination.[13]

I don't seem to get anywhere listening to the drumming. What am I doing wrong? Sometimes it takes a few attempts to get underway. The idea of non-ordinary reality can be quite different from your current way of thinking. It also conflicts with normal views of what is reality. It helps to suspend disbelief before you journey. Make it an experiment. Spend some time relaxing with the drumming. Really focus on your familiar place in nature at the beginning of the journey. Use all your senses to make it feel more real to you. Experiment by venturing down a tunnel. Having a clear intention to reach the lower world of non-ordinary reality is important. You can even narrate your journey out loud. What are you seeing in your mind's eye? Do you smell the dirt and rocks in the tunnel? It might take several tries. Persistent practice working with the drumming does eventually result in a successful journey for most people.

---

[12] From *The Co-Creation Handbook.*, copyright © 2014 by Alida Birch. Luminare Press. Reprinted by permission of author. P. 26
[13] From *The Co-Creation Handbook.*, copyright © 2014 by Alida Birch. Luminare Press. Reprinted by permission of author. P. 27

Meet a Power Animal

Once you have successfully journeyed down the tunnel to the lower world, your next step is to meet a power animal. Power animals are one form of non-ordinary spirit helpers who can bring you vitality. They assist you in your day-to-day life. It's essentially the same process as the lower world journey we just discussed. The only difference is to start with the intention to meet a power animal. The power animal can be a spirit helper on your journeys. After you have met a power animal, dance your animal as discussed in Chapter 10.

Recommended Shamanic Journey Resources

Many can learn to journey just by following these simple instructions. If you feel unsure of your journey results, you can get more training. The references in Appendix A and listed below will help you deepen your journey experience.

Harner, M. *The Way of the Shaman*. HarperOne, 1990.

Ingerman, S. *Shamanic Journeying: A Beginner's Guide*. Sounds True, 2008.

You can download mp3 shamanic drumming tracks at our website: www.reidhart.com/tsh-resources

If you are interested in a more complete introduction, consider this online course: *Introduction to the Shamanic Journey* with Alida Birch. You will learn step-by-step what is needed for a successful Shamanic Journey with these lessons:

- Introduction and basis for the shamanic journey
- Preparation and calling in the Spirits
- The lower world journey
- The upper world journey
- Suggested practice journeys
- Power animal retrieval
- Power animal integration

To learn more about this course, visit: www.reidhart.com/tsh-resources

Chapter 2 Recap

Chapter 2 was all about learning how to take the shamanic journey. If this is new territory for you and it was successful, great! If you are an old hand and are just brushing up on the technique, wonderful. If it has not come together for you yet, have patience. Give the journey process several tries, and remember that the journey information can come to you in many ways: as telepathic information, through non-visual senses, or just as a feeling. The exercises in the next chapter are likely to enhance your visual journey experience. If you work better with a meditation approach, you can use that instead of the journey. And you can check out resources on how to journey listed at the end of the chapter and in Appendix A.

3: Bridging into the Otherworld

In this chapter, we overview the fundamental pathwork you will complete with the Tarot Spirits. Then create an Otherworld bridge. It is a consistent place to start all your journeys. Then you experience Pathwork A. You use a scanning technique to begin your work with each Tarot Spirit. You will receive a personal message.

Pathworks A/B/C: Individual Tarot Spirits

In your fundamental work with Individual Tarot Spirits, you complete pathworks A, B, and C in order for each Tarot Spirit. It's as simple as A, B, C.

A. Tarot Scanning: After scanning the card for one of the Major Arcana, enter the shamanic journey and go onto your bridge to receive a message from the scene of the Tarot Spirit.

B. Meet a single Tarot Spirit. After crossing the bridge with your tarot guide, you travel to the Tarot Spirit's home. You engage, accept a gift, and express your eagerness to collaborate.

C. Get to know an individual Tarot Spirit in their place, after crossing the bridge with your tarot guide. Learn about them, finding out about their powers, territory, and sphere of influence.

Which Tarot Spirits Do I Work With?

This main connection to each Tarot Spirit (Pathwork A, B, and C) is an individual connection. Which Tarot Spirits are your initial focus? It is great to work eventually with all the 22 Major Arcana or key spirits, but focusing your efforts on the ones that can contribute to immediate practical or spiritual benefits is helpful. If you add up the basic A/B/C pathwork journeys, or 3 x 22 totals 66 journeys, it can feel overwhelming at first. Benefit from this work by connecting with the Tarot Spirits you're attracted to. There is no need to meet all 22 right away.

Start with accessible Tarot Spirits, such as the Sun or the Empress. Dealing with Death, the Devil, or the Tower can be intimidating. For more challenging Tarot Spirits, it's important to include a tarot guide, as discussed in the next chapter. You do not need to work with all 22 Tarot Spirits immediately to reach the goal of resolving potential challenging astrological aspects as discussed in Part 3 of this book.

It's crucial to develop a personal connection with each Tarot Spirit before advanced work in pairs or groups. A valid approach is to start with the Sun and Empress. Then, journey to your personal special Tarot Spirits found in Chapter 7. Then expand to the Tarot Spirits representing planets as discussed in Chapter 12 of this book. You can limit the number of planetary Tarot Spirits further by reviewing the potential challenging aspects based on your natal chart as revealed in Chapter 13.

The final point here is that it is important to establish the primary engagement with individual Tarot Spirits using Pathworks A, B, and C before you work shamanically with them in pairs or in larger groups.

Creating Your Bridge

Bridge pathwork as a meditative practice is an ancient mystery lodge exercise. Why a bridge? In Latin, the root of bridge is *pont*. Notice the similarity to Pontiff or Pope. As a brief aside, understand that the Hierophant card in the tarot represents a ritual leader or high priest. While earlier Marseilles decks called this card "the Pope," the original meaning of the card is not based on the Catholic Pope. The "Hierophant" was the name of the ritual leader at the Greek Elysian mystery gatherings that occurred before the birth of Christ, hence the name precedes Christianity. The bridge symbolizes a bridge between the ordinary person and divinity, or a connection between the ordinary world and the magic of the Otherworld. This idea of a personal to divine connection is reinforced in Nordic lore, where an ice bridge forms a link between this ordinary world and the Otherworld.

You can use this bridge motif in your work with the Tarot Spirits. The bridge creates a reliable place to begin each journey. Repeatedly connecting with the bridge creates a stronger, easier path to the Tarot Spirits. In the shamanic approach, you yourself cross the bridge to find your own truth rather than relying on a religious authority as an intermediary.

Figure 3. Here's a possible glimpse of your Otherworld bridge. Your own bridge may be quite different based on your personal journey. The bridge is a consistent access point to the Tarot Spirits in the Otherworld.

You begin by finding the bridge location in the shamanic lower world. Your power animal can guide you. Begin at your sacred garden or grove in the lower world, if you have one. If not, let your power animal guide you to a future sacred grove or garden location with a river or stream nearby where you can create your bridge. One option is to deepen your experience by repeating the bridge creation daily for a week.

Steps to Creating the Bridge

Your intention is to create a bridge in the otherworld you can return to for your Tarot Spirit journeys. Rattle, drum, or play a drumming track[14] during this process.

---

[14] You can download shamanic drumming tracks at: www.reidhart.com/tsh-resources

1. Set sacred space in your preferred way. Turn off distractions. Light a candle.

2. Focus on the candle and while breathing slowly, focus on the candle flame that represents the three Suns (see Appendix D). Say "I welcome the flame of the three Suns."

3. Look through the flame and close your eyes. Witness spirits or angels constructing a bridge beyond the flame. The bridge may be built from wood, stone, rainbow light, glass, or other material. Following a Western Mystery lodge tradition, you may see the bridge shining with inner light.[15]

4. Let your awareness be with the bridge. If your awareness drifts, just return your focus to the image of the bridge.

5. Contemplate the qualities of bridging, the purpose of the bridge, crossing under, crossing over. Commune with the core essence of the bridge. Just look. Do not cross the bridge at this time. Let the meaning of the bridge settle into your consciousness without words.

6. Once finished, step back from the bridge and reorient yourself. This will help you find your way back when you visit the Otherworld again.

7. Thank your power animal and retrace your steps, arriving at the place where you started in ordinary reality. You may wish to use a call back rattle or drumming passage. Become fully aware of your body and open your eyes slowly.

8. Journal about your bridge's description, location, and any meaning or messages you received from or about the bridge.

Pathwork A: Tarot Scanning and Message

Your journey with the Tarot Spirits starts with Pathwork A. The purpose of Pathwork A is to develop visualization skills and have direct experience of each Tarot Spirit. You may also receive messages from the Tarot Spirits. Select one of the Major Arcana tarot cards.

---

[15] Stewart, R. J. *The Miracle Tree: Demystifying the Qabalah.*

Figure 4. Just before your journey, scan the card in strips and focus on the details with your eyes open. This helps you see the Tarot Spirit in the journey with your eyes closed. *Credit: DruidCraft Tarot.*

Steps for Pathwork A: Message

Journey intention: See a particular Tarot Spirit at your bridge in the Otherworld and receive a message from that spirit.

1. Opening: Set sacred space and light a candle. Be aware of the directions and rattle or drum for a bit.
2. Tarot scanning: Scan the card visually in strips from top to bottom a few times. Notice all the details.
3. Look at the flame of your candle, then close your eyes. See yourself journeying to your bridge in the Otherworld.

4. At the bridge entrance, see or sense the card image you scanned as a life-sized scene on or beyond the bridge.

5. Cross onto the bridge, entering the scene of the card.

6. Listen for or watch for a message from the Tarot Spirit or from an element that appears in the scene. Use all your senses. You may hear the message or receive a telepathic message. You may receive it through some other sense.

7. When complete, thank the Spirit, retrace your steps, arriving at the place where you started in ordinary reality. You may wish to use a call back rattle or drumbeat. Become fully aware of your body and open your eyes slowly.

8. Record how the card scene appeared and the message you received in your journal, along with any other impressions. Summarize the message on your Tarot Spirit tracking forms (see Appendix B) for pathwork A.

It is best to do Pathwork A as a separate journey before the other pathwork with a Tarot Spirit. If short on time, you can combine Pathwork A with Pathwork B, moving from the scene observation and message of Pathwork A to a live first interaction with a Tarot Spirit in Pathwork B, as discussed in Chapter 5.

Questions About Pathwork A: Scanning and a Message

Should I do the scanning pathwork A with all 22 Tarot Spirits before going on the Pathworks B and C? Its better to do them sequentially. So you might do Pathwork A one week with a couple of the Major Arcana, and then do Pathwork B the next week with the same cards, and then do Pathwork C the following Week. Appendix B has some suggestions on long term planning. You may choose to do Pathworks A, B, and C all in one day or one week as separate journeys with the same Tarot Spirit. Pursue it in whatever timing feels right to you. Most get more satisfaction out of working with a limited set of Tarot Spirits at first, so they can move on to the advice and healing journeys with them and start to see some impact in their life (see Chapters 9 and 10). Then they can examine their astrology and focus on the Tarot Spirits needed to clear their astrological challenges. Getting to all 22 of the major arcana can be spread out over time, with no rush.

What if the image at the bridge was visually unclear? Keep in mind that visualization of the Tarot Spirit may be limited. They may not look just like the tarot card. As we talked about with journeying, other senses than visual may be more important. You want to have a sense of the Tarot Spirit, whether it's through touch, kinesthetic, or even telepathic means. They may appear in some other symbolic way. Just be open to different ways they can show up and communicate with you.

Chapter 3 Recap

In Chapter 3 you connected with the bridge, your jumping off place for future Tarot Spirit journeys. After getting a message from the Tarot Spirits with Pathwork A, you can meet them with Pathwork B. Before you engage in Pathwork B, it's time to meet your tarot guide.

4: Your Tarot Guide

Conversation 2: Each Tarot Guide is Different

One week later, Isabel was waiting at the picnic bench by the taqueria food cart. She had bodywork clients all morning, so she was hungry and she'd already started munching on some tasty street tacos. She spied Rachel sauntering her way, dressed sharply with a new close cropped "power" haircut. After ordering the vegan burrito special, Rachel plopped down next to her.

"Isabel, you didn't tell me this shamanic book had anything to do with tarot! I was curious about the journey and gave it a go. And, you know, I was surprised it was not at all like transcendental meditation or a guided visualization. It felt like I was transported to a different but very real world." She took another deep breath and locked eyes with Isabel. "I met a hawk as a power animal, and he had so many wise things to say. I was stunned!"

Isabel smiled broadly; happy her friend was curious enough to experiment with something new. "Oh yeah, the tarot mix with the journey is quite interesting. When I did it, I just started asking for messages from the Sun and the Empress. I like the Empress—she is pretty down to earth. She gave me a message about Ron. That I should just ignore those jealous remarks he makes. I mean, he just needs to get used to the idea that as a massage therapist I touch people in my work. He needs to trust me."

"Oh, how true!" Rachel nodded. "I've been listening to the High Priestess. She agrees I am being undervalued at work. My boss keeps saying 'you need more experience before you get more pay,' but to me it looks like I am doing most of the work, while they just shmooze and take the clients to lunch."

"You know, I think you are pretty valuable to your firm. From what you have said, you're really at the core of their productivity. Back from when you were just clerical, to especially now that you have that paralegal training."

"Thanks." Rachel looked thoughtful. "One thing I do like about the shamanic journey is that it is pretty well defined. You get a question or intention and do the journey with the drumbeat. Then it's over in 10 or 20 minutes. This fits into my life. It's not like that time we did magic mushrooms together where the day slipped away. While it was an amazing experience, I couldn't do that very often. I have to hold down a job." They both smiled, remembering that magic mushroom day. Then Rachel added, "Have you done the tarot guide journey yet?"

Isabel reflected on the tarot guide. This was a spirit entity who helps you work with the Tarot Spirits. "Yes, I did that journey. I got the gift of a sunbeam in my forehead from the Sun." Isabel had an expression of joy on her face that Rachel rarely saw anymore. Isabel leaned in close and whispered, "You know that tarot guide is kind of a hunk! He may wear a loose tunic, but I swear he works out. Broad shoulders, firm chin: this guy could be a movie star!" She giggled mischievously.

"Well, don't tell Ron about him. That guy can get so jealous."

"Good advice! I'll keep this all to myself for now. Ron can be so skeptical, anyway . . ." She sighed, "I want to see where this goes without his influence."

Rachel recalled her journey to the guide a few days ago. "But my tarot guide seems aloof. She is tall and thin, with a thoughtful face. She seems wise and speaks in soothing tones. I felt very safe with her and get a strong sense she will take care of me if these journeys ever get difficult."

Meet your Tarot Guide

Your tarot guide is a very important part of working with the Tarot Spirits. You can work with easy Tarot Spirits like the Sun or the Empress without a guide. However, it can be intimidating to work with Death, the Devil, or the Tower. Over time, your goal may be to develop a strong relationship with all 22 of the tarot Major Arcana, by meeting them as Tarot Spirits. Some of them may intimidate you, invoking high anxiety so that you need another person to say, "OK, you've had enough of this; let's move on with your journey and get some space." The tarot guide is essential there.

The tarot guide and the sonic drive together provide tremendous safety as you journey into the Otherworld. The tarot guide also enhances meaning. You may struggle with some Tarot Spirits and require assistance.

Or, you may need to hit the escape hatch. That's not everyone's experience, but sometimes it takes a while to connect with a particular Tarot Spirit.

Also, you are trying to get information from the Tarot Spirits. You might need someone to interpret the message or help press with questions for clarification. The tarot guide can help with that.

What are the desirable attributes of a tarot guide? The tarot guide is almost always a humanoid spirit. They may be dressed in ancient clothing. You might consider them an ascended master; however, they should **not** be:

- a power animal
- an angel or archangel with wings
- a god or a goddess
- someone you would consider a guru
- someone currently alive in the world

Also, if the guide is one of your ancestors, they should be someone who died before you were born. If you knew your grandmother or grandfather when they were alive, they are not suitable candidates. The relationship is too familiar. If the guide is an ancestor from five or twenty generations ago, that's fine.

Most importantly, you want someone who shows a loving interest or compassion toward you. In this journey, hold that as your primary criteria. If you encounter a potential tarot guide who doesn't meet the criteria, kindly thank them and continue searching for a guide who resonates with you. As you search, look to the right for the next candidate. Retry the journey later if you don't find an appropriate tarot guide.

You will connect with the Sun in this journey. Scan the Sun card bit by bit before the journey, as in Pathwork A. Use the candle flame as well. See yourself going through the candle flame into the journey. Close your eyes and go down the tunnel into the lower world and look for a power animal. If you don't have a power animal connection already, either repeat the power animal journey in Chapter 2 or send out an invitation for a power animal to come join you. A power animal is not absolutely necessary, but it helps.

It's important near the end of your journey that you get the name of your guide so that you have a way to communicate with them. Introduce yourself and determine a signal, like calling their name, to meet your guide in future journeys. You will go to the bridge and meet up there. Remember, Spirits are always available as they operate outside of time. They'll be there for you whenever you require assistance.

Figure 5. The Sun is key 19 (XIX) in the tarot Major Arcana. The Sun represents the luminary, our Sun, and carries the archetype of conscious representation and healing. The Sun is often the first Tarot Spirit you engage with. *Credit: DruidCraft Tarot.*

In this journey, you are looking for an ascended human who died before you were born, perhaps dressed in ancient clothing. Someone who you feel expresses love or compassion for you. If the guide is disqualified (has wings, is a god, goddess, or famous guru, is an ancestor alive after you were born) then continue walking to the right to find another guide. If you do not feel love or compassion, or if they will not see the Sun in the Otherworld sky, continue walking right, searching for another candidate.

Steps to Meeting Your Tarot Guide

Journey intention: to meet an Otherworld tarot guide to work with you and the Tarot Spirits.

1. Remove distractions and create sacred space. Light your candle.
2. Play a 20-minute drumming track.
3. Briefly scan the Sun card.
4. Look at the candle flame and close your eyes.
5. Observe yourself traversing the flame and journeying through the tunnel to the lower world. Meet a power animal. Ask the power animal to take you to where you will meet a tarot guide.

   - From where your power animal takes you to, move to the right and wait for a human guide to appear to your right.
   - Get impressions of the guide, beginning with their feet; their face may not be clear. Ask them, "Are you my true guide and can you protect me while working with the Tarot Spirits?"
   - Take the guide's hands if they agree. If you feel acceptance and love or caring, continue.
   - If they answer no, they don't answer, they leave, or they are not sending a caring vibration, keep looking to the right until you find a guide who does.

6. Stand alongside an acceptable guide, hand in hand. Ask your guide to point to the Sun in the Otherworld sky. If they refuse or dissemble, keep looking to the right for a different guide.
7. When your guide points to the Sun, call it down as the first Tarot Spirit you will meet. The Sun will appear in human-like form; accept its first appearance.
8. When the Sun has appeared, ask the Sun two questions:

   - "What request do you have of me to work with you?"
   - "Do you have a gift for me that I need in my life?"

9. Give the Sun permission to send you light and power. Be open to receiving a gift. Thank the Sun.
10. Create a signal or get clear on a name or way to call your guide. Let the guide know that you will meet them at the step entering the bridge next time.
11. Then return to ordinary reality, tracing your steps back through the tunnel. Merge completely back into your body and slowly open your eyes.

12. Journal about your journey to find the guide. Include information about how the guide looked, what their name is, what the gift from the Sun is, and what is required to work with the Sun.

Seeking a guide to the right is proven in practice. However, any guide that exudes love and support toward you, meets the earlier criteria of being humanoid, and will point to the Sun in the Otherworld sky is a true guide for you.

Reports on the Tarot Guide Experience

Others' actual reactions to this journey are included below. These reports are from actual participants in workshops and trainings on the Tarot Spirit process. Only the first name is included for anonymity. Similar actual reactions are included for other exercises and pathworks throughout the book.

The purpose is to give some idea of the breadth of experience for this journey, not to indicate what you should experience. Your experience may be different as everyone has a personal relationship with the Otherworld and the Tarot Spirits. Honor the truth of your own experience, rather than comparing your experience to others.

Paulette: My guide is a Druid male. He is a guide to all the esoteric arts. I know him. I just call out his name and he comes. My gift from the Sun was the light of truth. It will sharpen my discernment.

Rhonda: I met Cann, my gate keeper. He said he is my protector. In the first journey he was there making sure the bridge was safe, then filled me with light in the heart. This time he split the Sun and he filled my third eye.

Questions or Issues About Finding a Tarot Guide

I did not find a guide during this journey. No guide? Repeat the journey steps or seek one with an open journey, guided by a strong intention. Although this format is designed to assist you to find a guide, you can also find a teacher or guide by journeying to the Otherworld and simply requesting a compassionate guide.

What if the guide was visually unclear? Keep in mind that visualization of the guide may be limited. The face might be initially unclear. The key is to have a sense of them, whether it's through touch, kinesthetic, or even telepathic means. So be open to different ways the guide can show up. Look for their presence, compassion, and communication, regardless of how they appear.

The guide that appeared would not talk to me. With a tarot guide it is important to ask them questions directly and insist on an answer. So, you can journey again and be more insistent about getting a straightforward answer or search for a different guide. At times, it will be your tarot guide's job to help interpret unclear messages from Tarot Spirits, so you need them to be communicative with you. That being said, you do need to ask the guide to help you receive an answer. They will not always volunteer information. You definitely want an affirmative answer to the question: "Are you my true guide and can you protect me while working with the Tarot Spirits?" If you don't get a clear answer, look for another guide.

I did not find a power animal to show me where to meet my guide. If you do not already have a power animal, you might do a separate journey to call for a power animal to work with you as described in Chapter 2. You should ask an animal that comes in the journey if they are a helping spirit who can work with you. Once you have a power animal, repeat the above journey to find a guide, and call the power animal to show you the place to meet a guide once you exit the tunnel into the Otherworld. While a power animal is good to have, if you do not have one, you can complete the journey yourself by searching for a place to meet a guide in the lower world.

Why do I move to the right when looking for a guide candidate? Experimentation with this process has found that moving to the left and connecting with a power animal, then moving forward to the right place to meet a guide, then moving to the right until you find an appropriate guide works the best for finding a compassionate guide. If you find the appropriate guide in a different direction, that is fine. The most important quality is that you have a sense of compassion from the guide.

What observations indicate a false guide? Often the first guide you meet will be your true tarot guide. Signs that you should keep looking to the right for your true guide are that the false guide:

- Refuses to point at or acknowledge the Sun.

- Will not answer your question "Are you my true guide and can you protect me while working with the Tarot Spirits."
- Does not emanate a loving or compassionate presence toward you.
- Does not work well with you when contacting the Tarot Spirits.

What other disqualifications exist for tarot guides? We recommend that you not work with any of the following as a tarot guide: gods, goddesses, power animals, Gurus, Archangels, Angels, or non-humanoid entities. Living relatives or recently-deceased ancestors that lived during your lifetime are also disqualified. These entities are either too close to you or too elevated to have the frank discussions and interactions you need from your guide.

Do I work with this guide forever? Maybe five years down the road, it's time for a new guide and you can repeat this basic initiation journey. Your current guide will let you know if it's time to change and will help you to vet the new guide. For more than a dozen years, I've used the same original guide.

Chapter 4 Recap

Meeting your tarot guide is an important initiation. You will have a long-term relationship with your guide. If the connection did not happen in the first journey, repeat it until the connection is made. The tarot guide is one of the important keys to successful AstroTarot work.

5: Meet the Tarot Spirits

In this chapter, you learn how to make a strong connection with an individual Tarot Spirit using Pathwork B. We will delve into: Exactly what is an Otherworld Spirit? What roles do they have? How can you contribute to a worthwhile and balanced relationship with them? How do you use gifts from the Tarot Spirits?

Conversation 3: Gifts from the Spirits

In the back of the elevator, Isabel rode up to the new rooftop lounge in town. In front of her was a broad-shouldered guy with a woman she assumed was his girlfriend. The intense look he gave her when they entered the elevator made an impact. There was a surprising but subtle vibration emanating from his body. As she entered the fancy rooftop venue, she saw Rachel staring wistfully out the window, sipping on a margarita. She gave her friend a quick hug and sat down at the window table, admiring the view of the city below. It was cloudy and gray, but through a break in the clouds, she could still just make out the snowcapped mountains—the Three Sisters—to the east.

"Hi there, good friend. What's going on?"

"Oh, just wondering where I'm at in my life. I've got an OK job—interesting but short on pay—but no 'Mr. Right.' Maybe I'm depressed about the gathering clouds and rain this fall."

"That's a bummer. How can we cheer you up?"

Rachel stared down at her glass. "Am I just expecting too much? After all, I'm healthy. I've got friends. I appreciate you." She shrugged her shoulders and gave an enormous sigh. "Sorry, I'm not more fun to be with."

Isabel reached out and gave Rachel's hand a reassuring squeeze. "Should we drown our sorrows in good food? I hear they have a great tortilla soup here."

"Sure, sounds like a plan." They picked up the menus and placed their orders. "Did you continue with those journeys?"

A strawberry margarita arrived, and Isabel took a sip. She reflected on what she had learned about receiving gifts from the Tarot Spirits. These gifts were whatever was needed to move forward in life with spiritual or practical goals. "Well, yes, I did. I went to meet the Empress Tarot Spirit, who gave me a gift. She put a small bird in my right ear. She said the bird can give me the advice I need as I go along in life. I just have to ask. And it did! It tweeted a couple of times this week. The bird told me to skip late night ice cream after I had not heard from Ron for yet another day. Another time, I was eying a really cute top at Nordstroms and the bird reminded me I was over budget for the month and suggested that I could find one at the vintage clothing store. And she was right."

"Hmmm, shopping advice from a bird . . . Who'd have thought?" They both laughed.

"I suppose. But hey, if it's wise advice, I'd even take it from a hippo. And it feels strange to be more responsible about money. Quite a change for me. What about you? Did you give the 'gift' journey a try?"

Rachel said, "Yes. I met the High Priestess with my tarot guide in a gorgeous marble hall. She made me promise to stop loaning money to those guys we worked with from our restaurant days. They are sweet talkers, but never seem to get around to settling up. Then she put a screen over my eyes. She said it's a screen of truth. And the next day I was getting some promises from my boss, and I could just see that it was all B.S. So, I'm feeling off balance with this new perspective. It's like when you see something new that was there all the time, but you never noticed it. Now I can't stop noticing! I've been there for seven years, and now I'm seeing clearly that I'm being taken advantage of. I can't ignore it any longer."

"Wow, that's huge!" They were both silent as the impact of Rachel's new perspective dawned on them.

Their tortilla soup arrived, vegan with jack fruit for Rachel, and the beef brisket version for Isabel. They dug in and enjoyed the spicy flavors. With the edge off their hunger, Isabel said, "What did you think about the idea of meeting all the Tarot Spirits and receiving gifts from them?"

"Seems like a lot. I think I will focus on just a few of them."

"I guess that makes sense. In the introduction, the book presented the whole idea of working with tarot and astrology together. So, I've just started reading about it, and it looks like each planet is represented by a Tarot Spirit. You can work with the ones that have challenging aspects in your birth chart to clear blockages in your life. So, you don't need to work with all the Tarot Spirits."

"I'll have to read up on that." Rachel noticed Isabel was looking off in the distance and not paying attention. She clinked her spoon gently on the stem of her glass. "Earth calling Isabel! Where are you?"

"Oh, sorry. It's just that guy over there. I rode up in the elevator with him. There is just something about his vibe that is hitting me."

"Oh, he's caught your attention, I see. Of course, he's with that skinny woman in the red dress. What about Ron?"

"Yeah," Isabel snorted, "what about Ron? I'm starting to wonder . . ."

Tarot Spirits vs. Archetypes

Many who explore the connection between tarot and astrology treat the tarot keys as archetypes. Edwin Steinbrecher, a pioneer in using tarot to access astrological issues, refers to the Major Arcana as living energies that have culturally important ideas.[16] These archetypes can be accessed and reflect parts of our own psyche, while being impersonal and part of the collective unconscious.

This psychological approach refers to the collective unconsciousness identified by Carl Jung.[17] Working this way gives you insight and expands your knowledge of unconscious motivations. It does not have the spiritual assistance of a shamanic approach. When you work shamanically, you see the tarot keys as independent and living spirit helpers. You acknowledge them as sovereign beings rather than projections of your subconscious or as archetypes from the collective unconscious. You will learn how to create this direct relationship to Tarot Spirits here and in Chapter 6.

Spirit vs. "a Spirit"

The question of "a Spirit" versus "spirit" as a general concept comes up as you learn to relate to the Tarot Spirits. Some people feel that "spirit"

---

[16] Steinbrecher, E. *The Inner Guide Meditation*, p.6.
[17] Jung, C. *The Archetypes and the Collective Unconscious.*

generally works in their life as a positive influence, but they are not really relating to an individual Spirit. To work shamanically means having a direct relationship with spirits as living entities. You meet the spirits as individual entities whom you talk to, have a conversation with, receive healing or advice from, or negotiate with. To develop trust with them is important. You will build trust with the Tarot Spirits when you engage Pathworks A, B, and C as outlined in Chapter 3.

For most, there is an abstract concept of spiritual unity. We may call it Goddess, God, "the All," or "the Great Spirit." We might call it "nature" or Gaia. Michael Harner taught[18] that connecting directly with such a large and overarching spiritual power can be challenging or even dangerous. Working with more approachable individual spirit helpers is safer and produces more practical results. These spirits include power animals, Tarot Spirits, ancestors, or spirit teachers. These relatable spirit helpers act like transformers. They take that big global all-knowing power and chunk it down to a power level we can work with personally. In shamanic work, we typically do practical work with individual spirit helpers.

Roles of the Tarot Spirits

Let's touch on the idea that the spirits we are working with— specifically the Tarot Spirits—have multiple roles.

For some pathwork, they could represent a general archetype. You could work with the High Priestess, for instance, to understand her role in the world. What is her meaning as a tarot card when doing a reading? Compare that to her being a Tarot Spirit that you have engaged for advice, healing, or initiation. What power does she possess in each of these roles? What can she teach you?

So, the living Tarot Spirits can take on many different roles as follows:

- They might represent a planet or a zodiac sign, either in general or in your chart specifically. These are two different things. In your chart, there are a lot of influences and interactions with other planets and signs. So, this role of representing a specific planet or

_____

[18] Harner, M. Lecture in Foundation for Shamanic Studies course: Three-Year Program of Advanced Initiations in Shamanism and Shamanic Healing™

sign in a specific chart might be a different role than when they represent the planet or sign in general.

- They might be teachers, with something to teach you. You can also experience a learning construct approach based on multiple Tarot Spirits, as described in Chapter 15.
- They might be advisors. You might have a question you want to take to them either individually or as a group (Pathwork H in chapters 9 and 14).
- They might be a healer. You might receive direct healing from them. We engage with that in Chapter 10.

Different Roles, Like a Parent

The roles of Otherworld Spirits are like the different roles a parent has. Parents are providers, putting food on the table for a child. Then they are teachers for the child, either helping with their homework or teaching them to ride a bike. They often are disciplinarians. Or they are cheerleaders, encouraging the child to improve a skill. They arrange activities for children. At a core level, they provide the first experience of unconditional love. Just as a parent has multiple roles, you'll engage with the Tarot Spirits in diverse ways.

Gifts from on High

In this work, we are asking to be connected to a compassionate spirit who can fully understand our experience and touch it in a healing way. We are open to the Spirit seeing us for who we are, experiencing us in a positive way, touching us with their compassion, and healing us with their power. This invokes a positive and healing claim to our own power. The focus is about the personal triumph of moving past being a victim into being one's own champion and truly accepting one's own power. We are asking the Tarot Spirits to have a personal relationship with us. We want them to provide direct healing power that will shift our lives for the better.

Pathwork B is the crux of the matter. It is where the personal engagement with the spirit occurs. There is an exchange. To collaborate with this Spirit, you must make a commitment. They give you a gift. Then you are both connected. You are, literally, engaged. You are in reciprocity with the Tarot Spirit.

You might wonder what kind of gift is likely. It can be anything. There is often a symbolic object placed in your astral body. It could just be a power or ability. You will often be surprised. Its use or value may be instantly obvious. It may be a bit of a mystery. It may be passive, and provide benefits without input. It may require some work on your part to understand how to use it. Be open to receiving whatever the Tarot Spirit offers. Be sure to record it on your list of Pathwork B journeys, so you have a long term reference to look back on.

Figure 6. Water is an age-old symbol of divine gifts that are delivered to a supplicant with their hands out. *Credit: Peter Herman, Pixabay.*

The Tarot Spirit knows which gift will aid you now. You are not posting a wish list. The gift will have spiritual or practical qualities, or both. Usually, the Tarot Spirit will place the gift in your astral body. Then it is up to you to learn about how to use it, either in the Otherworld or in ordinary reality.

A Common Journey Opening and Conclusion

You can start all your Tarot Spirit pathwork journeys with the same opening and conclusion. Having a familiar pattern for your Tarot Spirit work grounds you in a safe connection to the Otherworld. Suggested opening and closing steps are listed below. These steps are universal for all pathwork, eliminating the need for repetition of opening and closing instructional steps each time we describe a pathwork. You can start by using the full range of steps as listed several times. Then experiment with what works for you and customize your own personal opening and closing. You may already have your own approach to creating sacred space. Appendix D has more detail for several of the steps.

Opening Steps

Your personal Tarot Spirit opening:

1. Have clearly in your mind the purpose or intention of your journey. Get any preliminary questions or activities resolved. Take out the cards for the Tarot Spirits you are planning to meet.
2. Light a candle (be sure it is safely on a fireproof base that will be secure while you journey with eyes closed).
3. Smudge yourself, use incense, or if you are odor sensitive, use a feather to smudge yourself with air.
4. Call the directions, drum for a bit, or do the Shamanic Crossing (see Appendix D).
5. Say the following invocation aloud:

   I offer this flame to the Spirits and it is of the three stars
   Earth fire below
   Sun and Star fire above
   The Moon reflects the Sun
   The Earth is in my feet
   The Moon is in my loins
   The Sun is in my heart
   The Stars about my head

6. Start the drumming track, or drum or rattle for yourself.
7. Visually scan the tarot card(s) for the Tarot Spirits you plan to work with in narrow strips from top to bottom a few times. Notice all the details.
8. Focus your eyes on the candle flame that represents the three Suns. While breathing slowly, say or think, "I welcome the flame of the three Suns."
9. Look at the flame of your candle, then close your eyes. You may want to lie down at this point. See yourself journeying to your

place in nature, then down the tunnel to your bridge in the Otherworld.

10. Stand at the entrance to the bridge.

11. Call your tarot guide to meet you there.

12. Have any discussion with the tarot guide needed about your journey intention, which Tarot Spirits to meet, or where to meet them.

13. With your tarot guide, walk through the flame of the three Suns onto the bridge and continue to where you will meet the Tarot Spirit(s).

14. Continue with the steps of the particular pathwork.

In future pathwork steps, we will refer to the above sequence as a simple single step: "Complete your Tarot Spirit opening steps."

Closing Steps

Your personal Tarot Spirit closing:

1. When complete with your Tarot Spirit pathwork, thank all the Tarot Spirits present and thank your shadow-self (see Chapter 8).

2. Retrace your steps with your tarot guide back to the bridge, walking backwards off the bridge through the flame with the guide. Thank your guide and converse about any debrief needed.

3. Retrace your journey steps back through the tunnel to your place in nature and then back to where your body is in ordinary reality.

4. You may wish to use a call back rattle or drumbeat. Become fully aware of and connected to your body and slowly open your eyes.

5. Journal about your encounter with the Tarot Spirits. Note any messages, advice, or healing instructions. If this is your first A/B/C journey to a particular Tarot Spirit, record it on your tracking forms (see Appendix B). Include the message, gift, or instructions in abbreviated form.

6. Optionally, close with the Shamanic Crossing.

7. Blow out your candle, thanking the Spirits of place.

8. For some journeys, you may take appropriate action in this reality and act on the advice by honoring the spirit who helped you. Make

an offering, clean your altar, sing a song, or complete a ritual. Also, follow any appropriate instructions you received in the journey.

In future pathwork steps, we will refer to the above sequence as a simple single step: "Complete your Tarot Spirit closing steps."

Making the Opening and Closing Your Own

Once you have followed the suggested opening and closing steps a few times, you can customize the steps into a personalized version that works best for you. For instance, you might find Raising Earth Power or the Shamanic Crossing powerful, or you may have a better way to create sacred space for Otherworld work—perhaps just calling to the four or seven directions. You may choose to omit the flame of the three Suns from your journey. If you are doing this journey somewhere you do not have a candle, you can always imagine the flame.

You may use an abbreviated opening when your time is limited. Choose the steps that ring true for you. Create a reliable familiarity with your own customized version. Repeating the same steps into and out of the journey creates a ritual that connects with the power of prior journeys. It takes you deeper and more quickly into a shamanic state of consciousness.

One important reminder for everyone is not to be too concerned with getting the sequence perfect. If your intention is to create good and have respect for the spirits, then minor variations or mistakes are not a problem. You may forget a step for one journey or even reverse some directional information. That is fine. It is the intention in your heart that matters. If you enter this with a good heart and a clear focused intention, it will turn out fine. So, be easy on yourself.

Pathwork B: Meet a Tarot Spirit

The next step on your journey with the Tarot Spirits is Pathwork B. The purpose of Pathwork B is to engage directly with a Tarot Spirit and have a mutual exchange.

Remember that you want to complete a separate Pathwork B journey for each Tarot Spirit you plan to do deeper work with. It is best to complete Pathwork A previously with the same Tarot Spirit as discussed in Chapter 3, although once you have done Pathwork A with a few Tarot Spirits, you can combine Pathworks A and B into one journey. You should also have connected with a caring tarot guide in Chapter 4 who goes with you on these journeys. You can review the discussion about which Tarot Spirits to work with in Chapter 1 to help prioritize your AstroTarot work.

Steps for Pathwork B: Meet a Tarot Spirit

In Pathwork B, you will negotiate what each Tarot Spirit needs from you to work harmoniously with them, and likely receive a gift from them.

Journey intention: Connect with the individual Tarot Spirit named _____[insert Tarot Spirit name].

1. Complete your Tarot Spirit opening steps from earlier in this chapter.
2. Optional: If you have not previously done Pathwork A (get a message) with this Tarot Spirit, you can do it now, and then continue with Pathwork B in the same journey.
3. See the flame of the three suns at the entrance to the bridge. Pass through it with your guide to the center of the bridge. See the tarot card scene, and walk together across the bridge into the scene, meeting the Tarot Spirit. Alternatively, you may walk through the scene and transport to a special place where the Tarot Spirit resides.
4. On the first visit, ask the Tarot Spirit two questions:

   - "What do you request from me to work with you?"
   - "Do you have a gift for me that I need in my life?"

5. Work with the Tarot Spirit and your guide to get clear on the answers. If needed, negotiate the necessary actions to collaborate. The gift is usually placed some place in your astral body. Your guide can help you get more information about how to use the gift.
6. If at any time your guide tells you to leave, or you feel that you should "get out of there," do so with your guide's help (discussed further below under "safety").
7. Complete your Tarot Spirit closing steps from earlier in this chapter.

Pathwork B is the key to connecting with each unique Tarot Spirit. Do complete Pathwork B with each individual Tarot Spirit before pursuing other work. Do Pathwork B before you ask for healing, advice, or teaching. Do it with each one before working with a pair or group of Tarot Spirits to resolve astrological tension (Pathwork K in Chapter 13), or before you complete the power balancing circle of hands (Pathwork I1 in Chapter 9). You only need to do Pathwork B once with each of the 22 Tarot Spirits.

Reports on the Pathwork B Experience

Reports from those who have done Pathwork B are included below. Again, honor your own true experience. Do not compare your experience to others.

> *Shawn.* I traveled to the High Priestess. It was really lovely seeing her. She gave me a triple Moon necklace as a reminder that I need to do more to honor the Moon, like follow the Moon cycles more. And that's also what she asked me to do. This is like, OK, we're going to start at the beginning.

> *Renee.* I journeyed to the Hermit—in my deck it's the Hooded Man. It was very interesting because I hadn't journeyed to him before. He said he was the key that unlocks all of the teachings. He welcomed me as the daughter of the Dagda [a Celtic ancestral good god] and asked me to land in my embodied heart. Then the gift given was a torch to carry to see through to the true path in dark places. It will illuminate and light up when I am tracking clearly.

> *Christine.* In the beginning of my journey there was a lot of confusion. A centaur appeared and I didn't feel safe. I thought, "What is going on?" My guide was with me, and I realized my legs were crossed and my fingers were interlocked. I felt tension in my body. The minute I released the crossed legs and interlocked fingers the centaurs ran away. Then I was able to connect back with my tarot guide and trust her to take me to the High Priestess. So that was interesting for me. Just as soon as I got to the High Priestess, she put a big snake around me. It felt very comforting and loving. It was filling me with confidence and just peace and acceptance of all of the cycles of life. Then she went on to infuse one of the rings that I own that I didn't have on—I don't know why she chose that particular one. It's a labradorite ring. She asked me to wear it for the

rest of the week. She infused it with a protection shield. So, I enjoyed that journey.

Kate. I chose the High Priestess as I felt connected to her. I did both A and B journeys together. In the A portion of the journey, I told her that I felt very connected to her, and she said "You were once one of us. You were a priestess, and that's why you feel such a strong connection." When I moved on to the B part of the journey, her message to me was to "open up your heart to love." When I told her, "I'm not quite sure how to do that," she said, "Yes you do, you remember, you remember." Then she put her hand flat against my chest and said, "Here. This is your heart. Open it up." This was a warmly personal experience and left me wanting to meet with the High Priestess again.

Carol. What came through was my tarot guide was standing quite away from the back of me and holding space for me. The Spirit came through and put their hand on my third eye and just said that was my gift. That the third eye was being opened. Then I had a flood of colors coming through. It was very peaceful and clear.

Questions about Pathwork B: Receiving the Gift

When I ask the Tarot Spirit, "What do you request from me to work with you?" their request was more than I could commit to. What do I do? The next section covers this, but please remember, it's a request, not a command. In your work with the Tarot Spirits, both sovereignty and reciprocity are recommended. So, while you should likely give some commitment in exchange for the gift you receive, it is up to you to negotiate it clearly. You can let your tarot guide help you have the discussion. Commit only to what you can actually deliver. Keep in mind that Tarot Spirits live in the Otherworld and may not always grasp what suits your everyday life.

What happens if the Tarot Spirit doesn't show up? Consider returning another day for the journey. It is best to have done Pathwork A first. Be sure to scan the card before you close your eyes. Also, be open to receiving information through all the senses. Rather than seeing and hearing the Tarot Spirit like in a movie, you may have more of a sense of their presence or a telepathic knowing of their gift or message to you.

What if I lack the understanding to practically apply the gift in my life? Ask the Tarot Spirit the gift's purpose and how to use it. You can ask for your tarot guide's help in getting answers. The gift details might be disclosed gradually. Go test it in ordinary reality, see the outcome, and journey again for further instructions. You might receive the information kinesthetically as a felt sense in the body.

Tarot Spirit Considerations

When working with Tarot Spirits, keep in mind the important factors of sovereignty, reciprocity, incremental progress, safety and mutual respect. Engender a partnership approach. It helps create a successful spiritual relationship.

Sovereignty

It is best to work with the Tarot Spirits as partners. Have a relationship of mutual respect. If you approach them in a worshipful way, you may simply follow their suggestions or commands without considering what is best for you. Remember that Tarot Spirits are Otherworld spirits. They may not have a clear idea of your personal reality in this world. They can provide valuable insight and healing, but sometimes their advice needs to be filtered to be useful and practical in this world. Both you and the Tarot Spirits are sovereign individuals. Sovereignty is the center of the Celtic wheel of directions. It is important that each others' sovereignty be upheld through mutual respect.

To be powerful in your life, you must be the driver, and not just follow the instructions from another entity. The entity could be a boss, a spouse, a partner, a Tarot Spirit, a god, or a goddess. In a relationship of mutual respect and mutual sovereignty, you might receive advice from a Tarot Spirit. Then it is up to you to either choose to follow that advice directly or modify it. You may choose to make some modifications to the advice to fit your situation and circumstances more appropriately. Don't just follow spiritual advice blindly.

Reciprocity

In balance to sovereignty is reciprocity. It is important to have a balance and fair exchange. So, you don't just ask for a gift from the Tarot Spirit. You first ask: "What do you request from me to work with you?" You may work with your guide and the Tarot Spirit to negotiate that request. Their initial request may not always be right for you. Arrive at a commitment you can fulfill in exchange for the offered gift. This is reciprocity. Reciprocity is the balance needed as you take the gift of resources, yet make accommodations that sustain balance and work for you.

Figure 7. The Hermit is key 9 (IX) in the tarot Major Arcana. The Hermit represents the zodiac sign Virgo and carries the archetype of meditation, knowledge and personal retreat. This resonates with the inward journey we take to explore the Tarot Spirits. *Credit: DruidCraft Tarot.*

Incremental Progress

In addition to sovereignty and reciprocity, the idea of incremental progress is important. As you engage with the Tarot Spirits and work on some of your life issues and conflicts, you need to respect the pace at which it is appropriate to heal. You may need to walk before you run. As an introvert, you may be advised to step out of your comfort zone and embrace an extroverted lifestyle. That may not work and may push you further into your shell. Aim for a compromise. Rather than going out and talking to 20 people this week, it might be best to talk to just one. Making gradual progress is crucial. Steady movement toward a goal is better than smashing against it and being pushed backwards.

One reason you are working with a tarot guide is to have an intermediary who is focused on your best interests. Tarot Spirits can help with bigger life issues, but they may just see the final transformation or goal rather than the incremental steps needed to get there. Or one Tarot Spirit may work with part of the issue, while another one works in a different area for you. Your tarot guide sees the big picture and is sensitive to how fast you can move. If a Tarot Spirit insists on moving too fast, the guide can slow things down, negotiate, or if necessary, just give you a break from a fast transformation. You can come back later when you are ready for the next step.

Safety

The main reason you go to meet the Tarot Spirits with a compassionate guide is safety. The lower and upper shamanic worlds are safe places where you encounter loving and compassionate healing spirits, whether they be in the form of power animals, guides, teachers, goddesses, gods or Tarot Spirits. When we talk about safety, it is primarily the safety of your process that is important. While the Tarot Spirits are at their core loving and compassionate, some of them can be strong and confrontational. For example, working with the Sun or the Empress is usually easy, while working with the Devil, the Tower, or Death may be more challenging.

You may have to work with several of the easier Tarot Spirits first, in order to build your confidence. Then you can face some of the more challenging Tarot Spirits who may use tough love, bring forward challenging concepts, or call you out on your weaknesses. As discussed under "Incremental Progress" you want to build your strength gradually so you can deal with deeper or more painful issues. The tarot guide helps with that. They know your learning threshold and what you can handle. They can negotiate to back off from a change you are not quite ready for. But remember, safety is not an excuse for staying stuck. While it is appropriate to move forward based on each individual's history and strength, staying in past patterns that have held you back does not help. As you identify issues you want to resolve in your life, use the power of the Tarot Spirits to address them. They are powerful healers and helpers.

Engaging with them at least once a week will help you maintain steady progress.

Mutual Respect

In conclusion, the core idea is respect: respect of both you and the spirits, respect of your own process, and respect of the advice and healing you will receive. Learn from journeys and implement changes that work for you. There is also respect for the shamanic process. Often in the shamanic way of working, issues can resolve without the usual problem solving or psychological process we have been taught needs to happen. It is important for you to let that resolution carry through and show up in your life. Be open to change happening, even without the luxury of seeing a logical connection. Be open to positive things happening and be aware when parts of you sabotage progress with old thinking, like:

- "This can't be resolved this easily."
- "I must fight this change."
- "I can't move out of my comfort zone."
- "I don't deserve this good fortune."

Allow your mind to have these thoughts as you purposefully move forward in life. Just acknowledge those thoughts and move ahead both practically and spiritually. Be grateful for the Tarot Spirits' assistance and embrace the potential for miracles and positive change. As evidence emerges that the thoughts are not in line with actual progress, you can release them. You can also realize that even with spiritual help, you need to do your part and take the actions needed to move your life forward.

Chapter 5 Recap

In this chapter you learned a bit more about the relationship to Otherworld spirits and the roles they play. You had an opportunity to meet a Tarot Spirit and make a connection. With Pathwork B, you likely received a gift you can explore to see how it can be applied in this world. Give some thought to how you can work with the Tarot Spirits in partnership and balance. In the next chapter you can deepen your relationship.

6: Know the Tarot Spirits

For Pathwork A, B, and C, the term "pathwork" refers to a Western Mystery tradition of connecting with particular parts of the Otherworld. Your goal is to build your understanding and power. For each Tarot Spirit you plan to work with, it is best to complete Pathwork C after completing Pathwork A and B. See Chapter 3 for Pathwork A: Tarot Scanning. See Chapter 5 for Pathwork B: Meeting a Tarot Spirits.

Pathwork C: Know a Tarot Spirit

Pathwork C is not always mandatory for every interaction, as Pathwork B may be enough. Completing Pathwork C deepens the relationship with each Tarot Spirit and makes deeper journeys go more smoothly.

However, Pathwork B is the key to making an initial connection with each Tarot Spirit, so don't skip it. You also need a connection with a caring tarot guide who goes with you on every Tarot Spirit journey.

If you have trouble with one of the other healing, advice, learning, or reconciliation pathworks, go back to Pathwork C for the Tarot Spirits involved. Pathwork C builds a greater level of trust with the Tarot Spirits involved in other pathwork.

Steps for Pathwork C: Know a Tarot Spirit

The purpose of Pathwork C is to better know and connect with each individual Tarot Spirit through personal experience.

Journey intention: Get to know better the individual Tarot Spirit _____[insert Tarot Spirit name].

1. Complete your Tarot Spirit opening steps from Chapter 5.
2. When you arrive at the Tarot Spirit's place, hang out and get to know the Tarot Spirit. Its like having tea, beer, coffee, or wine with a friend. Useful questions for the Tarot Spirit:

    • What is your connection to my external world?

- What aspect of my reality do you create or sustain?
- Show me your territory in non-ordinary reality. Where do you live in the Otherworld landscape?
- Why are your clothes as they are?
- Why is it hard to see, hear, or touch you?
- Ask about the gift you received in Pathwork B and how to use it practically in your life.

3. Work with your guide for help to interpret answers.
4. If at any time your guide tells you to leave, or you feel that you should "get out of there," do so with your guide's help (see "safety" in Chapter 5).
5. Complete your Tarot Spirit closing steps from Chapter 5.

Questions about Pathwork C, Knowing a Tarot Spirit

Should I study the meaning of each tarot card in the literature before meeting a Tarot Spirit? It is best to enter Pathwork A, B, or C naively, without much historical information about each tarot card. Then you can have a fresh experience of the Tarot Spirits' qualities directly from them. If you are already a student of tarot or an experienced tarot reader, put your learning aside and meet the Tarot Spirit freshly. Be open to receiving some new or surprising information about this key in the Major Arcana. Once you have had the initial experience of getting fresh information about one of the Tarot Spirits, it can be interesting to read what one of the experts says about a card, and then go ask the Tarot Spirit what they think. You may be surprised at what they have to say.

What if the Tarot Spirit appears quite differently than the picture on the tarot card? This is quite possible. Be open to how the Tarot Spirit appears. Feel free to ask them what their appearance means? What does it symbolize? Get your tarot guide engaged in the conversation. You may learn something new and interesting about this particular Tarot Spirit. Remember, you may have other senses engaged, like feeling the shape of the Tarot Spirit, or engaging with their sound or smell.

Reports on the Pathwork C Experience

Reports from those who have done Pathwork C are included below. Again, honor the truth of your own experience. Don't compare your experience to others.

Shagufta: Pathwork C: The Empress told me she creates the part of my reality that is ease and abundance. She said ease is a shelter, a place of power. She said she works in a seated position because what she does is not born out of laborious efforts but with ease. In Pathwork B, she gave me a cluster of purple grapes and said that I can freely take.

Nancy: I journeyed to the High Priestess. She was in a beautiful moonlit temple wearing shimmery blue and silver robes. The area of my outer reality she creates and sustains is my intuitive learning and she helps with my book learning as well. I asked her if her Moon crown was heavy, and she laughed, saying it was as light as air. The atmosphere was all silvery and light. I danced for her.

Chapter 6 Recap

Pathwork C takes you deeper into your relationship with a Tarot Spirit. It can help you build trust as you both work together. Go back and repeat Pathwork C if you are having difficulty with a Tarot Spirit in other pathwork.

Part 1 Recap

In Part 1, you learned how to journey, connected with a tarot guide, and learned the basic Pathwork A/B/C that creates engagement with individual Tarot Spirits. This initial engagement is very important. The connection with Tarot Spirits built with the A/B/C pathwork may seem a bit trivial; however, it is the important basis of the AstroTarot work. These steps allow you to build trust with the Tarot Spirits and for them to build trust with you. Your tarot guide is also a very important player in this work. Look to them to help you progress with the Tarot Spirits and make positive changes in your life.

Honor Your Personal Experience

Hopefully, you have done the pathwork exercises so far and made a connection with one or more Tarot Spirits. Remember, reading and thinking about the exercises does not produce the results of actually doing the exercises. While you have a time investment in doing the A/B/C pathwork with the Tarot Spirits, it is the base work needed to produce lasting personal life results. Strive for incremental progress every week. You do not need to connect with all 22 of the Tarot Spirits.

The reason we will look at your personal astrological aspects in Part 3 is so you can see which Tarot Spirits to really focus on. We will discuss this more in Part 3. The greatest life improvement can be made working with Spirits who represent those potentially challenging natal aspects. For now, doing Pathwork A/B/C for the Tarot Spirits representing the traditional planets prepares you for the astrological work. Those planetary spirits are the Sun, the High Priestess (Moon), the Empress (Venus), the Magician (Mercury), the Wheel of Fortune (Jupiter), the Tower (Mars), and the World (Saturn).

Figure 8. The Moon is key 18 (XVIII) in the tarot Major Arcana. The Moon represents the zodiac sign Pisces and carries the archetype of the lunar cycle. Getting to know The Moon can open the door to better understanding of your unconscious. *Credit: DruidCraft Tarot.*

Work Incrementally

Your purpose in working on the exercises in this book is not to resolve every issue in one journey, but to learn how to do the pathwork journeys, so you can work with specific Tarot Spirits over time. The Tarot Spirits you work with will depend on your personal needs and interests. Set a goal for how many journeys you want to do each week. Then do them on a regular basis. Creating a plan for your basic pathwork journeys is discussed in Appendix B.

Now that you have learned the basic pathwork journeys to make a foundational connection, you can move on to meeting your special Tarot Spirits, meeting your shadow-self, and receiving advice, healing, and learning from individual Tarot Spirits.

Get your free resource material!

If you haven't already, check out the online resources that support the book *Tarot Spirit Healing*. They include:

- Shamanic journey drumming tracks for 10, 20, and 30 minute journeys.
- Blank forms for tracking pathwork and *AstroTarot mapping*.
- High resolution color graphics in pdf format.
- Video lessons: *Tarot Spirits: Who's on Deck?* and a *Tour of the Major Arcana*.
- Video lesson: *Shamanic Crossing*.
- Join the mailing list for updates on Tarot Spirit books and courses.
- Discounted offers for related online courses.

Check out these book resources at
www.reidhart.com/tsh-resources

Part 2: Advice and Healing from the Tarot Spirits

Figure 9. The Sun is key 19 (XIX) in the tarot Major Arcana. He carries the archetype of illumination and is a great healer. *Credit: DruidCraft Tarot.*

Now that you have learned how to engage with the Tarot Spirits in Part 1, Part 2 starts you on the path of healing with the Tarot Spirits:

- Find your special Tarot Spirits in Chapter 7 and make a connection with each of them. You'll learn about the cycle of becoming.
- In Chapter 8, take a journey to meet your shadow-self with Pathwork N. They are an important character that will be part of your Tarot Spirit journey.
- Receive advice or guidance from selected Tarot Spirit(s) in Chapter 9 using Pathwork H1. You'll learn to balance power with the Tarot Spirits using the circle of hands Pathwork I1.
- Receive personal healing directly from one Tarot Spirit in Chapter 10, using Pathwork J1.

The main section of this book will give you the information you need to move through the process of meeting the Tarot Spirits, receiving healing and advice, and resolving your astrological challenges. Additional background for Part 2 is in these appendices:

- Appendix A has resources and recommended books with descriptions.
- Appendix E has detailed directions for finding your special Tarot Spirits, as discussed in Chapter 7.

7: Special Tarot Spirits

Special Tarot Spirits are unique for each individual. You find them using a numerological treatment of your birthdate. They form a special relationship to your personality and soul path. Angeles Arrien[19] developed the concept in the 1980s and Mary Greer popularized it in her book *Tarot for Yourself*.[20] Mary Greer expanded the concept to include the hidden factor cards and tarot constellations.[21]

Your Special Tarot Spirits

There are four (or more) special Tarot Spirits you can work with:

- The **personality** card shows what lessons are here for you in this lifetime. This Tarot Spirit can be an outstanding teacher for practical matters related to your life.
- The **soul** card shows your purpose through all lifetimes. This Tarot Spirit can inform you of your long-term multi-life purpose. They can bring you lessons about how to engage in this lifetime related to this cosmic purpose.
- The **year** card is based on your annual birthday each year. You can consult them for practical matters during the year in question.
- The **hidden-factor** card(s) can be helpful in exploring shadow material or deeper lessons for yourself.

Working with these cards as Tarot Spirits can be enlightening. The Tarot Spirits discovered here have a special relationship with you and can support your optimum life. After working with them individually in Part 2, you can combine these spirits with spirits related to your natal astrology to form Tarot Spirit circles in Chapter 14. These personally unique circles help you improve different areas of your life.

---

[19] Arrien, A. *The Tarot Handbook.*
[20] Greer, M. *Tarot for Yourself.*
[21] Greer, M. *Tarot Constellations.*

Find Your Special Tarot Spirits

Section 1 of your *AstroTarot mapping* lists your special Tarot Spirits. The example below shows a portion of the mapping from the *My AstroTarot Report* in Appendix G.

		Personality	Soul	Hidden Factor
Month	3			
Day	4			
Year	2010			
M + D + Y Total	2017			
2 + 0 + 1 + 7 =	10			
1 + 0 =	1			
1 + 0 =	1			

10	*Personality Card*	**Wheel of Fortune**
1	*Soul Card*	**Magician**
19	*Hidden Factor T.S.*	**The Sun**

Figure 10. The image above shows the Special Cards section from a personalized *My AstroTarot Report*.

In this example, the personality, soul and hidden-factor cards are unique. In many cases some cards may be the same. Sometimes, a pair or three cards serve multiple shared functions, as discussed in Appendix E. If you do not get your *My AstroTarot Report* as described in Appendix G, find your special Tarot Spirits following the instructions in Appendix E.

Work with Your Special Tarot Spirits

Once you go through Pathwork A/B/C (Scan / Meet / Know) with your special Tarot Spirits, you can work with them and your tarot guide in journeys to get personal questions answered.

Questions for your designated **personality** Tarot Spirit include:

- What qualities can I manifest and reinforce in this lifetime?
- How do I contribute to those in my community?
- What is my lesson on the current earth walk?
- What can I do to develop a full range of positive interactions with others?

Questions for your designated **soul** Tarot Spirit include:

- What is my long-term soul's purpose?
- How do I make the best of my natural talents?
- What growth should I strive for in this life?
- What can I do to grow spiritually?

Questions you can ask your current **year** Tarot Spirit:

- What is my lesson for the year?
- What should I focus on this year?
- What opportunities should I prepare for this year?
- What obstacles should I prepare for this year?
- What practical changes can I make right now

The Hidden-Factor Spirit and your Shadow-Self

In Chapter 8, you will meet your shadow-self. They will join all your journeys with the Tarot Spirits. They offer insight and an alternative viewpoint. Connecting with your shadow-self helps reveal untapped potential, address imbalances, and reconcile difficult planetary influences.

Your **hidden-factor** Tarot Spirit relates to the numerological family of your personality and soul cards. They can help you work with your shadow-self. To better understand your shadow-self, ask your hidden-factor Tarot Spirit questions like:

- Do parts of me have hidden agendas to reveal?
- What shadow parts of myself need recognition now?
- How do I best work with my shadow parts or selves?
- How can my shadow-self contribute to my healing?

You can invite any of these special Tarot Spirits into circles you will work with in Chapter 14. Your special Tarot Spirits add their insight and healing to your AstroTarot work.

The Cycle of Becoming

Before we dive into the theory of the cycle of becoming, let me share my story related to this concept:

> *Reid:* As I reflect on my life, I remember that when I practiced Tibetan Buddhism intently, the meditation practice would have almost a numbing effect. With the stress of my day-to-day life, in meditation, it would be like a shower of honey pouring down over the pain. Relief came, but the root cause remained unaddressed. At this time, I started digging deeper into my psychological history with four-years of personal growth through Hakomi psychotherapy, followed by Hakomi therapist training. Finally, there was enough psychological material cleared to continue pursuing a spiritual path. As I worked shamanically with my Tarot Spirits, hidden personal tendencies were revealed: fear of authority, challenges in close relationships, and overfocus on work. The Tarot Spirits aided me in personal and spiritual growth. Subtle changes resulted in increased life satisfaction.

I have discussed with my spirit teachers the purpose of engaging in shamanic work. They have told me about "the cycle of becoming." This is a pattern that initiatory shamanic work follows. The cycle of becoming has three phases:

- **Healing.** The first step is to let go of past hurts and move forward. To release past hurts, you must first recognize and heal them. Shamanic healing brings many methods to remove lingering pain and support your more empowered self. Remember that, in addition to shamanic healing at the spiritual level, you might need psychotherapeutic or medical aid.
- **Transformation**. Transformation helps you release what no longer serves you. Then you can bring in what you need next in your life. You move forward on an enlivened trajectory toward an intentional future. You create intentional manifestation. You can ask spirit helpers to use ancient magic traditions to aid in your transformational process.
- **Initiation.** After you attain the next level of healing and transformation, you are ready for initiation. Spirits help you find a deeper connection to the true nature of the universe. Instead of

adopting a rigid belief system, you receive direct revelation from the spirits. Your connection with the spirits often leads to service for your community and your world.

The cycle of becoming is not linear, but a cycle. You work incrementally layer by layer. The Tarot Spirits heal what is present, then move you to the next incremental level of transformation. The Tarot Spirits initiate you into the next spiritual space available. Then the cycle can repeat, working at a higher level of vibration: healing, transformation, then initiation.

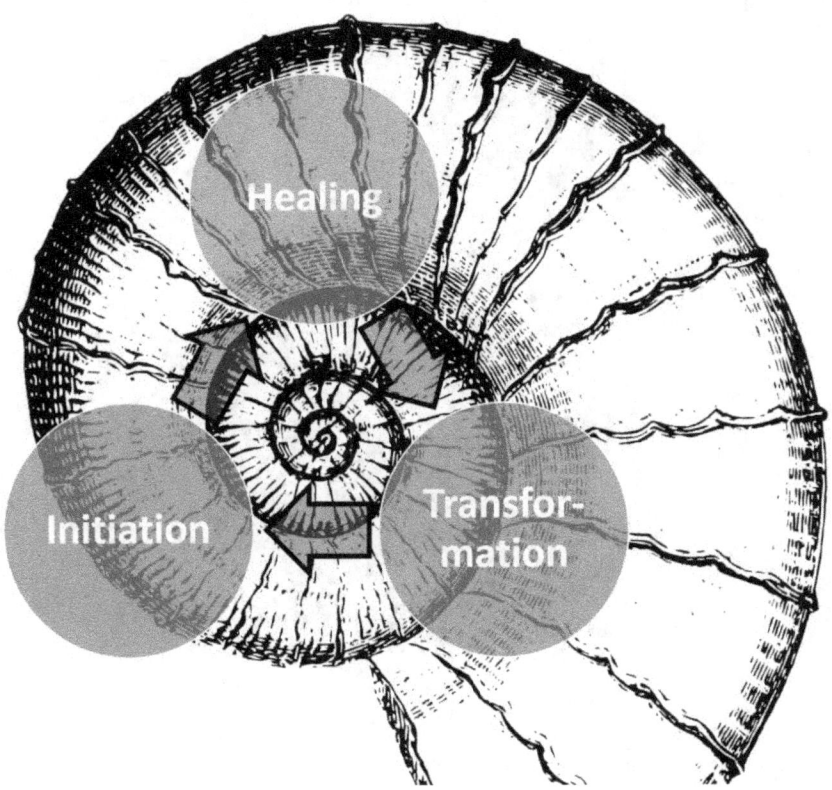

Figure 11. The cycle of becoming continues in a circle, moving from healing to transformation to initiation. Then spiraling up to the next level. *Background image credit: Emmie Norfolk at Pixabay.*

Be aware that a spiritual approach can be wonderful, or it can be an escape. It is important to deal with base level psychological pain, bring the shadow into the light, and move forward. That can be done in either a psychological context or a shamanic context. As you work with the Tarot

Spirits, they bring transformative healing, which differs from layering over pain with a balm of meditation or spiritual escape. We each have our own path. Mine had a period of psychological introspection, although it went beyond basic talk therapy. Others may more easily receive healing directly from the spirits. When the spirits bring healing, it is pure and brings divine light into the soul. It is different from covering up wounds of the past and putting off resolution for another day. When the divine light comes into your being, you'll notice it brings truth and relief. Forgiveness and gratitude are important parts of this process. Healing from the spirits is a vital step in the cycle of healing, transformation, and initiation.

Figure 12. Temperance is key 14 (XIV) in the tarot Major Arcana. Temperance, called the *Fferyllt* in the *DruidCraft Tarot,* represents the zodiac sign Sagittarius and carries the archetype of balance and alchemy. *Fferyllt* means alchemist in Welsh. Temperance often provides transformation in the cycle of becoming. *Credit: DruidCraft Tarot.*

For effective Tarot Spirit work, first work with healing. Then focus on transformation. Then engage shamanic initiation by the spirits. Healing with the Tarot Spirits can be direct. Shamanic healing is discussed in more detail in Chapter 10. Healing can also result from reconciling challenging aspects in your astrological chart. Along the way, transform your relationship to your shadow-self, as discussed in Chapter 8. Once challenges are cleared, pursue initiation into the mystery of the tarot and planetary powers, as discussed in Chapter 15.

Each individual has their own path to their spiritual evolution. The spirits know what's next that is helpful. There is not some overarching manifesto or plan that everyone must follow. The cycle of becoming follows your own unique path so you can achieve your unique personal destiny and spiritual realization.

Chapter 7 Recap

Now that you have learned how to make a connection to the Tarot Spirits in Part 1, you have found a few special spirits that are important players in your life. The numerological approach to finding these special Tarot Spirits is less complicated than mapping your astrology. It directs you toward a few Tarot Spirits to start doing practical work with. You also learned about the cycle of becoming, a process you can apply for continuous personal improvement. Next we find your shadow-self, then pursue advice and healing from the Tarot Spirits.

8: Meet Your Shadow-self

The reason you want to meet the Spirit representing your shadow-self is so they can be present in your Tarot Spirit circles. They may speak up about something that might otherwise be overlooked. No need to delve too deeply into shadow work right now. Meeting your shadow-self in the Otherworld lets you invite them to the rest of your pathwork. When the shadow-self is present, they can reveal information about one of your shadow parts. This may help the Tarot Spirits give healing and support for that shadow part.

You may get some advice from the Tarot Spirits and say, "I could never do that." And then the shadow-self says, "Well, wait a minute, why not?" Or maybe you have an angry part that you don't want to act out. Yet, it's beneficial to connect with your anger as a motivating force. For example, many of us were taught that anger is not acceptable. Sometimes that anger is necessary—not to act out against someone, but to make sure that you are assertive enough or to move things in the right direction. You can channel anger either for personal boundaries or for social justice.

Considering the shadow-self often prompts questions like:

- Who is my shadow-self?
- What is the shadow?
- Is it scary?
- What does it mean?

Many people who may not have engaged with shadow work may feel a little trepidation about getting into it. You can start by just acknowledging or witnessing your shadow-self. You can save the deeper shadow work for when we take it up later in the book series.

Your shadow-self is an important personage to have involved in these journeys with Tarot Spirits. Your shadow-self brings in another perspective about your inner workings. You might present a pleasant face and the shadow-self may bring in some information that you weren't quite ready to divulge. They can move things along with better transparency. The presence of the shadow-self can get you closer to what you need to heal.

The shadow includes anything hidden or repressed, spanning a broad range of material. It's a psychological concept, but it could also cover areas of your life you gave up on. Examples of identifiable shadow material include:

- Sports or other abilities never pursued.
- Hobbies or interests you wanted to pursue, but never did, like learning to knit or going fishing.
- Repressed anger at unfairness or perpetrators. Dealing with dynamic family situations. It can be pretty heavy. Maybe to survive as a child—as someone without power in a strong family dynamic—you had to bite your tongue or go along with things you didn't want to do.
- Debating abilities or being kept quiet, like "Girls don't talk that way" or "A gentleman doesn't say that." So, you repressed it.
- Financial pressure that kept you from pursuing a career of genuine interest, since you have to put food on the table.
- Sexual repression because of shame or religion.
- Musical pursuits or talents dropped because of criticism or lack of opportunity.
- Internal tendencies that show up as projection onto others when their behaviors bother you.

Unfolding over time, the discovery of your shadow-self will be beneficial. It's like peeling back the layers of an onion to get to the core material. It's a process that you can pursue gently. Be sure to have this character, this aspect of yourself, available for your pathwork. As you move into larger Tarot Spirit groups, present in the journey will be yourself, your tarot guide, several Tarot Spirits, and also your own shadow-self.

The shadow-self's job is to call you out if you're presenting something that is not really true. The shadow-self provides another viewpoint to consider. In a way, the shadow-self is the opposite of your persona. What act have you put together to survive in this world? Perhaps you adopted the goody-two-shoes act. If it was important to be agreeable, then the rebellious part would be the disavowed shadow part that you did not allow to come forward. Perhaps you chose to be the rebellious one, leaving the cooperative one hidden in shadow. When cooperation is hidden, you cannot be helpful when needed. Working with the shadow is not about acting inappropriately in real life or creating damage to others. It is about recognizing honestly those parts of yourself that:

- Are repressed
- You can bring forward into the light
- You can find out more about
- You can understand better
- You can embrace and bring into your circle of knowing

It does mean you want to accept and forgive internal tendencies that may be socially unpopular. Where possible, you can redirect those tendencies to a more positive purpose. The result is the ability to work with more of your inner self present.

So, the shadow-self isn't tied to a particular Tarot Spirit or to a particular shadow part. It's a separate Spirit representing the hidden things in your life. It will be a Spirit in non-ordinary reality that represents the fusion of all of your shadow parts. In contrast, your tarot guide shows up at the bridge and takes you to meet the Tarot Spirits with a role of guidance and protection. Your shadow-self's role is to be there with the Tarot Spirits to remind you of things you may have left behind, things you may not have pursued, or things that are hidden, repressed, or buried. It's just another character to have in the circle as you're having these interactions with the Tarot Spirits.

We all wear masks in society, projecting what we think others want to see. The shadow-self can be the minority report. While you may not be ready to reveal shadow parts publicly, it's OK to have them present in these private sessions you're having with the Tarot Spirits. You'll get a better understanding of your full motivations by hearing what the shadow-self has to say.

Pathwork N: Meet Your Shadow-self

To help you get in touch with the shadow-self, bring along the hidden-factor Tarot Spirit that you found in Chapter 7. Be sure to complete Pathworks A, B, and C with them first if you have not already done so. The hidden-factor card does not represent your shadow. Your shadow-self is a spirit entity unto itself, just like your astral spirit is present as yourself in the journey. The hidden-factor Tarot Spirit is there to help find and understand your shadow, answer questions about your shadow, or help you draw out your shadow. Its role is to ask questions to help you understand your shadow-self. It's like a shadow teacher who teaches you about your shadow-self or how you might bring that part of yourself out into the open constructively.

So, you may touch on some sensitive areas. You will get into conflict and issues related to the shadow. You need to get these things out in the open—at least into your conscious mind—so you can get this shadow character to engage with this process in your Tarot Spirit group work. The shadow is an important part of yourself to engage with. If you've been touched by something that you feel could use some healing, you can do Pathwork J1 in Chapter 10: going to a Tarot Spirit and requesting healing. You can use that process for healing around shadow issues. Many Tarot Spirits have remarkable healing abilities. You can work with them directly. First, though, you need to meet your shadow-self and let them help bring shadow parts into the light.

Steps for Pathwork N: Meet Your Shadow-self

Journey intention: Meet your shadow-self who brings another point of view into your Tarot Spirit pathwork. Use the hidden-factor card from Chapter 7 as the one you scan for this journey.

1. Complete your Tarot Spirit opening steps from Chapter 5.
2. Ask your guide to take you to meet your hidden-factor Tarot Spirit and your shadow-self.
3. Introduce yourself to your shadow-self and ask what is true but hidden; consult with the hidden-factor Tarot Spirit if needed.
4. Complete your Tarot Spirit closing steps from Chapter 5.

When you return from this journey it may be helpful to write a description of your shadow-self, or even make a rough sketch or draw a symbol for them. Another option is to sort through the court cards in your tarot deck and see if one of them reminds you of your shadow-self. We explore this approach in more detail in a later book in the series. If you find yourself working specifically with the shadow-self in a future journey you can read your description, scan your sketch or symbol, or scan the court card that resonated with the shadow-self just before the journey. You only need to do this when you are focusing on shadow aspects. Your shadow-self will be along for all your other journeys, but you only need to scan them or review their description when you are really focused on shadow material in a particular journey.

Reports on Pathwork N: Experience of the Shadow-self

Reports from those who have done this pathwork are included below. Honor the truth of your own experience. Avoid comparing your experience to others.

Renee: In the journey I returned to the place where I have visited my shadow-self before. It is a round, mirrored room beneath the Healing Water's Pool within the High Priestess's Temple. There are stairways going down on both sides of the Healing Pool that lead into a pitch-black space that houses the shadow-self. When I first visited this space, the shadow-self was cast face down upon the ground amongst broken shards of mirror that held images of fragmented selves. Her eyes were shut tight. Now, after working with the Tarot Spirits and the shadow-self for some time, I find her sitting upright in the center of the space with her eyes open. I notice that large parts of the mirrored walls are now intact and there are fewer fragments of broken shards on the ground. I realize that as the work is done, more of the scenery of seeing through the mirrors is coming into view, integrating more of the whole picture of my soul's incarnation, intentions, and gifts being received into this lifetime. I ask the shadow, "what is most important for me to know at this time?" She answers she is the greatest wisdom-keeper I will ever meet, and it is worth my time and energy to honor her and learn from all that she will reveal.

Reid: I probably would not have chosen to go down the road to becoming an engineer in my life, although I needed to put food on the table and engineering paid pretty well. It did fit with some of my abilities. So, I went down that road. The esoteric subjects covered in this book are much more what I'm interested in doing: working with spiritual and Western Mystery traditions. When I met my shadow-self, he pointed out that I can not hide my mystic side. When I was an engineering supervisor at an electric utility, the word somehow got out about my shamanic work. People came to me for healing support if they were going in for an operation. So, I learned that I might try to hide my true avocation, but it came out anyway.

Rhonda: The overall paramount for me at this time is procrastination, and I saw that clearly. I've got a bit to do and also the High Priestess talked to me about that earlier this morning when I did Journey C with her. It's interesting. I need to work on that one. Anyway, thank you. That was really good for me.

Kate: I didn't meet my shadow-self. Tinker Bell showed up as a stand-in. She has been a special figure in my life, a magic creature. I was told that my shadow-self was afraid to meet me because I had not been very kind. Even though my shadow-self didn't want to have anything to do with me, but I found it positive that she sent Tinker Bell to check me out. I see that as a good omen for the future, but there is more work to be done here. More trust to build. I'm not quite sure how to build it, but I'm sure it will come. I'll learn.

Laurie: My shadow is just the creative force. The things that happen to us in our life become instrumental in our teaching. The things that cause us pain, we learn from. Then we create through that learning, and it becomes our badge of honor. We're able to teach others through it.

Questions about the Shadow-self

What benefit comes from working with the shadow? The biggest benefit is to notice something you may not be paying attention to: repressed, hidden, or unheard parts of yourself. Bringing a shadow part into acceptance may take time and effort, but it always will start with awareness. That is an important part of resolving whatever it is you're working with. Maybe it's simple, like, "I was never given the opportunity to do X." Unless the part that "wanted to do X and didn't" shows up in your awareness, you can't really get to resolution around that lost dream. The shadow-self can voice those hidden truths.

Does the shadow-self represent just one aspect of what is hidden or all of them? The shadow-self represents all of them. While individual aspects may surface at different times in your journeys, the shadow-self is the voice of all things hidden or repressed. In a later book in the series, we will learn to use one of the 16 royalty cards in the tarot deck to represent a particular shadow facet when scanning the cards at the start of the journey. We will work more with the idea of shadow parts and shamanic psychodrama in a later Tarot Spirits book.

How do you handle conflicts between two extremes when working with the shadow? If assertiveness is repressed, you might manifest as an accommodating or pushover person. How do you resolve that? Perhaps this is the classic feminine issue of being accommodating versus being assertive. Both could be seen as extreme. And whichever one is repressed could even lead to a physical illness. When you realize this and start being assertive, it may be awkward at first. It may be rough in the beginning as you bring something forward that has been hidden and could help you out. For example, you might have cramping stomach pains every time you assert yourself. Part of you might back away from assertion because it backfired once when you were a child. Your assertive nature got repressed. There is a gradual process of getting used to a new behavior like asserting oneself.

Is there a shadow aspect to not pursuing an interest? For example, instead of pursuing a musical career, someone could go into a nursing profession because they were not competitive enough in music. Yes, this has a shadow aspect. As a specific personal example: in elementary school I sang a French song in the talent show and got teased so mercilessly by a few students that I never pursued singing. After that, I went into theater arts. I later did acting, but I didn't do musicals. That musical part got shamed and shut down by my peers in a way that caused me never to pursue it. So that's a type of shadow. While I might pursue singing now, I haven't done that, although I do chant when doing ritual work. So, consider what level of emotional energy it has. To work with this missed musical career, you don't need to quit nursing and start a rock 'n roll band. But is there some grief over the missed career that needs expression? Or you might join a local choir? This question focuses on music, but it applies to other activities dropped because of outside pressure.

Do we heal ourselves through our shadow? For example, is it unlocking an emotional code that could hide in a physical illness? Maybe something buried from childhood traumas? Sometimes repressed emotional material will somatize in your body. You could carry it unconsciously. There can be deep body, mind, and psychological connections. As you pursue missed activities, you may feel less impact from suppressed trauma.

Is it possible to do a healing through the Tarot Spirits of your shadow-self? The idea of the shadow arises from suppressed and rejected parts. Those parts didn't get us forward in our life or they might have been a detriment to survival. They literally might have been something we couldn't express, because if we did, we wouldn't survive. It might be that extreme, but often it's not. Yet it's something that was just easier to repress to get along in life. So, the first step is to just acknowledge the truth about the shadow. That releases the energy taken to repress it. You can discover these shadow aspects working with the Tarot Spirit circles and bring them into awareness. Does that part need to be healed? It depends. Once discovered, you can ask for healing from the Tarot Spirits you are working with or the hidden-factor Tarot Spirit. Then you can engage with one of the healing pathworks if needed.

When you say the shadow-self unfolds over time, does that mean it shows itself over time, it's resolved over time, or both? Probably both. You met a representative of the shadow-self in Pathwork N so that the shadow-self will be along with you on your later journeys, as you continue your pathwork with the Tarot Spirits. Having the shadow-self present is like getting a minority report. Possibly you're looking at something with rose-colored glasses. Then the shadow-self might come up with a comment that goes deeper—closer to the truth. You might be asking for advice, and there may be a deeper question underneath your asked question that is important. The shadow-self can reveal hidden dimensions or considerations that would otherwise not get attention.

Chapter 8 Recap

Next to your tarot guide, your shadow-self is an important Otherworld Spirit for successful AstroTarot work. Being open to hearing from the shadow-self about shadow parts that may need attention provides a counterbalance to the persona who needs to look good. With the guide and shadow-self on board you can move on to receiving advice and healing.

9: Advice and Circle of Hands

You have two general goal areas in your work with the Tarot Spirits:

- Spiritual and personal growth
- Practical matters

Spiritual and personal growth proceeds with the cycle of becoming we discussed in Chapter 7: healing, transformation, and initiation. A parallel path involves practical matters that include:

- Having a life of abundance
- Having safety
- Skill development
- Creating a just and vibrant community

Figure 13. To allow for personal and spiritual growth, you need to work with the practical matters in your life, such as skills, abundance, safety, and community. *Photo credit: Graham H. at Pixabay.*

Shamanic work often involves practical work with the Spirits on behalf of the individual, the family, or the community. In true service, you expand your circle of concern out to the entire world family and all beings. The practical path requires work in several areas:

- **Advice.** In your life, or the life of the community, you are often given several choices, but no clarity on how to proceed. Connecting with the Tarot Spirits for advice and clarity can help. This advice can cover a broad range, from what vegetables to plant, what relationships to pursue, what stock or mutual fund to buy, where to live, what home remodeling to invest in, or what career path to pursue. The advice can also be spiritual in nature: what practice to pursue, which spiritual paths to study, or what mysteries to explore.

- **Learning.** You can seek learning from teachers in non-ordinary reality. The learning can relate to practical or spiritual aspects. Practical items include how to fertilize your garden or manage your investments. Spiritual aspects include how to move your vibration to the next level or how to improve your divination accuracy. The spirits may channel ancient information from human history on practical to esoteric matters. They could help you cook a spectacular dinner or do shamanic weather working responsibly. Of course, you must adapt ancient information to current times, but you may find power in rediscovering ancient ways.

- **Manifestation support**. You can reach into the Otherworld and bring support to a project or process that will benefit yourself, your family, your community, or the world. Balance your own needs with community needs. Use the Otherworld support of the Spirits to direct divine, mental, and astral energy into manifestation of your will to support the greater good. We will discuss this in more depth in a later book in the series.

- **Improvement of your world.** There are so many places to put your energy in the world community that you need direction to where you can achieve the greatest improvement with the time, resources, and energy you have available. Your goals may also benefit from direct spiritual intervention, rather than going about things in the normal way.

Pathwork H1: Tarot Spirit Advice

So far, you have worked with Tarot Spirits individually with Pathwork A/B/C. You can work with any Tarot Spirit, doing Pathwork H1 for advice and problem solving or Pathwork I1 for a general power tune up. You can combine these into one journey. We append the number 1 to H here to distinguish it from the very similar Pathwork H2 or advice from a Tarot Spirit circle and Pathwork H3 or advice on mysteries. These related pathworks are discussed in Chapters 14 and 15.

When asking for advice, you want to keep your power as discussed under Sovereignty in Chapter 5. Rather than asking for a yes or no answer to the question, "Should I move to New York?," ask: "What would be the outcome of me moving to New York?" The first question gives away your power and asks the Tarot Spirits to decide for you. The second question asks for information about how it might turn out. Keep your power by making a personal choice. Remember that the spirit's advice may need to be filtered by practical reality to be useful in your world. Your tarot guide can help filter their answers. The spirit's point of view is of the Otherworld, and you know more about how to operate in ordinary reality.

Steps for Pathwork H1: Tarot Spirit Advice

Journey intention: Get guidance, aid, or advice from Tarot Spirits.

1. Formulate your question, then use one of the three ways to determine which Tarot Spirit(s) to seek advice from:

   - Review the qualities of the Tarot Spirits as listed in Chapter 1 and choose one that fits with your topic.
   - Give your question or issue to your guide and ask which single Tarot Spirit should give you advice. Later, you will learn how to meet with multiple Tarot Spirits for advice.
   - Draw tarot cards from a shuffled deck until you get one of the tarot keys (Major Arcana). You can optionally keep the Minor Arcana cards that turned up in mind, as they may bring some additional information to your issue.

2. Complete your Tarot Spirit opening steps from Chapter 5.
3. Stand in a circle, holding hands with the Tarot Spirit, your guide, and your shadow-self. Discuss the issue. In addition to verbal advice, you may receive direct interventions or power from the Tarot Spirit. Ask the Tarot Spirit or your guide for clarification whenever needed.
4. Ask for a clearing or supporting mantra, phrase, or gesture. You can use this later when working with the question or encountering doubt or concern about it.
5. At this point, you may want to complete the circle of hands (see Pathwork I1 in the next section).
6. Complete your Tarot Spirit closing steps from Chapter 5.

Pathwork I1: Circle of Hands

The circle of hands is a powerful way to balance and exchange power with the other participants in a pathwork journey. The circle of hands process allows power to be shared and balanced with all participants in the circle. It helps you share power with the Tarot Spirits in a more direct way.

You can do Pathwork I1 alone as a separate journey with a single Tarot Spirit, spirit circle of choice, astrological challenge group, or other group of spirits. Alternatively, you can incorporate the process with another one of the pathworks as a conclusion for the journey. It works well as a follow up after pathworks for advice (H), healing (J), planetary reconciliation (K), or learning (L). Incorporate Pathwork I1 by calling for the circle of hands after completing the other work in the journey.

We add the number 1 in Pathwork I1 to distinguish it from the very similar Pathwork I2 or gratitude circle and Pathwork I3 or blessing circle. These related pathworks are discussed in Chapter 14.

A circle of hands can create a powerful and beautiful experience. You, along with your guide, shadow-self, and other Tarot Spirits, are present in the circle for the pathwork. The shadow-self you met in Chapter 8 is there as a witness. Their purpose is to contribute to group problem solving.

Power vs Energy

In Steinbrecher's original instructions for the circle of hands, the focus is on moving energy around the circle to where it is needed. Here, let's focus on letting power move. Power is distinct from energy as it has spiritual intelligence and intention. When the compassionate spirits move or deliver power it is for a healing purpose. It has the compassionate intelligence of the helping spirit integrated into the power. Energy can be moved for good or ill by practitioners, as it does not have that compassionate intelligence. So when we do the circle of hands, we should consider it a power rebalancing, where helpful power is moving in the circle to where it is needed. This distinction was important in core shamanism teachings.[22] During that three-year training, there were many times we were corrected when referring to "spirit energy" rather than "spirit power."

The distinction between energy and power may seem subtle. We will probably continue to use the word "energy" when we actually mean "power." That's OK. But do give this distinction some thought, and see if you can feel the compassionate spiritual intelligence as you receive power in the circle of hands pathwork.

During the circle of hands, make sure that you focus on your body, and notice sensations and changes in your physical body as power moves around the circle. As a personal example, when I have focused on my body in the circle, I have felt strong changes in my body as compassionate power from the spirits entered to provide healing, balance, or reinforce the advice received.

Steps for Pathwork I1: Circle of Hands

Journey intention: Balance power & synergy with one or a group of spirits.

1. Select a Tarot Spirit or group as in Pathwork H1.
2. If done as a separate journey, complete your Tarot Spirit opening steps from Chapter 5. If not, do the circle of hands in the same journey, immediately following the other pathwork.
3. Stand in a circle, holding hands with the Tarot Spirit(s), your guide, and your shadow-self. Sense the power balance and if you or any participant in the circle are out of balance or alignment. If

---

[22] Lecture by Michael Harner in Foundation for Shamanic Studies course: Three-Year Program of Advanced Initiations in Shamanism and Shamanic Healing™

so, seek guidance from the group on actions needed to restore life balance. In the circle, give permission to balance power with each other and do it. Feel any shifts in your physical body while you stay focused on power moving through the circle in the journey.

4. Complete your Tarot Spirit closing steps from Chapter 5.

Reports on Pathwork H & I Experience

Reports from those who have done this pathwork are included below. Honor your own experience. Avoid comparing your experience to others.

Shawn: I found the circle of hands to be very comforting. I felt that energy with the relationship circle. Because I'm starting a whole new life here—even though I have family here—I still need to have my own life. So, I'm doing a lot of relationship building and questioning a lot. My question was, "how do I tell if I'm in the right place?" The advice was: I don't need to compromise; If red flags come up, trust them.

Karen undertook several journeys on this advice topic: My guide, dressed in deep purple felt robes with jewels, is holding a jeweled staff, very regal. He has a snowy owl perched on his shoulder. We travel to the High Priestess. I asked the High Priestess (HP), "What would be the outcome of continuing down the shamanic, healing, psychic path?" HP answers, "Great healing and comfort for others. So many animals helped that are in need. You will help others. Be strong in your commitment." I ask, "Which psychic abilities?" HP: "All of them. They will be made available to you. Do you know why you are here? It is to continue to do the work you do when non-incarnated. We are merging the two of you back together. You always complain about how much is forgotten when you incarnate. Here is your chance to fix that. Connect back to yourself and your wisdom, your learning. You will be helping a great many along the way as you are helping yourself. Take others on the ride with you. They will benefit too. So, yes, continue. Continue your education, your learning. Read, take classes, explore, journey. It is all there to support you. We will open the doors for you. You just have to step through them and commit. Leave it to us, the synchronicity will occur. You just need to allow it, to welcome it. Are you prepared to do this?" I say, "Yes." HP: "Yes, that's right. It's like coming home, isn't it? That's what you've been feeling. It's time to come home."

At this point, we are in the circle of hands. It is me, my tarot guide, my power animals, my shadow-self, one of my main teachers from the upper world, and the High Priestess. My hands heat up, start tingling, there's a pain on the left side of my neck. The High Priestess gives me a crystal for my third eye, crown chakra, and heart chakra. This incredible power is put into the crystals, and I can feel the energy going from above my head, to my crown, to my third eye, and heart, infusing and fusing them together with such power I thought I was going to pass out. My eyes rolled back and are moving really quickly. I could feel the heat of the energy moving through these crystals so much that I became incredibly hot. At the end, she took the power back and balanced it amongst all of us in the circle. The High Priestess said I will be safe, secure, and watched over. When I returned to my place in nature, I noticed my robes changed color from white to deep purple. My robes now look like my guide's robes without the jewels and staff.

Karen completes several more journeys to the High Priestess over several weeks and experiences more crystal initiations, culminating in a connection with the cosmos: I expand. I see the cosmos and I keep expanding larger and larger . . . There are so many planets and stars, there is so much! It's overwhelming, the expansiveness. I'm brought back to the place with the High Priestess. It's like the cosmos I just witnessed was brought back with me and put into a sphere that keeps turning and turning. HP: "There is so much out there. So much to know." I am back up in the cosmos, way high up. There are lights and light beings flying past me in all directions. There's so much color swirling out in the cosmos. It's so beautiful. No matter where I journey, upper, lower, wherever, I experience incredible things and the wisdom I'm given is so amazing.

Questions about Pathwork H & I

What can I do if I feel lightheaded, shaky, or tired after a strong Tarot Spirit interaction? The first thing is to make sure you come fully back into your body after the journey. If you do not feel fully back after a journey, repeat the call back sequence with your drum or rattle. You might eat food or drink something neutral to help ground you, especially if you need to drive. We are dealing with powerful spirits and sometimes they have a strong initiation for you. You can ask them to tone it down or possibly spread it out over several journeys, but the initiation may need to be powerful to have the desired impact. There is an effect called shamanic ecstasy, where you may experience shaking or tears after a journey. Fortunately, those encounters are usually rare. When they happen, give yourself space or rest for a day or two. Sometimes, the strong reaction is a rebirth and you need time to integrate.

What do I do with instructions from the Tarot Spirits that make little sense to me? There are two varieties possible. If you don't understand, ask for clarification during this journey or in a follow-up. Your guide can help. Asking for examples and "what if" scenarios can help you get clear. If you're given inappropriate commands or advice, assess their relevance to your life and discuss them further. Remember the idea of partnership with the spirits and sovereignty we talked about in Chapter 5. Do not give up your personal power. Just like advice from a friend: listen to it, think about how it fits into your life, and then make **your own choice** about the actions you will take.

Chapter 9 Recap

Now that you have made a good connection with Tarot Spirits, you can create some practical impacts in your life. Throughout human history, the role of the Shaman was to bring back practical information or help for their community. This work is no different. The spirits are there to help, through advice, healing, and teaching. It is important to respect what they have to offer and apply the advice they have in your life, tempering it with judgement as needed. The circle of hands is an important pathwork that allows spiritual power to affect us outside of rational thought. Be open to receiving power from the spirits and thank them for helping.

10: Healing from the Tarot Spirits

As we discussed in Chapter 7, the cycle of becoming starts with healing. In this chapter, we provide specific steps for Pathwork J1: Receiving Healing from one Tarot Spirit.

Conversation 4: Healing from the Tarot Spirits

Rachel and Isabel had been waiting for a table in the new Thai restaurant for almost half an hour. It seemed everyone in town wanted to try it. Finally, they got seated. Rachel ordered the green curry with tofu and Isabel ordered Pad Thai with chicken. They noticed it was already getting dark outside.

Rachel said, "What are your plans for Thanksgiving?"

"I think I'll just stay here. You know, my family is just hard to be around with all their opinions and judgements. And the politics!" Isabel rolled her eyes. "The airfare back home is pretty high this year. It's hard to shell out all that money. How 'bout you?"

"I think I'll fly back east. Of course, it's a challenge with Mom and Dad not really speaking. It's just uncomfortable hanging around with them. I call it shuttle diplomacy, divorced family style." She grimaced.

"I hear you." Their appetizers arrived and they eagerly picked up their forks, happy for the distraction. After a few more bites, Isabel broke the silence. "I was wondering, did you do any more of that journey work?"

"Yes, indeed." Rachel put down her fork. "I did the healing journey. I met the Empress. Remember when we talked about how I feel like I'm drifting? I asked her for help around that. I want to feel more focused."

"And what happened?"

Rachel took a deep breath. "Well, at first, I thought nothing was going on. Then my tarot guide suggested I tell more of my story. I went on for a while and the Empress looked at me and started humming. Her one voice created a strange harmony like those Tuvan throat singers we saw last year. She even lit up with a halo of light. Frankly, I did not know what to think. This is usually the kind of story you have that I question." She smiled knowingly at Isabel. "My tarot guide said to breathe, and after several breaths, the light from the Empress grew and focused on my heart. Suddenly, I felt sad, and I cried right in the middle of my journey. Then there was this lightness, as if something old had left me. My heart started radiating light on its own, and I felt ten pounds lighter. The next morning, I was excited about getting up. The day breezed by. Gosh, I don't know what to think of it. I'm not my usual sarcastic self . . ." Both of them laughed at this.

"Wow! It sounds a bit like a movie where they have a mystical experience or an initiation. But, of course, without the drugs." Again, they both laughed.

"Yea, I know, more your kind of thing than mine. But I feel lighter and less worried. So, I'll just go with it." She shrugged. "What about you?"

The entrees arrived, and after she smothered her Pad Thai with peanut sauce, Isabel took a bite. "Umm, that's good." She wiped her mouth with her napkin. She thought about the idea of a hidden-factor spirit. This AstroTarot process teaches about shadow tendencies—the unconscious things you do that might get you into trouble. "I also did a healing journey. I worked with the Temperance Tarot Spirit, who is my hidden-factor spirit. Now, I know you think I am all connected spiritually—and I follow things like tarot and astrology—but when I really focus on my spirituality, I do not feel an emotional connection to the spirit world. It's just abstract thoughts in my head. So, I asked her to help me create a greater feeling of spiritual connection."

Rachel, intrigued, thought about how her skepticism about all this spirit stuff was waning. She asked, "And what happened?"

"Well, when I met Temperance on my journey, I was in a dark forest. I was a little nervous. My tarot guide suggested I touch the ground. When I did, I stopped shaking and could breathe more easily. Temperance came closer and mixed white and red liquid together. That mixture was making a very faint buzzing sound. I knelt down and Temperance poured the liquid over my head and then the buzzing got very loud, like a swarm of insects. There was a shaft of energy coming up from under the ground to the top of my skull, right through me! A green mist glowed all around me. Temperance asked me to stand, and I did, even though my legs were wobbly. I returned from my journey and when I opened my eyes, there was a change in how I saw the world. Even the air felt more alive. I had an immediate sense that I was part of a greater whole, a part of the web of life. I felt more at peace, and that has stayed with me all week." Isabel paused and added, "So, there must be something to this Tarot Spirit work."

"Well, I guess we will have to keep checking in with the Tarot Spirits. I'm glad I can talk about it with you. I'm not sure my co-workers would think I was sane if I shared this with them."

"Yeah, me too . . ."

What is Shamanic Healing?

Shamanic healing is a direct intervention from spirits in the Otherworld to aid an individual. When you visit a shamanic healer or shamanic practitioner, they do not personally do the healing work. They act as an intermediary on behalf of the client to encourage spirits to provide healing to the client. The practitioner usually meets the spirits in a shamanic state of consciousness, journey, or a trance. In the Otherworld, they work with power animals, spirit teachers, and helping spirits to achieve the requested healing.

In core shamanic work, shamanic healing is considered being just part of the client's overall process. It is not faith healing, where other forms of intervention are discouraged. It is a complementary art that works in tandem with standard care. Standard care might include mainstream or alternative medical care, physical therapy, massage, or psychological counseling. Over time, shamanic practitioners observe that when shamanic healing is applied, the more standard forms of healing modality often work better.

There are many forms of shamanic healing outlined below. Once I thought that shamanic healing was more effective for psychological rather than physical conditions. Even though I had this idea, frequently over the past 40 years, the spirits proved me wrong. Clients requested healing for physical concerns and then came back later to report significant progress or pain reduction for physical issues.

When you ask for healing from the Tarot Spirits, it may take one of the forms listed below. Alternatively, it may be a unique approach to your situation. The spirits are creative. Sometimes you may get full relief. Other times a partial improvement results. If you do not feel completely healed, you might follow up with a shamanic practitioner who has deep experience working with the helping spirits. Generally, the forms of shamanic healing can include:

- **Spiritual extraction**. If a person has power loss or soul loss, a spiritual intrusion can enter uninvited to fill up the empty space. Intrusions are often generated by random negative emotions projected from others in the world around us. Intrusions cause physical illness, pain, or unexpected emotions. Extraction removes spiritual intrusions. They are moved to a neutral place. Shamans understand that illness often originates on a spiritual level. It is best to follow extraction with a power or soul retrieval.
- **Power retrieval**. A common healing practice is power animal retrieval. As we go through life we may lose power, evidenced by accidents or bad luck. The shaman finds lost power and returns it to the client. The result is a reconnection to the great powers of the universe that can guide, protect, and advise us. Besides power animals, power can be retrieved in other forms. Nature power retrieval is a direct infusion of the general power of the universe. Elemental power can also be applied intentionally.
- **Soul retrieval**. If you yearn for a fuller sense of vitality and connection to life, or you feel disconnected, soul retrieval may be the solution. Another indicator is never feeling the same after a traumatic event. Soul retrieval can put you on the path to healing your connections to self, loved ones, and to the earth. The shaman works with spirit helpers to find a lost soul essence, then returns the pure healthy essence to you. With the positive qualities of that essence returned, you can be more connected to and effective in your life.
- **Body part retrieval**. Sometimes, resulting from an injury or operation, qualities of individual body parts may be affected. The result can be pain or poor function. For this healing, helping spirits bring back the lost life force of the damaged body part.
- **Resolve astrological challenges**. As discussed later in this book, certain planetary aspects produce challenges. Tarot Spirits can

take on planetary roles and reconcile astrological conflicts for individuals. This can open up opportunities, reduce blockages, and help you live the life you love.

- **Other healing possibilities**. The helping spirits often use other spiritual healing modalities. They relieve suffering and address your unique needs. For example, a helping spirit may design a healing ritual for you. They may teach you how to work with the power of words or dance to bring healing.

Nature Healing

If you look at your tarot cards, you see that many have nature scenes. You can enhance your healing experience by paying attention to these nature elements in the journey when you visit a Tarot Spirit. In fact, the Tarot Spirit may work with nature power retrieval, bringing nature power to you from elements in the landscape.

Another way you can bring the power of nature into your healing is to go out in nature to do some of your journeys. Bring your rattle and cards to a peaceful and private place in nature. Take time to look around while rattling just before the journey. Take in the beauty of nature. Allow nature powers to support you during and after the journey.

Positive Healing Intention Statement

One of the more important methods in core shamanism is to create a clear and specific intention for each journey. What are you seeking? In healing work, it is important that this intention be a positive outcome statement. Usually, when we seek treatment for a problem, we focus on the problem—or what is **not** working. The problem statement is not a "positive outcome." Brain science and magical methods have shown us that focusing on what is wrong will give us more of what's wrong, rather than creating a positive outcome.

The importance of a positive statement is to receive a clear and desired outcome from the spirits, yet you want that question to be specific. You could try "I want my body to have perfect health," but that is not specific, even though positive. Start by zooming in on the problem with questions like: "What is out of balance in your life?" or "What do I need help with?"

Then working with the answer to those questions, transform the answer into a desired positive outcome. A couple of examples follow:

- You might discover that what is out of balance is an ongoing pain originating in the hip that refers down the outside of your leg to a pain in the top of your foot. That can be reframed to "My hip and leg are free from pain and I have full walking mobility." That is specific and positive.

- You might have high anxiety driving so that you need to avoid freeways. Maybe the fear of going through green lights leaves you anxious and breathless. You end up anxious in a parking lot, your trip incomplete. That issue could be restated as the positive outcome: "If this healing is successful, I will drive calmly and confidently, knowing I will be safe in my automobile."

Pathwork J1: Healing from One Tarot Spirit

The overall steps of Pathwork J1 are very similar to Pathwork B. The intention is different and focused on healing. We append the number 1 to J here to indicate we are working with only one Tarot Spirit. We will have slight variations to the healing pathwork in Chapters 14 and 15.

When asking for personal healing work, you have a choice. You can receive the healing directly into your body or have a representational object healed. For the representational approach, in your journey visualize an object or form that represents the problem, issue, or disease. See that form in the middle of the circle and watch it being healed by the Tarot Spirits.

You can complete this journey many times, focused on different healing requests each time. Focus each journey on a single issue for healing. Make your intention and request based on a positive result. Avoid dwelling on negativity or pain. Create an intention that states the positive outcome you want, as outlined above. Let's say your relationship with money is painful. Create a positive outcome statement like: "money flows to me easily and creates good feelings for all."

Steps for Pathwork J1: Healing from a Tarot Spirit

Journey intention: To receive healing from a Tarot Spirit.

1. Before you journey,

    *   Formulate your healing goal, as described under Positive Healing Intention Statement above: "_____ _____ is the positive outcome I want to receive from this healing."
    *   Select a Tarot Spirit to work with. Choose the Sun, Temperance, High Priestess, Star, Fool, or Empress. Or consult with (journey to) your guide to choose another healing Tarot Spirit aligned with your issue.

2. Complete your Tarot Spirit opening steps from Chapter 5.
3. Discuss your positive healing request with the Tarot Spirit. What needs to be healed? For the symbolic approach, see or sense this thing needing healing as a symbolic manifestation in non-ordinary reality. For example, if you came to heal anger, it might appear as a red flame at your throat. Ask the Tarot Spirits to heal the symbolic manifestation in you. You may also receive direct interventions or power from the Tarot Spirit into your spirit body.
4. You may also receive information on worldly actions you can take to help this healing process. Perhaps herbs or medicines will be suggested. Ask your guide to help with clarification if you are unclear about what follow-up is needed. Talk about these recommendations during the journey until instructions are clear.
5. If at any time your guide tells you to leave, or you feel you should "get out of there," do so with your guide's help.
6. When the healing process in the journey is complete, you can also do a circle of hands (Pathwork I1) with all who are present in the journey, as discussed in Chapter 9.
7. Complete your Tarot Spirit closing steps from Chapter 5.

Integration After Shamanic Healing

If you have recently had shamanic healing—especially power animal retrieval and soul retrieval—several activities can help you integrate after the healing session.

After Power Animal Retrieval

If you have received a power animal retrieval, the following activities will help you benefit from this helpful spiritual ally:

Dance Your Power Animal

When you consciously ask your power animal to join you in your physical body, this is called "Dancing Your Animal." You can dance indoors or outdoors. Take a rattle or something that can make shaker sounds—like a pill bottle with popcorn kernels in it. Start rattling with a beat of two to three shakes per second. Then move your feet in time to the beat. Move around in a sunwise or clockwise circle. As you move with the beat, think about your power animal and invite them into your body. Let the power animal dance through your body. You might feel the urge to make animal noises, flap your arms like wings, or move as the animal would. Continue moving, dancing along with the animal for 3 to 15 minutes with the rattling continuing. When you feel complete, thank the power animal. If you have more than one power animal, you may move on to the next one. When you are done, separate completely, feeling all residuals of the power animals leave your body.

This practice is a mutual exchange. The power animals receive a gift by being embodied in a physical body. You receive a gift by having the power of the animal in your body. Repeating this practice regularly will help retain the power the animal brings to you.

Call the Power Animal

If you are heading to an important meeting or an occasion where you need power, you can call your animal into you. Request the animal's power to be in your body. Walking down the street or in the woods, you can sense your animal being with you. You can also make subtle movements characteristic of the animal to feel them more present. You may get telepathic messages from your power animal in stressful situations.

Meet the Power Animal

You can use a drumming or rattling journey to the lower world to meet the animal. You can play with them, talk to them, and see how they are in their world. You can develop a relationship with them for power and healing. You can also ask your power animal to give you advice. You may receive this as a thought, hear them, or see them dance out a pattern that has meaning.

After Soul Retrieval

A soul retrieval brings back vital life force that may have been missing for some time. It brings back a positive aspect with gifts or empowerments you can use today in your life. Do make a gift to the earth—from a pinch of corn meal offered prayerfully to planting a tree—in the 24 hours after the time of the soul retrieval. Then wait for a week or two for the returning soul essence to integrate. If you notice large changes, positive or negative, contact the practitioner that did the retrieval for you or journey to the Spirit who brought back the soul essence. To aid integration, engage in these individual activities.

Meet Your Soul Essence

After waiting a week or two, arrange a meeting with your new soul essence to find the answers to two basic questions:

- What gift do you bring back to me I can use in my life right now? Common gifts are the ability to have better boundaries, more connection with the world, more involvement, greater emotional awareness, or love of self.
- What change can I make in my life to become more integrated? Common changes might involve more time outdoors, more exercise, stopping destructive behavior, starting positive habits, cultivating relationships that help you be your best, or taking more time for fun. The focus is on self-care and love of self.

Always remember the concepts of sovereignty and reciprocity we discussed in Chapter 5. You are in charge. You do want to integrate the positive essence that returned in your soul retrieval. Negotiate about making changes in your life appropriate for your circumstances. You can arrange a meeting in many ways, including the following.

- **Journey to meet your soul essence.** If you know how to do a shamanic journey (see Chapter 2), you can use a drumming or rattling journey to the lower or upper world to meet the soul essence. You might invite a trusted power animal, teacher, or

Tarot Spirit to be with you as a mediator. You can ask your questions about what gifts are available and negotiate what changes are appropriate in your life.

- **Meditation.** If you are unfamiliar with journeying, try meditation to connect with your soul essence. Have the strong intention that you will meet your soul essence and get answers to the two questions.

- **Journaling.** Get answers from spirits using right hand / left hand journaling. In this technique, you write a question with your dominant hand. Then hold the pen in your non-dominant hand, close your eyes or be quiet for a moment, then let your soul essence answer your question, writing with that non-dominant hand. You will be surprised at the answer.

Complementary Healing Modalities

After any shamanic healing, you should continue or pursue ordinary healing modalities. Remember that shamanic healing is a complementary art that works best in tandem with standard or alternative medical or psychological care. So pursue the proper medical treatment, physical therapy, massage, or psychological counseling. Standard therapies work in conjunction with the shamanic healing work. The shamanic healing at the spiritual level will make physical or mental treatments more effective.

Reports on Pathwork J1: Healing

Reports from those who have done this pathwork are included below. Honor your own experience. Avoid comparing your experience to others.

Shagufta: A spirit told me that when I don't ask for healing, I am not allowing them to fully do their job. They have even thanked me for asking.

Becky: I felt very empowered and strong because the High Priestess is standing up and that image stuck with me as a powerful image. The message was that I have everything, all the skills that I need, to do this . . . I mean, simple is not always easy, but it's as simple as lightening up my schedule basically . . . The raised arms were powerful for me as I was floating around . . . So, I was imagining that if I just move my schedule around with my own hands like that in the sky of my thoughts, it'll be a lot easier to manage things and rank things. So, my task is to do a mind map of all the things I'm committed to right now and all I have going on and just look at what that really looks like in my day. Is there a way to carve out time for tarot? Yes, I have to choose it instead of getting on my phone first thing in the morning, right? So again, simple, but not always easy. So that's what I gathered. I feel like I already have it in me. I just have to do something about it.

Reid: I received a guided visualization in an astrology conference focused on the current conjunctions of Pluto and Saturn. While my realizations were quite manageable on an intellectual level, I noticed that afterward I was short with my wife. I was resentful around some gardening tasks. I went into a healing journey with the Fool and the Sun, and they found an alien manifestation in me that they healed. During the journey, it became apparent that all the tension, concern, and grief around COVID-19 had been triggered by the astrological guided visualization. The personal response was at an unconscious level. The healing journey not only brought this into consciousness, but released the negative energy at a core level. As a result, I could be more relaxed and civil with those around me.

Nancy: I journeyed to the High Priestess, and I brought her some chocolates just to sweeten the deal. My guide took me there. She was happy to see me. That was just a really nice thing, to feel welcomed. She asked me to sit down by her side. I told her I needed help with a project I'm on the team for. She put her hands on me and told me that I was very capable of contributing to this project. It was a positive thing. She said I should look within and tap my intuition to help me. So, I felt a lot of love and a lot of strong compassion. She told me to come visit her when I felt my confidence wane. It was a very nice journey, a beautiful journey.

Kate: Shortly before this journey, I hit a bird while driving my car, and I was feeling guilty. I chose to go to the High Priestess for a healing and called on my power animal to take me to her. He quickly appeared and immediately embraced me in a loving hug, then carried me all the way to her. The High Priestess said to me, "You have to let go of guilt. You're a human living on earth and these things happen, but you forget. Love and forgiveness for you!" She reached out and put her hand on my heart and said "love" and then put her other hand on my heart and said "forgiveness" and went back and forth, "love, forgiveness, love, forgiveness" about three times. I felt a sense of rest and relaxation, somewhat peaceful. She focused on the areas where I struggle to heal, loving and forgiving myself and letting go of guilt. It was quite a powerful experience.

Questions on Pathwork J1: Healing

Do I need to do a formal journey to ask for healing from the Tarot Spirits? Generally, yes. The formal journey process activates a unique relationship with the Tarot Spirits. So, it's a good idea. But you can be open to receiving healing when you're involved in life processes. For example, if you're involved in a project or a task, or just having hard feelings, the Tarot Spirits can come in spontaneously and give you a burst of energy, healing, or a telepathic message. They'll keep working on things while you're going about normal activities. Doing a formal journey is not always required. While that focus certainly helps, remember that spirits can intervene directly in a situation as it unfolds.

Can I repeat a request for healing on the same topic? Of course! Feel free to return and ask for healing once again. Many times, full healing requires a layered process, creating a first level of progress before the next layer is addressed. Request healing whenever you need it. Don't be shy about it. It is a valuable method, and it's worth repeating. Remember, in this book we're just giving you techniques that you can come back to again and again as you need them. You won't wear the spirits out. Ask for aid when you need it.

Chapter 10 Recap

After 30 years of being a shamanic healing practitioner, I have no question that shamanic healing is beneficial. The pathwork in this chapter lets you access shamanic healing directly from the Tarot Spirits.

Part 2 Recap

In Part 2, you learned about your special personal Tarot Spirits in the areas of personality, soul, hidden factors and the year spirit. You met your shadow-self. You engaged pathwork to receiving advice, healing, and learning from the individual Tarot Spirits. The circle of hands pathwork allowed you to balance power with the Tarot Spirits. In many ways, these interactions with the Tarot Spirits can create great value in your life.

With this foundation in place, you can move on to Part 3, where you will learn which Tarot Spirits are active in your astrological chart and engage reconciliation of potentially challenging astrological aspects. You will also engage with personal Tarot Spirit circles and meet Spirit Constructs who will provide ongoing learning or initiatory opportunities.

Get your free resource material!

If you haven't already, check out the online resources that support the book *Tarot Spirit Healing*. They include:

- Shamanic journey drumming tracks for 10, 20, and 30 minute journeys.
- Blank forms for tracking pathwork and *AstroTarot mapping*.
- High resolution color graphics in pdf format.
- Video lessons: *Tarot Spirits: Who's on Deck?* and a *Tour of the Major Arcana.*
- Video lesson: *Shamanic Crossing.*
- Join the mailing list for updates on Tarot Spirit books and courses.
- Discounted offers for related online courses.

Check out these book resources at
www.reidhart.com/tsh-resources

Part 3: Clearing Your Natal Chart

Figure 14. The Magician is key 1 (I) in the tarot Major Arcana. He represents Mercury and carries the masculine archetype of magical knowledge. He represents sharp thought and magical power. *Credit: DruidCraft Tarot.*

Now that you have engaged shamanically with the Tarot Spirits in Part 1 and worked with them for advice and healing in Part 2, you can do the specific AstroTarot work in Part 3 as follows:

- Understand the power of AstroTarot, learn astrology basics, and tour your birth chart in Chapter 11.
- Map Tarot Spirits to your birth chart and learn the impact of astrological aspects in Chapter 12.
- Resolve potentially challenging astrological aspects in Chapter 13 using Pathwork K.

While the main section of this book is designed to provide you with the information you need to move directly through the process of meeting the Tarot Spirits, receiving healing and advice, and resolving your astrological challenges, additional background for Part 3 can be found in these appendices:

- Appendix A has resources and recommended books with descriptions of the books.
- Appendix F has a brief history of astrology, provides background on Hellenistic vs. modern astrology, and discusses the relationship between different cultural deities and the ancient planets.
- Appendix G has a sample of a personalized *My AstroTarot Report* you can order with all the *AstroTarot mapping* done for you.
- Appendix H has the forms and instructions needed to create your own *AstroTarot mapping*.

11: The Power of AstroTarot

Humans have used astrology since prehistoric times. Natal (or birth) charts developed around 2500 years ago. The natal chart outlines the tendencies, challenges, and opportunities of an individual's life. These markers unfold over the course of a lifetime. Transiting [23] planets, asteroids, and other sky objects influence the natal markers.

The counseling astrologer reviews the dynamics of the natal chart with the client. They point out potential challenges and opportunities that are part of the client's basic personality or are transitory phases in their life. This consultation provides helpful insight into beneficial and harmful tendencies in current life cycles. It provides an increased awareness of personality and dynamic influences from the sky. With this information, you can work more effectively with challenges or be aware of passing phases. You can better align expectations with what is realistic in life overall and at the current time.

AstroTarot takes the process one step further. It calls on spiritual intervention into astrological challenges or opportunities. These interventions either reduce negative impacts or enhance positive results. Interaction of the planets, signs of the zodiac, and the houses can be quite complex. In basic AstroTarot work, you focus on the aspects between the planets. You ask the Tarot Spirits to work out potential challenges in your Natal chart. This process could be through direct consultation with planetary spirits, but that is a challenging task. By building on your work with the Tarot Spirits in Parts 1 and 2, you expand a spiritual relationship, rather than starting over in the new area of planetary powers.

If you are new to astrology, read about the basics in this chapter, with more historical background in Appendix F. You do not need to go deep with astrological concepts to work shamanically with AstroTarot. You can

---

[23] A transit is when a current planet location forms a relationship to the location of a planet at the time we were born. In the basic AstroTarot work in this book, transiting planets are not considered.

just work with the general concepts presented here and use the *AstroTarot Report* discussed in Chapter 12 to guide your journeys. Several books on the reading list in Appendix A give more background for those interested.

Astrological Philosophy

There is a longstanding debate in the astrological community about how the position of planets in the natal chart affects the native. Is the impact of astrology based on direct electromagnetic influence from the planets? Do the planets represent messages from the divine about your life opportunities and challenges? Is astrology a pathway into psychological exploration? Perhaps all three have influence!

Fate and Free Will

Questions arise about the balance of fate and free will. Is the purpose of astrology to understand your fate so you can better withstand it?—a Stoic approach. Do you engage the stars so that you can create positive movement in your life?—a personally assertive approach. It could be a blend of both.

At first glance, astrology may seem fate bound: "The stars decree what will happen, and you are stuck with it!" Not so fast. Some may attribute this kind of thinking to Hellenistic rather than modern astrology. Although this thought is more like the Stoic school, there is variation in the approach to fate and free will by different Hellenistic astrologers. One way to hold the contradiction between fate and free will is to acknowledge "both/and."

We can use the analogy of a canoe trip down the river for your life path. The river represents fate, what is set and immovable. The wise ones say, "don't push the river." Yet you are in your canoe. You can move back and forth across the river. In fact, when I learned white water canoeing, I was trained to point the canoe toward danger—like large rocks or tree snags—and back paddle. The river current then pushes you to the side, so you avoid the danger. It is like getting caught in a rip tide. While the rip tide is there, your outcome is quite different if you struggle directly against the current rather than swimming at a right angle and getting out of the current.

So, astrology provides insight into the nature of the river. What is fixed in the current situation? Then you can work within constraints to get the best outcome. The Tarot Spirits can take your agency one step further. Working shamanically with them provides intervention for your planetary aspects. For example, once you see a challenging aspect between two planets in your natal chart, you can ask the Tarot Spirits shamanically to adjust the planetary enmity. This helps you understand what the best action is to take with your canoe on the river of life. The result is to improve your situation.

In the end, the idea is to understand the conditions that surround you— what is the map of the river—and then use powers that are already flowing to help you navigate the rough spots and speed through the areas where you can take advantage of forces that are already flowing in a favorable direction. You can smooth the path down the river by working with the Tarot Spirits. It makes sense now that you have spent some time working with those Tarot Spirits so you can get help from them. Using your astrological natal chart will help you focus on where the work needs to be done for your benefit.

Tarot Spirits and Your Chart

So far in Parts 1 and 2 of the book, you have introduced yourself to the Tarot Spirits through Pathworks A, B, and C. You have received healing and advice from individual Tarot Spirits through pathwork for healing (J1) and advice (H1). You have also exchanged power with the Spirits using the circle of hands in Pathwork I1.

Once you have completed Pathworks A/B/C with individual Tarot Spirits, you can work with them in pairs or groups. Tarot Spirits can help you resolve life conflicts, offer group advice or healing, or deliver education that will help you in your practical or spiritual life. So, your purpose in AstroTarot work is to focus on Tarot Spirits that are important to you personally. You can use your natal or birth astrological chart as a key to find which Tarot Spirits are the best fit for these different roles. This is your task in Part 3 of the book.

The greatest benefit you get from the Tarot Spirits is resolution of natal chart challenges. After we introduce AstroTarot here, you will find your challenging natal chart aspects. Then you use Tarot Spirit pathwork to resolve those challenges.

The Stars and You

This section reviews the basic elements of astrology. You learn the meaning of planets, zodiacal signs, and houses. Then you see example types of a sample birth chart. If you are already familiar with the basics of astrology, skim this section. The information provided here and in Appendix F is not comprehensive, but provides a basic understanding of terminology and general meaning. For a deeper understanding, please refer to the many worthwhile books and resources on the list in Appendix A. Appendix F includes a brief history of astrology.

Understanding Your Astrological Chart

Astrology is a large and complex subject. The good news is that when you use the Tarot Spirits to work with your natal chart, the process becomes simple. Rather than trying to understand or interpret what each planet, sign, and house combination mean, you can rely on the Tarot Spirits themselves to resolve challenges using the AstroTarot pathworks in a shamanic journey. You can get the information needed for personal healing and transformation directly from the Tarot Spirits. That being said, it is helpful to have at least a basic understanding of astrology terms. We will introduce the following topics here:

- Astrology basics
- Symbols for the zodiac signs and planets
- Getting your astrological natal (birth) chart
- Taking a tour of your astrological chart

Astrology Basics

Astrology is an important part of the Western Mystery tradition. Using astrological methods, we can interpret the impact of changing planetary cycles. Planetary interactions in zodiac signs narrate the stories of individuals, groups, events, or countries.

In AstroTarot, we focus on transformation rather than interpretation. There are a few terms you should be familiar with: zodiac sign, planet, natal chart, major aspect, ascendant, and house. We will briefly discuss these concepts here. The glossary contains definitions for terms that are unfamiliar.

The impact of planetary positions when we are born is often explained as electromagnetic field impact. I think it is more likely that there is an Otherworld field of creation. Another Western Mystery element, the Qabalistic Tree of Life, enshrines this. There are strong planetary influences in the Otherworld magical field. These planetary influences affect manifestation and what will show up on the material plane. The Qabalistic influences are directly impacted by both natal and transiting astrology. By working shamanically in the Otherworld, you can respond to and adjust the impact of astrological influences on your life. A full explanation of the interactions of astrology and the Qabalah are beyond the scope of this book. The point is that the astrological influences exist in an astral field that is beyond a simple electromagnetic explanation.

In each of our natal charts lies a map of cosmic and practical impacts on our approach to life that can be helpful or limiting. In many cases, just learning and growing in life, you may have moved past many of these limitations, but there may be lingering impacts that would benefit from further resolution. In the AstroTarot process, you can work directly on your astrological influences at the astral plane level and find out where you can still focus on releasing limitations or augmenting benefits. In actual life, the improvements at the astral level must be brought down to practical changes in our day-to-day life: adjustments in behaviors, relationships, and skillsets. We will discuss planets, signs, and houses separately. High-level meanings for planets, signs, and houses are listed here. More detailed significations are in the books on the reading list in Appendix A.

Symbols

Astrology is like a new language, with special symbols for the signs of the zodiac, the planets, and other chart objects. If you are new to astrology, take time to review these symbols. It's like learning a new alphabet! You might scribble them out on scratch paper to help get them into your brain kinesthetically. If the symbols are too foreign, you can use abbreviations for the names of the planets and signs on the worksheets.

Planets

Planets are called the "wandering stars." They can be seen at night to move along the ecliptic or path of the Sun in the sky. They move through a background of fixed stars that have a constant relationship to each other. In astrology, we refer to the Sun and Moon, or luminaries, as planets. The first seven ancient planets are easily visible without a telescope. We have interpretation of their movement that dates back to Hellenistic times and thousands of years earlier. Each planet has an astrological symbol and a general meaning listed in the table below:

Symbol	Planet	Basic keywords for each planet	In my chart, this planet...
☉	Sun	Will, individuality, spirit, identity	represents my true path, will, inner authority and creative power
☽	Moon	Personality, matter, emotions, physical body	demonstrates my emotional response, feelings, rhythms, self-nurturing, and security needs
☿	Mercury	Mind, writing, communication, intellect, opinions	governs how I think, communicate, learn, and make connections
♀	Venus	Personal affections, appreciation, art, beauty, romance	indicates my appreciation of aesthetics and capacity for attracting love, enjoyment, and pleasure
♂	Mars	Energy, initiative, courage, desire	brings forward my assertiveness, drive, and actions based on personal desire
♃	Jupiter	Prosperity, ethics, philosophy, good fortune, expansion	holds the key to my good fortune, meaning, ethics, and confidence
♄	Saturn	Boundaries, limits, structure, organized, contraction	channels my ability to create structure, have discipline, honor tradition, and work within limits
♅	Uranus	Independence, originality, change	channels rebelliousness, abrupt change, and opens me to uniqueness and individuality
♆	Neptune	Compassion, chaos, cosmos, illusion	opens me to dreams, transcendence, ideals, illusions, and fantasies
♇ ♆	Pluto*	Regeneration, purging, coercion, cooperation	represents how I regenerate, relate to mortality, and welcome transformation

* Pluto has two symbols in common use.

Into prehistory, these planets were observed and their meanings aligned with the gods and goddesses in ancient mythology. Their movement and aspect were interpreted as messages from the divine. More information about the planetary deities in different cultures can be found near the end of Appendix F.

When astrology was originally developed, the theory was that the earth was the center of the universe. So, in your astrological chart, the position of the planets is as viewed from earth, even though they are orbiting the Sun. While we call the Sun and Moon planets, they are also referred to as the lights or luminaries in ancient astrological texts. As the earth orbits the Sun, it looks like the Sun is moving through the sky against a backdrop of the zodiac. So, every month, the Sun moves from one sign of the zodiac to the next.

Signs of the Zodiac

There are twelve signs of the zodiac. The Sun takes about one month to travel through each sign. About 2000 years ago, the signs aligned with the visible zodiac constellations in the night sky. Vedic astrologers still use a "sidereal" zodiac system with that alignment. Due to precession, the physical zodiac has slowly shifted from the seasonal alignment in place during Hellenistic times. Since Ptolemy in about 150 CE, most Western astrologers have used the "tropical" zodiac system. The tropical zodiac aligns 0° of Aries with the spring equinox and maintains a seasonal alignment of the zodiacal signs.

Each sign has a symbol and multiple characteristics. Each sign of the zodiac connects to an element, a modality, a polarity, and a season. Three signs connect to each of the four elements: air, earth, fire, and water. Around the zodiac, the signs alternate between male (+) or female (-) in polarity. As gender becomes a more fluid concept, it may be better to think of the polarities as positive and negative (in an electric rather than judgmental sense), yang and yin, fast and slow, or assertive and receptive. Four signs align with each of the three modalities or quadruplicities. The modalities are cardinal, fixed and mutable.

It is probably easiest to remember the order of the signs of the zodiac and their modalities as they relate to the four seasons. Each season contains three signs with all the modalities. Each season begins with a cardinal sign. The first sign at the start of the season it represents the beginning of an action. The second sign is fixed. It aligns with the middle month of the season, where seasonal qualities are fixed and fairly constant. The third sign in each season is mutable or changeable. This mirrors the changing daily weather in the last month of each season. These modalities or quadruplicities of the signs also reflect tendencies the signs bring to the action of the planets. Cardinal signs impart an impatience or assertiveness. Fixed signs impart a constancy or steadiness. Mutable signs impart a changeable or variable nature.

The signs, their symbols, name, element, polarity, and modalities are listed below along with the approximate date the Sun enters each sign in the tropical zodiac. They are grouped by the season of the year.

Symbol	Sign of the Zodiac	Sign Element	Sign Polarity	Sign Modality (Quadruplicity)	Date Sun Enters Sign
Spring Season Signs (Autumn in Southern Hemisphere):					
♈	Aries	Fire	+	Cardinal	March 21
♉	Taurus	Earth	—	Fixed	April 21
♊	Gemini	Air	+	Mutable	May 22
Summer Season Signs (Winter in Southern Hemisphere):					
♋	Cancer	Water	—	Cardinal	June 22
♌	Leo	Fire	+	Fixed	July 22
♍	Virgo	Earth	—	Mutable	Aug. 22
Autumn Season Signs (Spring in Southern Hemisphere):					
♎	Libra	Air	+	Cardinal	Sept. 22
♏	Scorpio	Water	—	Fixed	Oct. 22
♐	Sagittarius	Fire	+	Mutable	Nov. 22
Winter Season Signs (Summer in Southern Hemisphere):					
♑	Capricorn	Earth	—	Cardinal	Dec. 22
♒	Aquarius	Air	+	Fixed	Jan. 22
♓	Pisces	Water	—	Mutable	Feb. 22

Zodiacal Sign Meanings

While we think of the planets as verbs, or the items that take action in your chart, the zodiacal signs can be thought of as adjectives and adverbs that give context, style, and direction for the planetary action.

Sym -bol	Zodiacal Sign	Key Word	General Meaning
♈	Aries	I am	Spontaneous, initiative, willpower, fast, assertive, courage, high-energy, direct
♉	Taurus	I have	Physically connected, sensual, grounded, steadfast, needs time, strives for security
♊	Gemini	I think	Adaptable, witty, communicative, mobile, pleasure in learning, quick, capricious
♋	Cancer	I feel	Emotional, stubborn, seeks safety, family oriented, intuitive, caring, shy, tenacious
♌	Leo	I will	Commanding, glamorous, generous, prideful, organized, showmanship, expressive
♍	Virgo	I analyze	Precise, analytical, practical, disciplined, efficient, focused, skillful, critical, sanitary
♎	Libra	I balance	Harmonious, considerate, cooperative, fair, aesthetic, refined, tactful, seeking balance
♏	Scorpio	I desire	Intense, passionate, piercing, extreme, resentful, desirous, probing, cathartic
♐	Sagittarius	I perceive	Optimistic, confident, needs freedom, wanderlust, big picture, ungrounded
♑	Capricorn	I use	Enduring, purposeful, traditional, proud, ambitious, deliberate, organized, bounded
♒	Aquarius	I know	Altruistic, detached, abstract, self-sure, communicative, humanitarian, progressive
♓	Pisces	I believe	Sensitive, imaginative, compassionate, helpful, sociable, adaptable, elusive

The Houses

The Hellenistic astrologers developed the idea of houses or places in the natal chart as they adopted the concept of the ascendant from the Egyptians. We introduce the houses here, although we will not work with them deeply in this book. We will delve into working with houses and house/sign rulerships in a later book in the series. The houses show what area of your life the energy of the planets is focused on—as shaped by the sign they are in.

Houses begin with the ascendant in the East—the rising zodiac sign at your birth time. So it is important to find an accurate birth time, preferably from your birth certificate. Fortunately, if you don't have access to an accurate birth time that will not impact the basic AstroTarot pathworking in this book.

The twelve houses continue counterclockwise from the ascendant in order around your natal chart. In Hellenistic astrology, the houses are aligned with the signs in what are called "whole sign houses." In modern astrology there are many systems to divide the houses. Most of them are quadrant house systems that align the 1st, 4th, 7th, and 10th houses with the horizontal and vertical angles of the chart, calculated based on the location you were born on the planet. The Placidus house system is the most popular in modern astrology. The table below gives basic meanings for the twelve houses.

House	Areas of life
1	Appearance, personality
2	Property, resources, finances
3	Thinking, communication, learning, siblings
4	Home, traditions, origins, family, parents
5	Self-expression, creativity, children
6	Work, skills, regular routine, physical illness
7	Partners, marriage (also business partners)
8	Inner values, sexual attraction, psychic abilities
9	Meaning, travel, religion, spirituality
10	Reputation, vocation, career
11	Community service, social ties, friends, associates
12	Transformation, transcendence, enemies, challenges

Interactions of Planet and Sign

While you are probably most familiar with your Sun sign, the most basic astrological interpretation will consider your ascendant sign, Sun sign, and Moon sign placements in your natal chart. Then the other planets are considered, along with their interactions. Each house has a "host" represented by the planetary ruler of the sign it is in. We discuss houses and rulerships further in a later book in the series. Interaction of the planets, signs of the zodiac, and the houses can be quite complex. In basic

AstroTarot work, you focus on the aspects between the planets and let the Tarot Spirits offer the opportunity to work out potential challenges in your natal chart. We will discuss available interpretive resources as you build your natal chart.

There are multiple astrological systems. They all include interaction of the planets with the signs of the zodiac. Since 200 BCE, the houses and the ascendant are also a factor in most systems. For individual planet considerations, the basic grammar[24] of astrology goes like this:

> In my birth chart **[planet]** shows how I will **[planetary action influence]** and this will express itself through **[zodiac sign significations]** in the **[house significations]** area of my life.

A blank form to fill out for your chart and examples for Sample Chart 1 are included near the end of Appendix H. Here is an example of how this might be completed for the Sun in Sample chart 1:

> In my birth chart, the **Sun** represents my true path, will, inner authority and creative power as expressed through the idealistic, poetic, and mystical qualities of **Pisces** in the **4th house** of establishing roots and foundations through connection to the land in my life.

Interactions between Planets

Planets have relations with each other in your chart. These are called aspects and can be positive, neutral, or negative. Planetary aspects, also known as configurations, are discussed further in Chapter 12. They are a very important part of AstroTarot and form the basis of the natal chart clearing in Pathwork K, as discussed in Chapter 13.

A Tour of Your Natal Chart

As discussed later in this chapter and in Appendix H, you can choose to work with either a modern or Hellenistic astrological chart, or both. If you are new to astrology, pick just one to start with. Before you can tour your natal chart, you, of course, must get it. You have three options:

1. Use a copy of your natal astrological chart you already have.

---

[24] This grammatical approach is inspired by the *Astrology for Yourself* workbook by D. Bloch & D. George. The workbook provides much more background than the discussion here.

2. Get your *My AstroTarot Report* that includes your natal chart as described in Appendix G.

3. Get your natal chart using online resources following the steps in Appendix H.

The tour of your natal chart can help you understand the parts of the chart even if you do not plan to learn how to get one on your own. Review the primary elements of your natal chart using the samples on the following pages to orient yourself. Hybrid, modern, and Hellenistic chart samples are shown. Working with either system—or even a Vedic system (not shown)—will be effective with the Tarot Spirits.

General Astrological Natal Chart Components

For all the charts shown here, the main circle is a map of the circle of the zodiac, along the Sun's ecliptic, with the top to the south, the left to the east (sunrise) and the right to the west (sunset). The chart shows each planets' zodiac sign location at the time of birth. The planets' location in the zodiac wheel is as viewed from your birthplace on earth. Look for these items in your own chart or in the example charts:

- Twelve signs circle the zodiac. This circle moves clockwise with diurnal motion following the large outer arrow in Figure 15. It completes a full rotation each day. The zodiacal signs rise in the east at the ascendent (abbreviated as AC, AS, or ASC) and move throughout the morning to the midheaven (also called top of the sky or *Medium Coeli*, abbreviated as MC). Then the sign sets in the west at the descendent, abbreviated as DC. The signs then travel down below the horizon, where they are not visible. They arrive at the "bottom of the sky" or *Illum Coli*, abbreviated as IC. The planets ride along with the zodiacal wheel and follow the daily motion, rising and setting with the signs.

- Your natal chart shows where the planets are on the zodiac wheel at the time of your birth. The planets usually move through the signs counterclockwise following the small inner arrow in Figure 15. When planets are retrograde, they appear to move backwards in the wheel or clockwise. As we go from one day to the next, the planets move through the signs more slowly than the daily clockwise cycle. The Moon takes a month to get around the full zodiac wheel and the Sun a year. The other planets' speed varies, taking several years to cover the full circle of the zodiac.

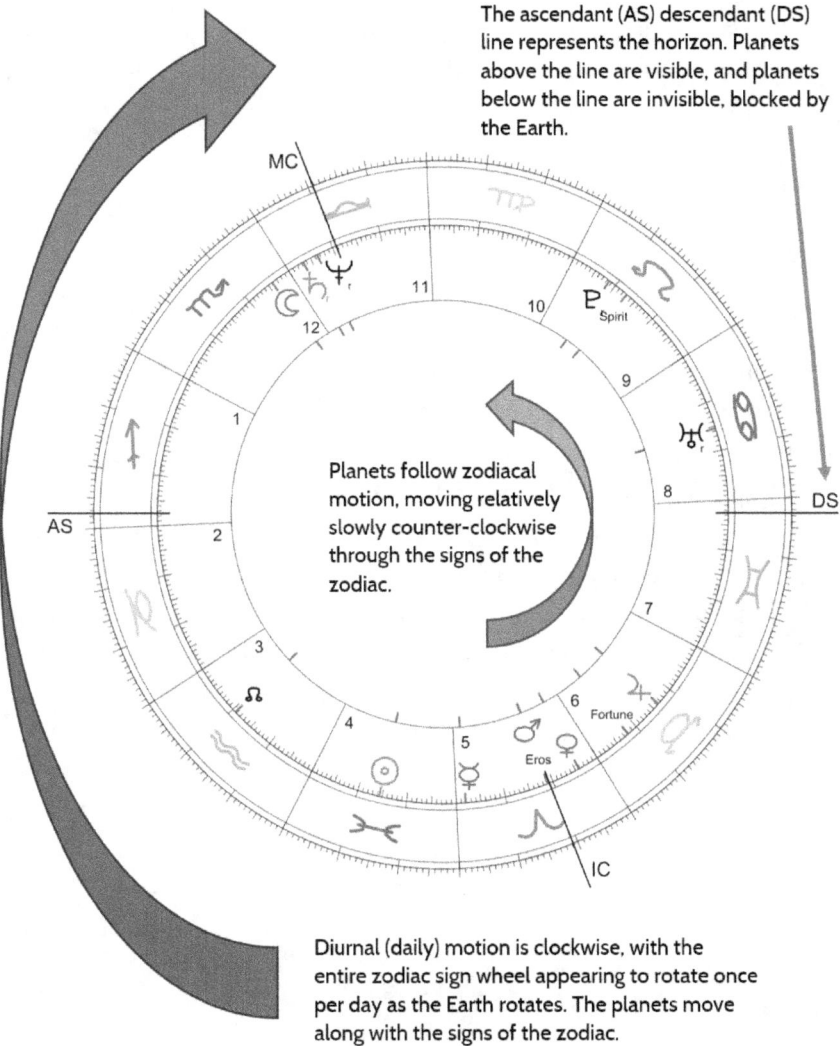

The ascendant (AS) descendant (DS) line represents the horizon. Planets above the line are visible, and planets below the line are invisible, blocked by the Earth.

Planets follow zodiacal motion, moving relatively slowly counter-clockwise through the signs of the zodiac.

Diurnal (daily) motion is clockwise, with the entire zodiac sign wheel appearing to rotate once per day as the Earth rotates. The planets move along with the signs of the zodiac.

Figure 15. The wheel of the zodiac turns clockwise with diurnal motion, rotating once every 24 hours. The planets move through the wheel in a counterclockwise motion called zodiacal motion. Each luminary and planet has its own speed that appears variable based on our view from earth.

- Your ascendant (abbreviated AS, AC, or ASC) is the sign rising on the Eastern horizon at the time of your birth.
- The aspect matrix in Figure 16 is usually included below the wheel chart. It shows the planetary aspects between the planets. These aspects are also called configurations. See the discussion of aspects in Chapter 12 and Appendix H for details of how to read the aspect matrix.

☉ Sun	♓ 14° 26' 2"	
☽ Moon	♏ 4° 3' 11"	Fall
☿ Mercury	♈ 1° 52' 57"	
♀ Venus	♈ 25° 44' 43"	Detr.
♂ Mars	♈ 18° 57' 58"	Dom.
♃ Jupiter	♉ 16° 22' 8"	
♄ Saturn	♎ 26° 37' 14"r	Exalt.

Figure 16. Many astrological charts include an aspect matrix. This summarizes the planetary aspects in a compact format.

- An element/modality matrix in Figure 17 shows the elemental quality and modality of the sign each planet is in. The sign elements (F = Fire, A = Air, E = Earth, W = Water) are in rows, with all the planets in each row sharing the same element. The sign modalities (C = cardinal, F = fixed, M = mutable) are in columns. Planets with the same modality align in one column. This matrix helps you to see the emphasis for each element and modality in a chart.

	C	F	M
F	☿♀♂	♇	
A	♄♅	♌	
E		♃	
W	♅	☽	☉

Figure 17. Many charts have an element/modality matrix with the elements listed down the left side and the modes listed at the top.

On each of the example charts, the previously discussed components along with the following components are annotated:

- Aspect lines in the central circle show the aspects between planets.

- The House numbers show which house each planet is in.
- The planet/zodiac sign list gives the sign of each planet and the degree location or ecliptic longitude in that sign.

Although not directly required for AstroTarot, the chart you produce may include other object positions on the zodiac wheel or other information, including:

- Lots or Arabic parts: Fortune (P. Fort., ⊗) Spirit, and Eros.
- The ascending node (North, *Rahu*, dragon's head, ☊) and descending node (South, *Ketu*, dragon's tail, ☋) show where the paths of the Sun and Moon cross and where eclipses occur.
- The other chart angles besides the ascendent (abbreviated as AC, AS, or ASC) including the midheaven (also called top of the sky or *Medium Coeli,* abbreviated as MC), the descendent, (abbreviated as DC), and the "bottom of the sky" or *Illum Coli,* (abbreviated as IC).
- The main centaurs and asteroids may be shown on the chart: Chiron (⚷), Ceres (⚳), Pallas (⚴), Juno (⚵), and Vesta (⚶). Asteroid meanings are interpreted similar to planets and have their own symbols and meanings.[25] There are thousands of asteroids.
- Wheel rings might be added for the decans and bound lords.[26]
- Essential dignities might be noted for planets, such as fall, detriment (Detr.), domicile (Dom.), or exaltation (Exalt.). Dignities are defined further in the glossary.

Hellenistic and Modern Chart Differences

Hellenistic and modern astrology systems share many of the same basic qualities. You can use the Tarot Spirits to work with either style of astrology. A Hellenistic chart is similar to a modern astrological chart with a few changes:

---

[25] Asteroid meanings are covered in *Astrology for Yourself: A Workbook for Personal Transformation* by Douglas Bloch and Demetra George.
[26] See Glossary for Decans and Bound Lords and the "Focus on the Basics" discussion.

- The ancient seven visible planets are emphasized, and sometimes the more recently discovered outer planets—Neptune, Uranus, and Pluto—are ignored altogether.
- Aspects are treated differently, being based on sign rather than degree. As a result, some aspects shift compared to a modern chart. Planets can have different aspects when comparing modern and Hellenistic charts. A trine (120°) aspect can switch to a square (90°) aspect or the other way round. Aspects are discussed in Chapter 12, with examples in Appendix H.
- Sign rulerships will be different for some signs, as Uranus, Neptune, and Pluto are not included in the Hellenistic ruler lineup. Rulerships are discussed in a more advanced book later in the series and in the glossary.

Hellenistic, Modern, or Both?—You choose!

Its up to you to choose between the two astrological systems covered in this book: Hellenistic and modern. These systems share many items, but differ primarily in aspect determination. Earlier we suggested those new to astrology pick one system, either modern or Hellenistic. Those with more advanced astrology experience can include both chart types in their AstroTarot work. It is easy to get both a modern and Hellenistic chart, as discussed in Appendix H, and review both chart types in comparison with each other.

The crucial difference is how aspects are determined. If you work with both, aspects both **by sign** (Hellenistic) and **by degree** (modern) will be found on your *AstroTarot mapping*. The difference is discussed in Chapter 13 and Appendix H. You can choose to focus on just modern or Hellenistic potentially challenging aspects. Either approach, or a combined approach, works for AstroTarot.

Focus on the Basics

In the explanations above and the charts that follow, many elements are discussed or shown that are not necessary to applying AstroTarot methods to your own chart. This information is included so that you can understand the symbols and items that may show up on the typical chart you will get from an online source. If you are an astrology beginner, just focus on the main items you will need for the AstroTarot work:

- The planets, especially the seven traditional planets
- The signs of the zodiac the planets are located in
- The aspects or angles between the planets (see: Chapters 12 & 13)
- Your ascendant sign

While the rest (sign rulers or lords, centaurs or asteroids, parts or lots, decans, terms or bound lords, nodes, angles, houses, dignities, etc.) are interesting, focus on the basics for now. Learn about the rest later, once you are comfortable with astrological basics.

Four Different Natal Chart Types

You can view the elements discussed above on the following four sample charts. Figures on the following pages show three types of wheel charts and one square astrological chart. All charts shown share identical birth details, referred to as chart "Sample 1" throughout. They all show the positions of planets in the sky for a particular person at the time they were born. Chart types shown include:

- Figure 18: A modern style astrological chart with quadrant houses
- Figure 19: A Hellenistic style chart with whole sign houses
- Figure 20: A hybrid astrological chart with whole sign houses
- Figure 21: A square Hellenistic style chart

An astrological chart is usually computer generated today, either with local software or via a website. In Appendix H, we include instructions for getting your chart at astro.com. When I first started casting astrological charts in high school, the process was manual. We consulted ephemeris tables with the planetary zodiac locations for each day. Then we used interpolation methods to adjust planetary locations for the client's time of birth. Finally, we used a protractor to locate the planets and draw the chart by hand. Computers have made the job of casting an astrological chart much easier.

While looking at the examples of natal chart types, it can be helpful to have your own natal chart handy so you can find the same items there as well.

Modern Astrological Chart with Quadrant Houses

This modern chart has quadrant houses, and some houses are wider than others. Aspect lines connect all the planets, including the outer planets. For this chart, extra objects include the ascending lunar node, the centaur Chiron, and the Part of Fortune. There is an aspect matrix and element/modality matrix.

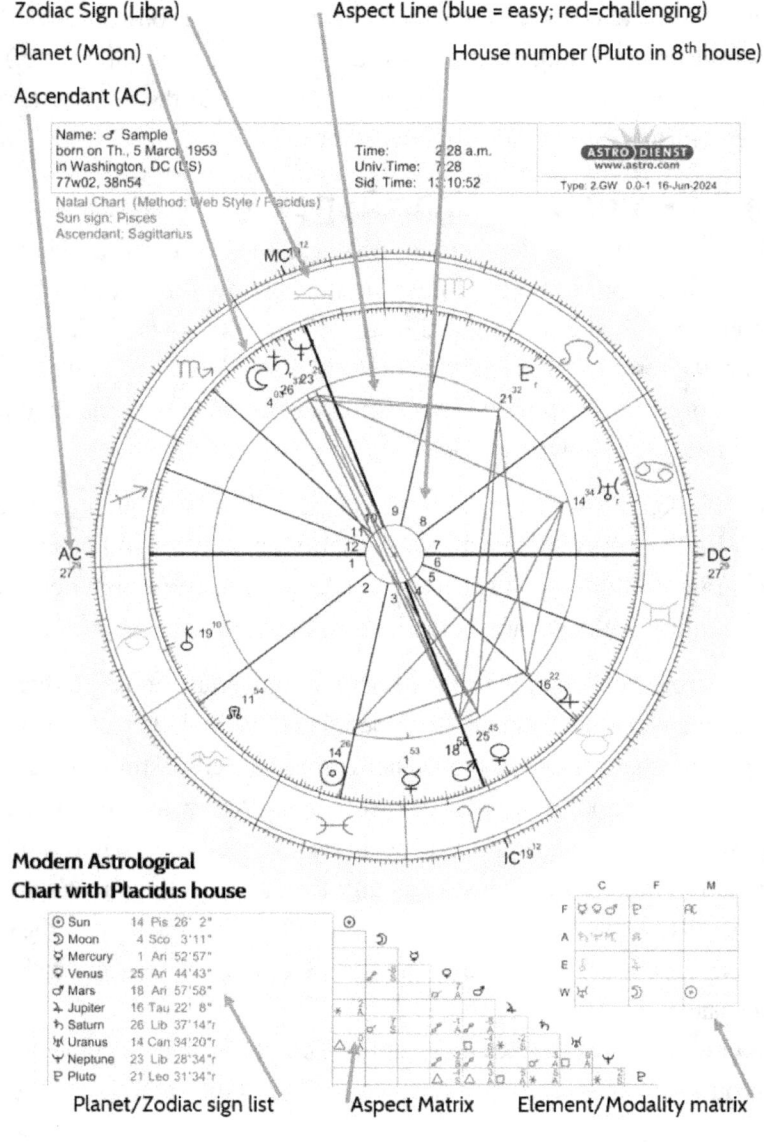

Figure 18. Modern astrological chart. *Generated at Astro.com.*

Hellenistic Astrological Chart with Whole Sign Houses

This Hellenistic chart is for the same person and the items on the wheel match the other charts. Hellenistic charts use whole sign houses, which are all the same width and aligned with the signs. Whole sign aspect lines connect only the seven visible planets. Outer planets without aspect lines and several Lots or Parts are included. There is an aspect matrix and element/modality matrix.

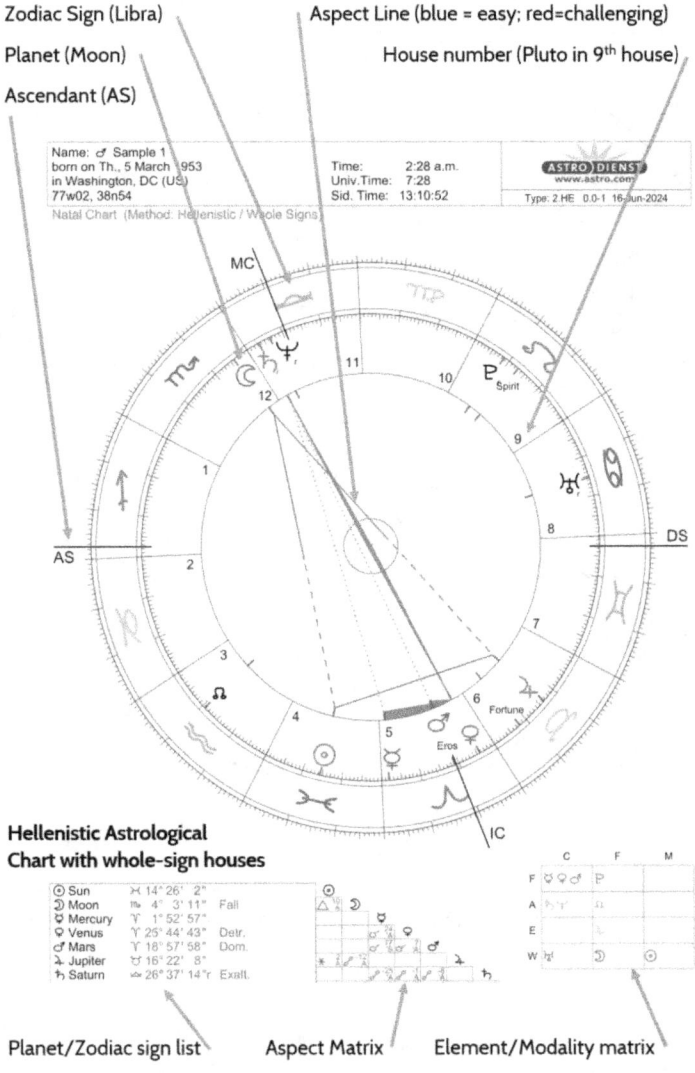

Figure 19. Hellenistic astrological chart. *Generated at Astro.com.*

Hybrid Astrological Chart with Whole Sign houses

This hybrid chart has whole sign houses, as is typical in Hellenistic astrology. As in a modern chart, degree-based aspect lines connect all the planets, including the outer planets. Unlike the earlier two examples, the ascendent/descendent line is not horizontal, but the ascendant (AS) is shown as an object in the ascendant sign of Sagittarius in the first house at the left side.

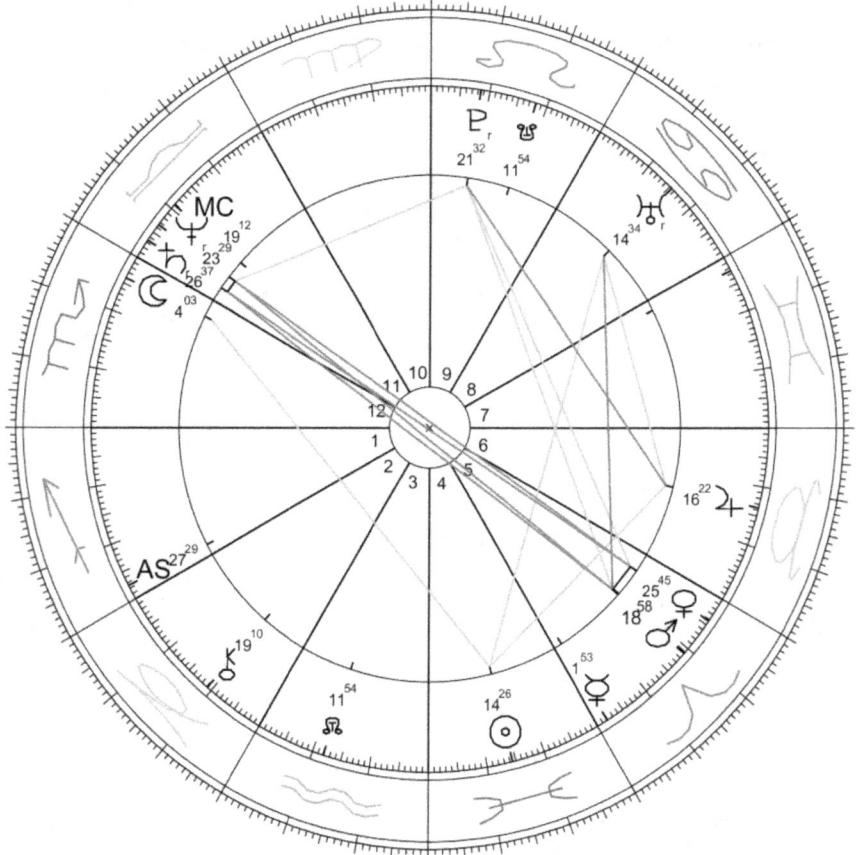

Figure 20. Hybrid astrological chart. *Generated at astro.com with vonXylander chart drawing style.*

Square Hellenistic Astrological Chart

This square Hellenistic chart was in use from the 2nd century BCE through the 7th century CE. It has whole sign houses and is drawn in a square pattern with straight lines dividing the signs. The ascendant sign (Asc) is always the box on the left center. There are three lots with circled planetary symbols: the lot of fortune is a circled Moon, the lot of spirit is a circled Sun, and the lot of eros is a circled Venus.

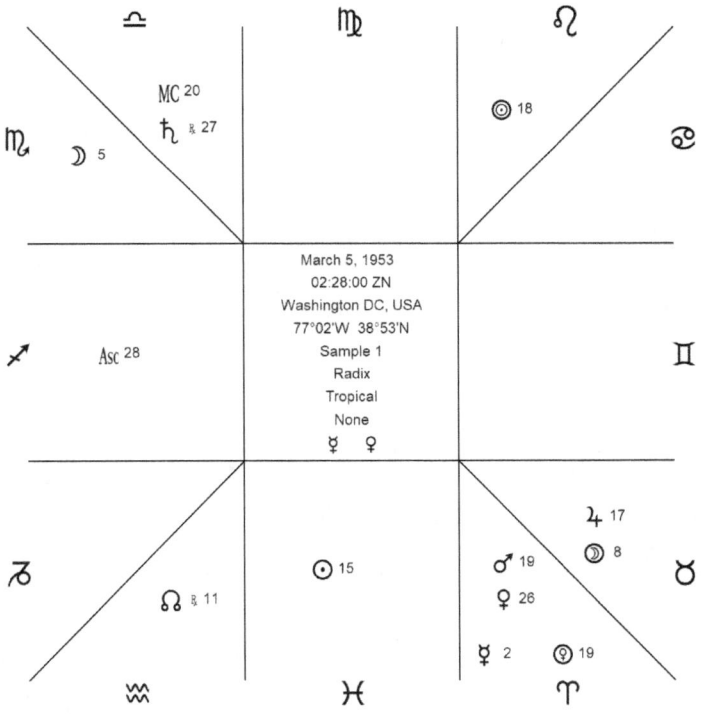

Figure 21. Square Hellenistic astrological chart. *Generated with Valens open source software:* sites.google.com/site/astrovalens/

Chapter 11 Recap

This chapter covered the basics of astrology. If that is new to you, it can seem a bit overwhelming. Just focus on the basics: planets and signs and how to find them in your chart. That's all you need for AstroTarot work. In the next two chapters we learn about the relationship between planets or aspects, and how to work with them in AstroTarot.

12: Tarot Spirits and Your Natal Chart

The Tarot Spirits are there to help you resolve challenges or enhance opportunities in your natal astrological chart. If you are new to astrology, its time to expand your knowledge to identify those challenges and opportunities. Your primary focus is on planetary aspects. Both harmonious and challenging aspects hold significance. Your first clearing of challenging aspects is the most profound part of AstroTarot work. The next chapter will discuss that topic. First, you must map the Tarot Spirits onto your chart and identify those potentially challenging aspects.

Your Own AstroTarot Mapping

Your mission now is to expand from the tour of a general natal chart and basics of astrology in Chapter 11 and find the important Tarot Spirits for you to work with based on your personal natal chart. First, you need to get an organized mapping of your personal astrological chart with the representative Tarot Spirits so that you can do reconciliation pathwork with them. There are two ways you can do this:

- Order a personalized *My AstroTarot Report* with all the mapping done for you, as outlined in Appendix G. If you feel overwhelmed by learning the details of astrology, this is the best path.
- Create your own *AstroTarot mapping* using the instructions in Appendix H. If you want to dig into astrological concepts and have the time to do so, you may want to do this yourself.

Either approach produces the same results, so choose whichever path makes the most sense to you. We will refer to the report or forms as your *"AstroTarot mapping"* from here on.

The Tarot as a Map to the Stars

Many Western Mystery schools emerged in the 17th through 19th centuries. The tarot emerged a few centuries before. In the mystery schools, astrological planets, signs, and Hebrew letters were assigned to each of the tarot keys. AstroTarot is a method to contact the tarot Major Arcana to work with astrology, specifically the astrology of your natal chart.

Astrology of the Spirits

The picture below is a relief of the zodiac from the ceiling of the Chapel to Osiris in the Hathor Temple at Dendera in Egypt. The Louvre in Paris houses the original, with a reconstruction at the original location in the ceiling at Dendera, Egypt.

Figure 22. The relief zodiac in the ceiling of the Hathor Temple. *Credit: Wikimedia commons, public domain.*

Dendera is north of the Aswan Dam, about midway to the Mediterranean Sea. It's near Luxor, which is where the ancient city of Thebes used to be. It's an amazing temple I visited with my wife in 2010. The day had just set a new heat record for March in Egypt and we were escorted by an army jeep with a machine gun to protect us from terrorists.

There is a big debate about a zodiac relief in the ceiling there. Was the relief made in the 16th century BCE or the 1st century CE? Different experts place it between 2500 BCE and 147 CE.[27] Astrological experts have probably proven that it was constructed just around the break point between BCE and CE. There is good evidence that there's both a solar and a lunar eclipse represented by the position of the planetary representatives in the relief. The eclipses happened about 51 or 52 BCE. This configuration with the eclipses occurs infrequently. This analysis shows that the astrological material is quite ancient.

Many of the symbols in the relief are familiar today. You can see the scorpion at about 11 o'clock in the circle. And there is an obvious lion and bull. Most zodiac sign symbols are as we use them today. If this was built around the turn of the millennia, that's when Hellenistic astrology was being formed. Its when information from Egypt was meeting up with information from Babylonia and the next implementation of astrology was forming, as discussed in Appendix F.

Another notable aspect of this depiction is several spiritual entities surrounding the zodiac circle. So not only do we have the symbols of the zodiac itself, but they are surrounded by gods and goddesses. We have support for the ancient idea that the zodiac and astrology are infused with the spirits. It is important to see that working with the Tarot Spirits mapped onto the zodiac is aligned with an ancient process. It is a wholly legitimate process. We aren't directly referencing the Egyptian gods and goddesses, but we are working with spirits who have a connection to the planets and the signs of the zodiac.

Your Natal Chart Mapping

Your *AstroTarot mapping* lists your natal chart Tarot Spirits, as shown in the example on the following page. If you do not get that report as described in Appendix G, you can determine your astrological mapping to Tarot Spirits on your own. Just follow the instructions and use the format in Appendix H. Either approach gives you the same reference guide.

---

[27] en.wikipedia.org/wiki/Dendera_zodiac

| Sample 1 | Planet & Sign Mapping | | Your AstroTarot Spirits | | 2 |

Mar 5, 1953 2:28 AM   Washington, D.C.   <<== Birthdate & Time & Location; printed on 06-Jun-2024

Note: "AS" = Ascendant; see tables below for symbol definitions.

The Planets in your Natal Chart:		Sign	Planet Tarot	Zodiac Sign Tarot	Whole Sign House	Quadrant Koch House
AS ruler; Sagittarius rising (AS)	♃	♐	Wheel of Fortune	Temperance	1	1
AS is the ascendant or rising sign. The planet associated is the ruler of the ascendant zodiac sign.						
Sun in Pisces	☉	♓	The Sun	The Moon	4	3
Moon in Scorpio	☽	♏	High Priestess	Death	12	10
Mercury in Aries	☿	♈	Magician	Emperor	5	3
Venus in Aries	♀	♈	Empress	Emperor	5	4
Mars in Aries	♂	♈	Tower	Emperor	5	3
Jupiter in Taurus	♃	♉	Wheel of Fortune	Hierophant	6	5
Saturn in Libra	♄	♎	World	Justice	11	10
Uranus in Cancer	♅	♋	Fool	Chariot	8	7
Neptune in Libra	♆	♎	Hanged man	Justice	11	10
Pluto in Leo	♇	♌	Judgement	Strength	9	8

Figure 23. The example shows planet symbols and their zodiac sign. To the right, planets and signs are represented by Tarot Spirits side by side. Houses are also shown for two house systems: whole sign houses and Koch quadrant houses.

So if we want to access the Sun in Pisces, we can look at the mapping and see that we work with the Sun Tarot Spirit who represents the Sun and the Moon Tarot Spirit who represents Pisces.

Recommended Tarot Mapping

While any consistent mapping between the tarot Major Arcana or tarot keys and the zodiacal signs and planets will work, most modern esoteric approaches use the English key attributions. They are used by Steinbrecher, Golden Dawn, Builders of the Adytum, and Waite. So, these are recommended for your use.

The English attributions are listed below in two tables. The first shows the mapping of zodiac signs to Tarot Spirits. The second shows how the planets are mapped to the Tarot Spirits. One unexpected mapping is that the Moon is represented by the High Priestess, as she has magical control of the Moon's qualities. The Moon Tarot Spirit represents the zodiac sign Pisces.

Tarot Spirit Mapping to Zodiacal Signs

Astrology Symbol	Sign of the Zodiac	Tarot Spirit or Key (Major Arcana)	Tarot Key #
♈	Aries	The Emperor	4
♉	Taurus	The Hierophant	5
♊	Gemini	The Lovers	6
♋	Cancer	The Chariot	7
♌	Leo	Strength	8*
♍	Virgo	The Hermit	9
♎	Libra	Justice	11*
♏	Scorpio	Death	13
♐	Sagittarius	Temperance	14
♑	Capricorn	The Devil	15
♒	Aquarius	The Star	17
♓	Pisces	The Moon	18

* In the *Thoth Tarot* and derivative decks, Justice becomes "Adjustment" at position 8 and Strength becomes "Lust" at position 11. The signs map to the tarot keys by name rather than number.

Tarot Spirit Mapping to Planets

Astrology Symbol	Planet	Tarot Spirit or Key (Major Arcana)	Tarot Key #
☉	Sun	The Sun	19
☽	Moon	The High Priestess	2
☿	Mercury	The Magician	1
♀	Venus	The Empress	3
♂	Mars	The Tower	16
♃	Jupiter	The Wheel of Fortune	10
♄	Saturn	The World	21
♅	Uranus	The Fool	0
♆	Neptune	The Hanged man	12
♇ ♆	Pluto	Judgement	20

Variants in Tarot-to-Astrology Mapping

There are alternative mappings of tarot keys to the planets and signs. Main approaches include the continental (French) and Spanish approaches, with multiple variations. If you want to pursue mapping methods other than the English occult mapping method shown in the tables above, then review the discussion on variant mappings in Appendix H. Whatever mapping method you choose should be used consistently after a period of experimentation.

Which Tarot Spirits Are Important for AstroTarot?

In your foundational work with Individual Tarot Spirits, you complete three pathworks for each Tarot Spirit individually—A: Tarot Scanning, B: Meet an Individual Tarot Spirit, and C: Get to Know an Individual Tarot Spirit. Once you complete the A/B/C pathworks, you can work with Tarot Spirits in pairs or groups. You can track the resolution of potential conflicts. You may also receive healing or advice. So, your purpose in AstroTarot work is to focus on Tarot Spirits that are important to you personally.

Which Tarot Spirits are important to prioritize? Your natal astrological chart is the place to start. It shows you where planetary powers are either in harmony or in conflict for you personally. In Appendix G or H, you identify which groups of Tarot Spirits are important to you personally, based on your personal chart. These Tarot Spirits are in several groups:

- **Potentially challenging natal aspects.** These pairs of tarot keys represent planets or signs in opposition or square in your natal chart. Challenges can also exist in other aspects. The pairs of potentially challenging Tarot Spirits are listed in Sections 4 and 5 of your *AstroTarot mapping*. In your life, they may work at cross purposes or be out of balance. Each pair can be reconciled and balanced using Pathwork K, presented in the next chapter.

- **Tarot Spirit circles.** These groups can be consulted as needed using Pathwork for advice (H), balancing (I), healing (J), and learning (L). These pathworks are discussed in Chapters 14 and 15. Work with each entire group as a whole—not in pairs—and include your guide and your shadow-self. These circles of Tarot Spirits are listed in Section 6 of your *AstroTarot mapping*. Bring them questions or issues for resolution and healing in the areas of relationships, personal projects, inner truth, current issues, life choices, and healing.

- **Circle of hands.** There are several groups of Tarot Spirits that, when brought together regularly using the circle of hands pathwork (I), ensure there is balance and synergy between these parts of yourself. They are listed in the circle of hands pathwork (I) and will be addressed in Chapter 14. These groups of Tarot Spirits are listed in Sections 7 and 8 of your *AstroTarot mapping*.

Natal Chart Planetary Aspects

The planets in your natal chart form aspects to each other. Aspects can be harmonious or challenging. While aspects are technically called configurations in Hellenistic astrology, we call them aspects here. You identify an aspect by the angular relationship between planets in the chart. Aspects are easy to recognize without a deep understanding of geometry or trigonometry. Luckily, online chart apps will calculate the aspects for you, so you don't need to find them yourself. You can ignore some of the technical information below, but it is important to comprehend the general meaning of the major aspects. Both modern and Hellenistic systems have similar interpretations.

As you work with AstroTarot, you will either reinforce harmonious planetary aspects or clear potential tensions between planets with challenging aspects. While aspects are generally characterized as challenging, harmonious or mixed, there is more than the aspect at play.

The level of challenge or harmony may be affected by planetary condition, house location, and other factors. These advanced concepts are beyond the scope of this book. We will take a simpler approach here. Also, a particular aspect's impact on you varies based on life experience. For example, you may have worked out how to manage the conflicts of a challenging aspect in the course of your life, reducing its negative impact.

We'll discuss the meaning of different major aspects: grouped as challenging, harmonious, and mixed. The matchups of sign element or modality discussed for each aspect below usually apply, but may not always apply in modern astrology when the planets are close to the cusp between signs.

Potentially Challenging Aspects

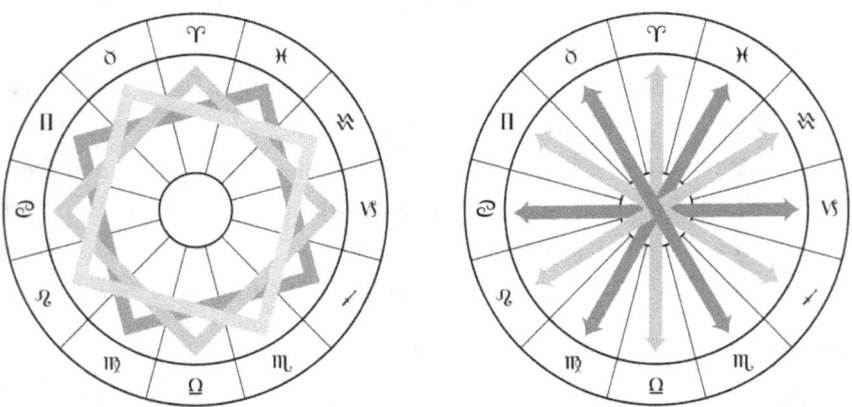

Figure 24. Challenging aspects. The left zodiac circle shows that two planets with a square aspect are a quarter way around the circle, 90 degrees from each other, or three signs apart. The on the right shows that two planets with an opposition aspect are half way around the circle, directly across from each other, 180 degrees or six signs apart. *Graphics credit: Ancient Astrology* by Demetra George.

A square aspect is challenging. So is an opposition aspect. The character of the square can be productive with beneficial planets, but stress or dynamic tension is involved. The relationship tends to be unsympathetic and harsh. It may lead to internal conflict. The opposition is definitely adversarial and often represents conflicting needs. There is a fixed tension between the actions of the planets and a need to impose balance. When Mars or Saturn are involved with either of these challenging aspects, the harshness, stress, or imbalance is amplified. More details about the two challenging aspects:

- **Square.** The planets are 90 degrees apart or three signs away. The planets are at right angles. This aspect is like rotating a square in the horoscope chart, with adjacent points touching signs or planets that have this aspect. There is usually some tension here, with the possible exception of the Moon, Venus, and Jupiter. When planets form a square, their signs will be opposite polarity and the same modality: cardinal, fixed, or mutable. They will have mis-matched elemental qualities. keywords for square aspects include: obstacles, produces stress with, and creates dynamic tension with.
- **Opposition.** The planets are 180 degrees apart or six signs away from each other. They are directly across the circle. There is usually tension here, with the possible exception of the Moon, Venus, and Jupiter. When planets are in opposition, their signs will be opposite polarity and the same modality: cardinal, fixed, or mutable. Keywords for oppositions include: awareness, opposes, creates tension with, and needs to balance with.

Harmonious Aspects

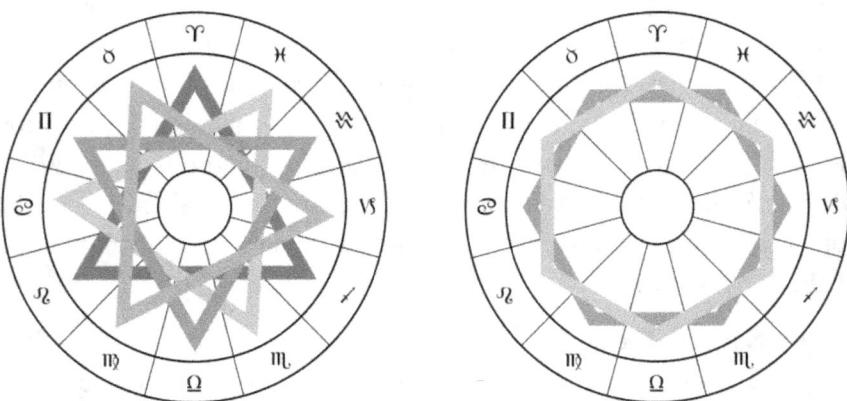

Figure 25. Harmonious Aspects. The trine aspect at left shows that the two planets are one third the way around the circle, 120 degrees from each other, or four signs apart. The sextile on the right shows the two planets are one-sixth of the way around the circle, 60 degrees or two signs apart. *Graphics credit: Ancient Astrology* by Demetra George.

The trine aspect is always highly harmonious. The energy flow between planets is easy. Planets support and cooperate effectively. They have a positive impact on the native. A sextile aspect is also harmonious, but much weaker than a trine. More details about the two harmonious aspects:

- **Trine.** The planets are 120 degrees apart or four signs away. This aspect is like rotating a triangle in the horoscope chart, with adjacent points touching signs or planets that have this aspect. There is almost always harmony here. When planets are in trine, their signs will be the same polarity and the same element (fire, air, earth, water). Trine aspect keywords include harmony, easily combines with, and creatively interacts with.

- **Sextile.** The planets are 60 degrees apart or two signs away. This aspect is like rotating a hexagon in the horoscope chart, with adjacent points touching signs or planets that have this aspect. Generally, sextile is a positive aspect, with the possible exception of Mars and Saturn. When planets are in sextile, their signs will be of the same polarity and matched as fire and air or earth and water. Sextile aspect key phrases include opportunity, productively combines with, and facilitates the expression of. The sextile function is weak and possibly ineffective compared to the trine.

Mixed Aspects

When planets are in the same sign or near each other, they form a conjunction aspect. The qualities of the planets get mixed together. When planets are one (semi-sextile) or five (quincunx) signs apart they are considered averse. Averse planets cannot be connected with one of the regular polygons. Hence, the planets have difficulty communicating.

- **Conjunction.** The planets are next to each other, within the set orb of degrees from each other or in the same sign. Conjunctions indicate support or merging of planet qualities. An exception is when Mars or Saturn are involved. Then there can be tension. Mercury or the Sun can also produce tension. When a planet is within 15 degrees either side of the Sun, the planetary qualities are considered suppressed in Hellenistic astrology. The Sun is so bright it blocks out the qualities of the planet. In conjunctions by sign, planets are in the same sign, so they are influenced with the same polarity, modality, and element of the sign. Conjunction aspect keywords include emphasis, merges with, and unconsciously identifies with.

- **Averse aspects**. Minor aspects in modern astrology include the quincunx and semi-sextile, among others. These aspects do not connect with regular polygons. These averse aspects have potential for disharmony or lack of connection, but are usually not a strong influence. So they are not usually included in the basic AstroTarot work.

Aspect Symbols and Matrix

You have just learned the symbols for the planets and signs of the zodiac, so it's time to learn the symbols for the aspects. These symbols appear in aspect matrices on most natal charts. The aspect matrix summarizes the planetary aspects in a compact format. A sample matrix is shown in Figure 26. The aspects are indicated using the symbols in the aspect symbol table. By simply finding the intersection of two planets on the matrix you can see if there is an aspect and what type it is. Alternatively, you can look for a particular type of aspect, like squares or oppositions, by scanning for the aspect symbol of interest. The sample matrix also shows the degree of the sign the planet is at and lists essential dignities.

The aspect between planets or other objects in the modern astrological chart is determined by degrees within an orb of the perfect aspect. In Hellenistic astrology the aspect is determined by the number of signs apart. Focus on the major aspects discussed above. While there are many minor aspects, we do not use them in AstroTarot work.

The following table shows the major aspects and the averse aspects between planets. The table lists the name of the aspect, symbol, degrees between planets for the perfect degree aspect, signs apart for a whole sign aspect, and a brief description.

Aspect or Configuration	Symbol	Degrees between	Signs apart	Description; Relationship Quality
Conjunction	☌	0°	0	Objects in the same sign; merging or unified
Sextile	✶	60°	2	Objects two signs away; mildly easy, harmonious
Square	☐	90°	3	Objects three signs away; challenging, conflicting
Trine	△	120°	4	Objects four signs away; harmonious synthesis
Opposition	☍	180°	6	Opposite each other; divisive, major challenge
Semi-sextile*	⚺	30°	1	Considered averse aspects as they are not formed by a regular polygon
Quincunx*	⚻	150°	5	

* Semi-sextile and quincunx are considered minor aspects. They are included here as they are recognized as an averse whole sign aspect in Hellenistic astrology.

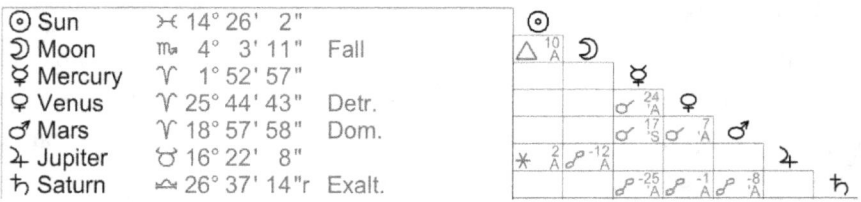

☉ Sun	♓ 14° 26' 2"	
☽ Moon	♏ 4° 3' 11"	Fall
☿ Mercury	♈ 1° 52' 57"	
♀ Venus	♈ 25° 44' 43"	Detr.
♂ Mars	♈ 18° 57' 58"	Dom.
♃ Jupiter	♉ 16° 22' 8"	
♄ Saturn	♎ 26° 37' 14"r	Exalt.

Figure 26. Many astrological charts include an aspect matrix.

Modern and Hellenistic Aspect Differences

To reflect different approaches to astrology, aspects can be evaluated two ways, resulting in three different categories of aspect:

- Aspects **by sign** are evaluated by the angular relationship between the signs the planets are in. This method is Hellenistic.
- Aspects **by degree** are evaluated by the actual degree angle between the planets on the zodiac wheel. This method is primarily modern and involves orbs as discussed below.
- Aspects **by sign and degree** meet the requirements of both evaluation methods.

Modern astrology focuses on aspects between planets measured by degree on the horoscope wheel. The software determines the aspects, so you don't need know the technicalities to do the AstroTarot pathwork. Each aspect **by degree** counts when the perfect aspect degree from one planet falls within an orb [28] of another planet. The software used to generate your chart in Appendix G or H accounts for the orbs appropriate for each planet and aspect.[29]

In Hellenistic astrology, the relationships of the planets are called configurations rather than aspects. In Hellenistic astrology aspects are based primarily on the sign each planet is in, rather than the exact degrees between the planets. So, planets that are four signs away would have a trine aspect (120°) even if the planets were not within an orb of being 120 degrees apart. That is because the signs they are in are 120 degrees apart.

We can refer to this difference as planets having aspects **by degree** (modern) or **by sign** (Hellenistic). Figure 24 and Figure 25 show the major Hellenistic configurations or aspects in which planets can bear witness and support each other. When an aspect meets the criteria for both systems, the

---

[28] In modern astrology the orb is measured plus or minus the degree from the exact aspect angle from the first planet to the second. If the orb was 7°, a square (theoretically 90°) would count if the angle between planets was anywhere between 83° and 97°. A traditional or Hellenistic astrologer would refer to that as a moiety of ±7° and would call the "orb" 14° or the entire arc that made a valid aspect.

[29] The allowed orbs vary by planet and aspect with larger orbs for the Sun and Moon (between 5 and 9 degrees) to smaller orbs for the transpersonal outer planets (between 2 and 5 degrees). The range indicates a variance by aspect with conjunctions and oppositions the largest, sextiles the smallest and trines and squares in between or sometimes the same as the conjunction.

aspect is valid **by sign and degree.** The point of this distinction is to prioritize your planetary reconciliation work. We discuss that in the next chapter. If you lean toward modern astrology, you are only concerned about aspects that are evaluated **by degree** within an orb. If you lean towards Hellenistic astrology, you are only concerned about aspects that are evaluated **by sign**. If you aren't sure, you can work with all the identified challenging aspects. Those **by sign and degree** are important to both modern and Hellenistic astrology. If you wanted to be thorough in AstroTarot work, you could just include all three types of aspects.

Astrological Aspect Patterns

In addition to looking at aspects between two planets, there are patterns of aspects in some charts with more planets involved. These are based on modern astrology with aspects by degree. Of specific interest in AstroTarot are the T-square, grand cross, grand trine, and Yod. Not every chart has these patterns. How to recognize the four main patterns is described in Appendix H with examples and graphics. The specific planets in each pattern of the examples are listed in Appendix H.

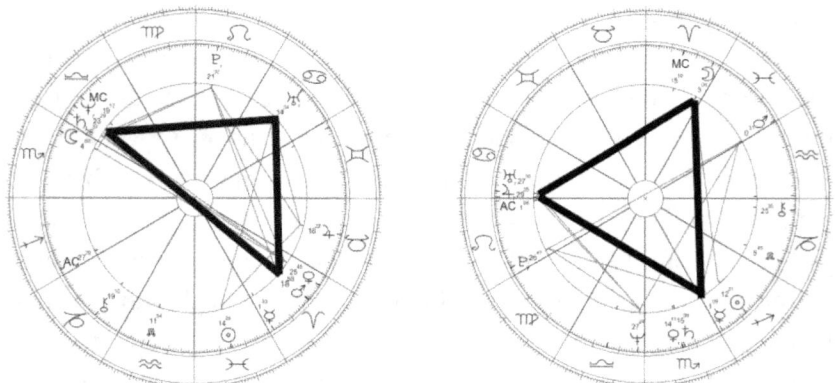

Figure 27. The T-square pattern at left from the sample chart is considered challenging, while the grand trine pattern at right from a different chart is considered quite harmonious. *Credit: Author using charts from astro.com.*

The meaning of the main challenging patterns is briefly discussed below:

- The T-cross or T-square pattern with two planets in opposition and each squared by a third implies drive and courage, but can have ongoing conflict or tension. If you have this pattern, you may find you experience frustration and focus on conflict in daily life (see Figure 27).
- The Grand square or grand cross pattern adds a fourth planet to the T-cross. There can be a sense of oppression and you might feel surrounded by conflict with this pattern in your chart. Lack of flexibility can be a challenge (see Figure 28).

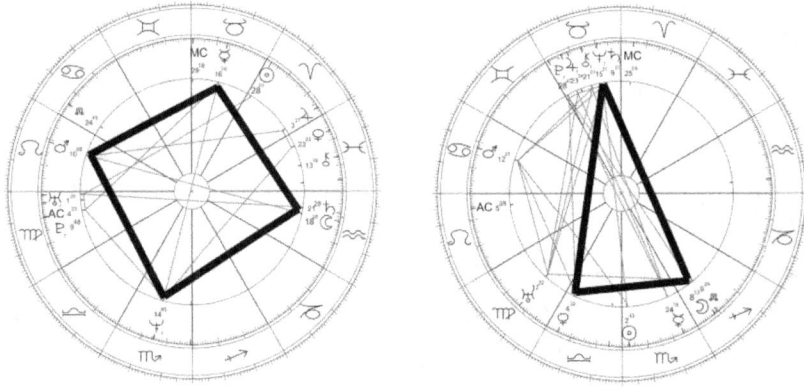

Figure 28. The grand-square pattern at left from Conan O'Brien's chart is considered quite challenging, while the Yod pattern at right from Pablo Picasso's chart is considered beneficial once integrated. *Credit: Author using charts from astro.com.*

The meaning of the main harmonious or neutral patterns is briefly discussed below:

- In contrast, the grand trine is harmonious and brings a blessed life. The pattern forms with three planets, each in trine to two others, creating an equilateral triangle in the chart. You can work with this group in AstroTarot to enhance positive opportunities, if applicable. Sometimes, the beneficence of this chart pattern results in a lack of motivation or challenge in the native's life (see Figure 27).

- Yod patterns have a mixed impact. A Yod involves three or more planets connected with an acute triangle. Two planets are in sextile and form the base of the Yod triangle. The planet opposite the center of that sextile base is in quincunx to the base planets. The quincunx aspect is also known as inconjunct or averse, and means that the planets cannot witness each other directly with a regular polygon. This leads to a possible hidden or difficult to see mystery. While, potentially wonderful once the mystery of one's destiny is discovered, there can be stress until maturity uncovers the deeper meaning of this planetary relationship (see Figure 28).

Other chart patterns could be included as well. For more information on patterns and their meanings, search the web for "astrological aspect patterns."

Chapter 12 Recap

Your natal chart is a map of the planets in the zodiac at the time of your birth. The planets are each located in a zodiac sign. Planets and signs can be represented by a Tarot Spirit. The planets have aspects with each other, based on their angular relationship. Some aspects (squares, oppositions, and some conjunctions) are potentially challenging. Other aspects (trine and sextile) are harmonious. Some charts have special patterns that amplify the impact of the aspects.

13: Resolve Challenging Natal Aspects

Conversation 5: Resolving Astrological Challenges

As she walked downtown, Rachel noticed the lights in the trees. There was a sense of winter seasonal spirit in the air. She slipped into the warmth of the Italian restaurant and spotted Isabel at a window table. As she sat down, Isabel asked, "How was your trip back East?"

"Well, I was able to ignore the tension between Mom and Dad and just enjoy my separate visits with each of them. I was fortunately distracted from their interactions because I was figuring out my *AstroTarot mapping*."

"Yes, I worked on mine, too. I now see that astrology is about much more than just having a Pisces Sun and Moon in Taurus."

After they ordered a bottle of their favorite Tuscan red wine, Rachel smiled and said, "Yes, finding the potentially challenging aspects between planets and doing journeys with the Tarot Spirits revealed surprising information for me. I explored the opposition between Saturn and Jupiter in my chart and wow! I had no idea it could be so intense! the World Tarot Spirit represented Saturn and Jupiter was the Wheel of Fortune. In my journey, they were almost spitting at each other. My tarot guide stepped right in and helped me get their attention so they would talk to each other. I let them know that my financial situation was not good. The World pointed out that I am disorganized around money. The Wheel suggested I could better promote my skills. They agreed to work together to improve my financial status. Just a week after I did that journey, I heard about some openings at two other firms. I've been updating my resume and realized that I am doing a lot more than my current job description—a lot more!"

"Wow, that's great! I wish you good luck with getting a more rewarding job."

The vegan cannoli for Rachel and Isabel's chicken piccata arrived, surrounding them with warm aromas. After a few bites, Isabel picked up the discussion. "It took me a while to understand the aspects in astrology so I could identify my challenging planetary aspects. I did a couple of journeys around that. The strongest impact came from a journey to the Tower for Mars and the Magician for Mercury. I think you know I can sometimes be a little fuzzy in my logical thinking. I go more on instinct or intuition. Well, the Tower was yelling at the Magician in my journey, just throwing insults at him. My tarot guide and I finally convinced the Tower that if he wanted me to be more assertive in the world, I would need to have clearer thinking and time to think without feeling so much pressure. As a result, I agreed to spend a little more time meditating while ignoring outside distractions so I could become clearer about my own thoughts."

The two women looked at each other thoughtfully. They raised their wine glasses and toasted each other with their favorite toast. "Here's to us!" they said simultaneously and smiled as they sipped their wine.

Aspects in Your Natal Chart

In your natal chart, the planets form aspects to each other that can be harmonious or challenging. As you work with the Tarot Spirit circles, you bring harmonious aspects into play. Using Pathwork K, you aim to clear potential tensions or stress between planets based on challenging aspects. The real reason to resolve challenging aspects comes down to clearing obstacles in your life path. You may be born with a "star crossed" situation, but in my view, you are not stuck with it. Using shamanic techniques with the Tarot Spirits, you can directly connect with and clear the more challenging aspects.

To apply this method, you do not need to be an astrology expert, but you need to cover the astrological basics discussed in Chapters 11 and 12. The steps include (1) getting your own natal chart, (2) mapping the astrology to Tarot Spirits, and then (3) reconciling the most challenging aspects. You will also work with harmonious aspects to increase your life force and make progress with your wishes when working with the Tarot Spirit circles and positive groups in Chapter 14.

You resolve challenging natal aspects in your chart by working with Tarot Spirits who represent the planets and signs in your chart. Where planets are in conflict, you can journey to the Tarot Spirit representatives and engage in a mediation process.

Some examples of challenging aspects in the sample chart are:

- There is a strong opposition by both sign and degree, from Saturn in Libra to Venus in Aries. There are also weaker oppositions by sign only: Saturn to Mercury and Saturn to Mars. These three pairs of planets have unique challenges and should be reconciled for this chart. Taken together, these aspects point towards a personal challenge and fear when working with authority. This interpretation resonates with Saturn's theme of structure. The approach is to reconcile the planets in pairs for each individual aspect. Then work regularly with all four planet Tarot Spirits in a circle of hands. After the reconciliation, issues around authority can fall into perspective, expanding life potential.

- Another opposition is the Moon in Scorpio to Jupiter in Taurus. This is a gentler challenge, as neither Mars nor Saturn are involved. There is a limitation on expansive wealth. When the High Priestess and the Wheel of Fortune reconcile, they help create a clear path to moderate financial success.

In these examples, the thematic nature of the planets and signs are considered. However, that it is not necessary. Just identifying the planets with challenging aspects and then using the Tarot Spirits for reconciliation in a shamanic journey is enough. The journey will reveal the areas of life affected by the conflict. The process itself creates the resolution of challenges. When you work with Pathwork K, follow-on effort in ordinary reality is required to achieve full reconciliation. Yet, you do not need to figure out what the challenging aspects mean ahead of the journey.

Mapping Potentially Challenging Natal Aspects

To reconcile challenging aspects, first you need an organized mapping of the representative Tarot Spirits to your personal astrological chart (Section 2 of the *AstroTarot mapping*). After that, you need a map of the potentially challenging aspect pairs. Then you can do the reconciliation pathwork with them. You can get your *AstroTarot mapping* in one of two ways:

- Order a personalized *My AstroTarot Report* with all the mapping done for you, as outlined in Appendix G.
- Fill out your own *AstroTarot mapping* using the forms and instructions in Appendix H.

Either approach creates the same *AstroTarot mapping*, so choose whichever makes the most sense to you. We will discuss the background of mapping and prioritization here, but the detailed steps to create your own map are in Appendix H.

Sample 1	Potential Challenging Aspects	Your AstroTarot
Mar 5, 1953 2:28 AM	Washington, D.C.	<<== Birthdate & Time & Location:

Potential Challenging Aspects

> Work these challenging aspects in pairs to identify and resolve conflicts. Prioritize traditional planets with aspects by both sign and degree. After exercise "A/B/C" with each separately, do pathwork "K" with the pair.

Planetary Oppositions and Squares

opposition; sign and degree	♀	♄	Empress <= => World
opposition; sign and degree	♂	♄	Tower <= => World
challenging conjunction	☿	♂	Magician <= => Tower
challenging conjunction	♀	♂	Empress <= => Tower
opposition by sign	☽	♃	High Priestess <= => Wheel of Fortune
opposition by sign	☿	♄	Magician <= => World
opposition by degree	☽	♀	High Priestess <= => Empress

Classic Planets above (Priority 1 & personal) / Outer Planets Below (Priority 2/generational)

opposition; sign and degree	♀	♆	Empress <= => Hanged man
opposition; sign and degree	♂	♆	Tower <= => Hanged man

Figure 29. A portion of Section 4 from the *AstroTarot Report* shows challenging aspects and the representative Tarot Spirits.

Now look at your own chart aspect matrix. You can use either a modern or Hellenistic chart. Look at Section 4 of either your *AstroTarot Report* or the *AstroTarot mapping* forms you filled out with the instructions in Appendix H. We will refer to both of those as your *AstroTarot mapping* from here on. You can see the potential challenging aspects to work with in Section 4 of your *AstroTarot mapping*. Each aspect has a pair of Tarot Spirits to work with. Priority 1 has only the seven traditional planets involved. Priority 2 expands to include the three outer planets. Figure 29 shows an example of challenging aspects in Section 4 of the *AstroTarot Report*.

Review the planets you find in Section 4 of your *AstroTarot mapping*. See if the aspect is an opposition, square, or conjunction. As we discussed in Chapter 12, aspects are "by sign and degree," "by sign," or "by degree." If you want to cover both modern and Hellenistic astrology, include them all. If your focus is only modern you can ignore the ones by sign only. If your focus is only Hellenistic you can ignore the ones by degree only.

First, you want to work individually with the Tarot Spirits listed in the Priority 1 potentially challenging aspects group at the top. Prioritize them in your A/B/C journeys. Then you can move on to reconciliation.

Focus on the Highest Priority Challenges

You may find many aspects in your chart, perhaps with several of them potentially challenging. Remember that even if you were unaware of astrological aspects, you have been working on coping with or overcoming any negative influence, just in the course of your life to date. Again, the aspects you identify are **potentially** challenging. So, you may work with a pair of Tarot Spirits on your list and find that everything is simply fine between them. This means you have already worked out some or all of the issues related to that challenging aspect.

Prioritization Method

The challenging aspects are unique for each individual. You may have many or few. I remember one workshop where a couple of attendees had only a few, while another had a two-page list. If you only have a few, reconcile them all. If you have many, then prioritize them. This helps you focus on the aspects with the highest potential reconciliation benefit. Not every aspect is so impactful. The *AstroTarot mapping* prioritizes the planetary aspect pairs into 5 groups, briefly listed here. More detailed prioritization instructions with examples are in Appendix H.

1. The top of Section 4 has challenging planetary aspects related to the seven traditional planets. Priority 1 includes all squares and oppositions related to the traditional planets. It also include conjunctions involving Mars, Saturn, and the Sun.

2. Priority 2 on the bottom of Section 4 has aspects similar to priority 1, but expands to aspect pairs that include the outer planets: Uranus, Neptune, and Pluto.

3. Section 5 has pairs of signs that oppose each other, rather than planets.
4. Section 9 is optional and for those who want to be quite thorough. It includes aspect pairs with conjunctions that were not covered under priority 1 or 2. It also has sextiles, semi-sextiles, and quincunxes. Planets with these aspects rarely create strife in your life; however conjunctions with Mercury can sometimes be problematic. Give higher priority to the seven traditional planets over the outer planets.
5. The lowest priority aspects are not listed in the *AstroTarot mapping,* but could include other minor aspects.

Priority 1 & 2: Section 4 challenging aspects. For most folks, working with just priority groups 1 and 2 and part of group 3 makes sense.

Any aspect pairs with outer planets (Uranus, Neptune, and Pluto) are priority 2. These planets move very slowly and are more generational than personal. Many people born within a few months of the same birthdate have the same aspects between outer planets. From an ancient astrological point of view, these planets were not visible. As the Western Mystery astrological traditions were developing, outer planets were not considered. They are not part of the long-term astrological tradition, so interpreting outer planets is not as well established as it is for the seven traditional planets.

We don't need exact prioritization, as the aspect pairs represent only potential challenges. The actual challenges are revealed when you do the Pathwork K journey. Establishing the priorities perfectly would require an analysis of planetary condition including rulerships, dignity, and other planetary aspects. A simplified prioritization is good enough without the added analysis needed for more subtle prioritization. The simplified prioritization works for both modern and Hellenistic astrology.

Adjustments for astrological style. If you are agnostic regarding modern vs. Hellenistic astrology, work with the priorities outlined above. If you have a strong preference, make these adjustments:

•   If your choice is modern astrology, then you can skip pairs identified as having aspects by sign only. You can also skip challenging conjunctions. Pay attention to pairs that have aspects by both sign and degree, as well as by degree alone.

• If your choice is Hellenistic astrology, skip pairs with aspects by degree only. Give emphasis to pairs connected by both sign and degree, as well as sign alone. Also include those with challenging conjunctions.

Priority 3: opposing signs. After you have completed the priority 1 and 2 pairs that are important to you, move on to the opposing signs. Sub-prioritization here can be simplified by working first with the pair related to your ascendant. Then you can add the pairs with your Sun sign and Moon sign. An alternative sub-prioritization approach is to focus on the signs with opposing planets in them. More simply, you can skip the sub-prioritization and just do reconciliation journeys for all six pairs of opposing signs. Pairs of Tarot Spirits to work in priority 3 are shown in Section 5 of your *AstroTarot mapping* with the ascendant pair highlighted:

Opposing Signs (Challenging)   **Your AstroTarot Spirits**   **5**

Opposing Signs - Work in pairs with Pathwork "K" (after A/B/C) as potential challenging aspects.

Prioritize the pair with your ascendant: Sagittarius Rising, represented by Temperance.

				Date
Signs: Aries vs Libra	♈	♎	Emperor <= => Justice	
Signs: Taurus vs Scorpio	♉	♏	Hierophant <= => Death	
Signs: Gemini vs Sagittarius	♊	♐	Lovers <= => Temperance	ASC
Signs: Cancer vs Capricorn	♋	♑	Chariot <= => Devil	
Signs: Leo vs Aquarius	♌	♒	Strength <= => The Star	
Signs: Virgo vs Pisces	♍	♓	Hermit <= => The Moon	

Figure 30. Section 5 from the *AstroTarot Report* shows opposing zodiac signs and the representative Tarot Spirits.

Priority 4 & 5: other aspects. Priority 4 and 5 aspects rarely have significant tensions that require reconciliation, but it is possible. How far you go depends on your desired depth and time commitment for this work. These aspects rarely reveal potent challenges. One possible exception is conjunctions with Mercury, which can be challenging in certain charts. Priority 4 is included in the mapping in case an issue exists. Priority 5 is optional, including only minor aspects. It requires expansion of Section 9. While these other aspects are not often a challenge, it may make sense to reconcile them by those who have very few aspects in Section 4. Another approach to Section 9 is to think thematically, and engage with planets that reflect a difficult situation in your life and have a minor aspect. For example, romantic difficulty may point toward a minor aspect between Mars and Venus. Financial problems can result from a minor aspect between Mercury and Jupiter or Jupiter and Mars or Saturn. Wait to look at thematic minor aspects until the main Priority 1, 2, and 3 aspects have been reconciled.

Prioritization is Approximate

The prioritization is not exact. More detailed planetary condition factors such as dignity and sect are not considered. In the shamanic Tarot Spirit process, fine tuning priority is not important. The prioritization is an indicator of higher potential for challenge. The actual tensions for each individual pair will vary for each person. The shamanic journey to the relevant Tarot Spirits is how you discover which pairs have the biggest current impact on your life. In the journey process itself, the actual level of challenge will become known. The needed personal remedies will come forth in the journey.

For most, working with just priority groups 1 and 2 and part of group 3 makes sense. Groups 4 and 5 rarely have pairs with significant tension that requires reconciliation, but it is possible. The depth of the work and the time devoted are up to you.

The Bad Boys vs. Good Boys & Girls

If you want to sub-prioritize, accelerate reconciling aspect pairs that contain either Mars or Saturn. These planets are considered "malefic" and can have a greater negative impact. This malefic tendency can be improved by sect or dignity. However, that analysis can be time consuming and requires a deeper understanding of astrology than we will consider here. Even though modern astrology places a positive spin on chart interpretation compared with Hellenistic, modern astrology still has a concern about the impact of Mars and Saturn. For example, Isabel Hickey points out that a conjunction of Mars and Saturn would be extremely difficult, while harmony would be found when Venus and Jupiter are conjunct.[30]

---

[30] Hickey, I. *Astrology: A Cosmic Science*. p 71.

In addition to the bigger challenge posed by aspects with Mars and Saturn, aspects with the Sun can also be challenging. They are prioritized after Mars and Saturn in groups 1 and 2.

The Moon, Venus, and Jupiter are always considered benefic, and are less likely to contribute to a stressful planetary relationship. They should be included in the journeys, in case friction exists. Just give them lower priority.

Figure 31. The Tower is key 16 (XVI) and represents Mars, one of the more challenging planets. Where Mars has challenging aspects in your chart, reconciliation is very important. *Credit: DruidCraft Tarot.*

All Potentially Challenging Aspects use the Same Method

No matter what the priority, any potentially challenging aspect will use Pathwork K to reconcile the pair of Tarot Spirits. This includes priority 1 & 2 pairs in Section 4 of your *AstroTarot mapping*, priority 3 pairs in Section 5, and priority 4 and 5 pairs in Section 9.

Pathwork K: Reconcile Challenging Aspects

Let's focus on Pathwork K. The purpose of Pathwork K is to refocus potentially challenging aspects into a more positive direction. You will work with the two Tarot Spirits representing the planets involved in each potentially challenging aspect. It is best to complete Pathwork A, B, and C previously with both Tarot Spirits individually, or at least A and B. You should also have connected with a caring tarot guide who travels with you on this journey. Select the pair of Tarot Spirits that represent the planetary or sign challenging aspect. Reconcile each pair in a separate journey.

Steps for Pathwork K: Reconcile Challenging Aspects

Journey intention: Create more harmony between the pair of Tarot Spirits
_____ and _____ who represent planets
(or signs) _____ and _____.

1. [Optional, before the journey] Review the interpretation of the impact of the two aspected planets. What life area could they affect? See the interpretation options discussed at the end of Appendix H.
2. Complete your Tarot Spirit opening steps from Chapter 5.
3. Tell your guide which Tarot Spirits you want to reconcile differences with. Ask your guide for any advice for this journey. Have your guide take you to a neutral place to meet with these two Tarot Spirits.

   - Ask: "Is it a good time to seek reconciliation?" If not, come back later after doing another pathwork C journey with each Spirit.
   - Inform the Tarot Spirits that their disagreement, opposition, or lack of cooperation affects your life and the world around you. Tell them you experience upset, difficulty, injury, pain (physical or emotional), and chaos. Give examples.
   - Make a sincere plea that you want to resolve any life challenges they are contributing to.
   - Ask what each one needs from the other to work together.
   - Ask whether they agree to fulfill each other's requests and work together.

- Ask the guide to mediate or interpret if needed.

4. When they have some agreement, ask what you need to do, or stop doing, in your life to help them stay in harmony with each other.
5. Stand in a circle, holding hands with the Tarot Spirits, your shadow-self, and your guide. Complete Pathwork I1, the circle of hands.
6. Work with your guide for help to interpret answers or clarify any commitments.
7. If at any time your guide tells you to leave, or you feel you should leave the journey for now, then do so with your guide's help, as previously discussed under safety.
8. Complete your Tarot Spirit closing steps from Chapter 5.

Pathwork K is the key to reconciling tension between pairs of Tarot Spirits. It is important to complete this with the high priority Tarot Spirit pairs listed in your *AstroTarot mapping* and then move on to circle of hands activities with groups of Tarot Spirits. Not every pair of spirits on the list of potentially challenging aspects based on your birth chart will have a high level of tension or stress. You may have worked it out already in your normal life growth. If the pair of Tarot Spirits both agree that "all is in harmony" then take them at their word and move on to the next potentially challenging pair.

Reports on Reconciling Potential Challenging Aspects

Reports from those who have done this pathwork are included below. Honor the truth of your own experience. Avoid comparing yourself to others.

Christine: I chose the Empress and the Wheel of Fortune. It was very difficult for me to connect in the beginning and then finally a hornbill, which is in the family of a toucan, appeared. It landed on my left shoulder. From there, my spirit guide came and took me on horseback to a place in a field. As soon as the Empress appeared, I felt very safe with her and very happy to be in her presence. And then when the Wheel of Fortune came, it was very weird, almost like a very cocky attitude. Like he was prancing around back and forth. All of a sudden, he built a wall. We were at a fire, and he built this wall up around it. And then the hornbill started singing and then slowly started tapping with his beak, breaking the wall down. Then memories of a longing when I was like a teenager came up like an old story. Then the hornbill just kept helping me and singing, to make peace. And then I just told them that I just want to experience real connections. They just held hands at the end over the fire circle and it felt very promising. Then they gave me advice to just follow what the hornbill has to say. So now I'm going to be researching what the hornbill has to say, connecting with a new power animal.

Kate: It was immediately apparent that the High Priestess and the Empress are at odds with each other. The High Priestess was quite clear that she prefers to keep a distance, to be an observer with a sacred attitude towards all of life. She feels she is the connection between the divine and me. The Empress, on the other hand, wants to be a lover of fun, wants to get down in the muck and roll around for the fun of it; act like a child and be silly; and have little regard for those things that are sacred to the High Priestess. They are both stubborn about their positions, but they gave me insight. I can see how their attitudes play out in my life, because I struggle with allowing joy and fun. I had a feeling that if I were more open to allowing silliness and laughter, I could build a bridge that would link the beliefs of each of them and give me the best of both. In retrospect, after this and other journeys, I have physically felt a softening in my heart chakra, and have noticed self-forgiveness comes with less effort.

Melody Bear: I went with my tarot guide to reconcile the opposed planets, Mars (The Tower) and Moon (The High Priestess). I was told I needed to bring in my other opposed planets, Jupiter (Wheel of Fortune) and Saturn (The World), as Mars and Jupiter were in Trine aspect, as were Moon and Saturn, so better all together.

The Tower, The High Priestess, Wheel of Fortune, and The World, agreed to seek reconciliation. My tarot guide chose, as neutral ground for the meeting, the red desert of Central Australia. We sat on small red boulders.

I asked them if they all agreed to the process. I was very nervous, and glad I had my shadow-self and tarot guide on either side to support me. The Tarot Spirits agreed, and I said to the World, "You told me you were angry with the Wheel as you feel he defamed you by the things he said about you, and you believe he destroyed your society. Can you tell him about that?" She said to the Wheel of Fortune, "You love explosions and destruction, and have no regard for who gets hurt." I asked the Wheel to respond, and he said, "If everything stays the same, things stagnate and decay. Everything needs to be shaken up to allow new things to arise."

I ask the High Priestess about her gripe with the Tower, and she says, "I work well with the World, because I like the structure and formality of ritual, but then the Tower comes along blasting everything to pieces. He's in too much of a hurry and creates chaos. He offends my dignity." I turn to the Tower. He agrees with the Wheel of Fortune, "Change and action are needed, or everything gets old and stale."

I tell them things can't go on like this; I've been stuck for a long time and I'm in a lot of pain. We must strike a balance: it's like a stream that needs the stagnant pools flushed out with a flow of fresh water. I need more action, energy, and expansion to clear out all the decay and mold of this stagnant pool I was living in, while preserving what is precious, and creating order and beauty. I asked them if they all agreed to the compromise between structure and ritual on the one side, and action and expansion of the other, in order to redress this imbalance. They agreed to give it a go if I do what I committed to, and we stood in a circle holding hands, and the energy flowed powerfully round the circle of hands.

Questions on Reconciling Potential Challenging Aspects

What if there is no friction between the two Tarot Spirits representing one of my challenging aspects? If you meet them on the journey and there is no friction, simply celebrate and proceed to the next potential conflicting pair. Many times, you have worked out the friction in your chart just in the process of life itself. While we all have challenging aspects in our chart, as we go through life, we may have already tackled the issues. Therefore, we call them "potentially" challenging aspects.

What happens if there is no resolution or communication between the two Tarot Spirits? If you sense strong conflict between the Tarot Spirits, but do not feel like they are willing to find resolution, you can try several strategies:

- Ask your tarot guide to assist as a mediator.
- Repeat Pathwork C with each Tarot Spirit on separate journeys to make sure you have a good connection to both Tarot Spirits individually. Then repeat your Pathwork K journey with them.

- You might invite one of the Tarot Spirits from the healing circle to the journey (see Chapter 14). Seek guidance from your tarot guide for recommendations.
- Look at your own willingness to reconcile. Is there attention or benefit you are getting from maintaining this friction in your life? Consider if you are truly willing to release this issue and find resolution.
- Do a separate Pathwork K for the Tarot Spirits of the signs the planetary Tarot Spirits are in. If there is clarity or relaxation from the sign Tarot Spirits, then you can invite them to a larger group with the recalcitrant planetary Tarot Spirits.
- Do Pathwork K for other challenged spirits, then come back to this pair to repeat Pathwork K.
- If you can't get full resolution, focus on a partial resolution. What small step could both potentially challenging aspected Tarot Spirits take to listen better to each other? Take baby steps.

Chapter 13 Recap

In this chapter, you worked with identified pairs of Tarot Spirits. They represent planets with potentially challenging aspects or opposing signs. You prioritized the challenges, if there were many. You used Pathwork K with pairs of Tarot Spirits to reconcile difficulties. Resolving potentially challenging aspects is an important step to releasing blockages to the life you want to enjoy.

Part 3 Recap

You built on the basic engagement in Part 1 and the foundational advice and healing in Part 2 with individual Tarot Spirits. In Part 3:

- You learned or reviewed the basics of astrology.
- You mapped which Tarot Spirits are active in your astrological chart.
- You engaged the Tarot Spirits for reconciliation of potentially challenging astrological aspects.

Now that you have your astrological framework, you can identify and engage with Tarot Spirit circles and delve into the mysteries in Part 4.

Get your free resource material!

If you haven't already, check out the online resources that support the book *Tarot Spirit Healing*. They include:

- Shamanic journey drumming tracks for 10, 20, and 30 minute journeys.
- Blank forms for tracking pathwork and *AstroTarot mapping*.
- High resolution color graphics in pdf format.
- Video lessons: *Tarot Spirits: Who's on Deck?* and a *Tour of the Major Arcana*.
- Video lesson: *Shamanic Crossing*.
- Join the mailing list for updates on Tarot Spirit books and courses.
- Discounted offers for related online courses.

Check out these book resources at
www.reidhart.com/tsh-resources

Part 4: Initiation into the Mystery

Figure 32. The High Priestess is key 2 (II) in the tarot Major Arcana. She represents the Moon, carries the feminine archetype of magical knowledge, and is a great teacher and healer. *Credit: DruidCraft Tarot.*

Now that you have engaged shamanically with the Tarot Spirits in Part 1, worked with them for advice and healing in Part 2, and resolved astrological challenges in Part 3, you can begin to work with them at a mystery level in Part 4 as follows:

- Connect with Tarot Spirit circles in Chapter 14, expanding the scope of advice and power balancing to multiple Tarot Spirits with Pathworks H2, J2, and I. Use these circles to maintain your personal growth progress and astrological reconciliation.
- In Chapter 15, use powerful questions to engage deeper mysteries with Tarot Spirit Constructs using Pathwork L.

The main section of this book is designed to provide you with the information you need to move directly through the process of meeting the Tarot Spirits, receiving healing and advice, resolving your astrological challenges, and exploring the Western Mysteries. Additional background for Part 4 can be found in these appendices:

- Appendix A has resources and recommended books with descriptions of the books.
- Appendix G has a sample of a personalized *My AstroTarot Report* you can order with all the *AstroTarot mapping* done for you. Your personalized Tarot Spirit circles are listed here.
- Appendix H has the forms and instructions needed to create your own *AstroTarot mapping*. All the details to identify your personalized Tarot Spirit circles are included.

14: Tarot Spirit Circles

Astrology is a large and complex subject. When you use the Tarot Spirits to work with your natal chart, the process becomes quite simple. You don't have to delve into astrological interpretation. Instead, you map your natal chart to the proper Tarot Spirit representatives for the planets and aid directly with conflict resolution, advice, and healing. These benefits can be expanded by working with groups of Tarot Spirits.

Expanding Tarot Spirit Pathwork

So far, you have worked with Tarot Spirits individually using Pathwork A/B/C. You have received advice or healing from a single Tarot Spirit through Pathwork H1 or J1. You have reconciled potentially challenging aspect pairs with Pathwork K. You met your shadow-self with Pathwork N. The next step is to work with a larger group of Tarot Spirits in circles and in groups.

In this chapter, you will learn which Tarot Spirits are in different circles and groups you can work with. Then you will learn how to work with them by adapting the pathworks you use with individual Tarot Spirits to a group. The pathworking you use for groups or circles of Tarot Spirits includes:

- Pathwork H2: Tarot Spirit advice or problem solving
- Pathwork I(1,2,3): circle of hands for: (I1) power balancing, (I2) gratitude, or (I3) blessing
- Pathwork J2: healing/empowerment from multiple Tarot Spirits
- Pathwork L: learning from a circle of Tarot Spirits (see Chapter 15)

Moving to Larger Tarot Spirit Groups

There are three types of circles and groups you can work with:

- Tarot Spirit circles based on your natal astrological chart. These are in Section 6 of your *AstroTarot mapping*.
- Tarot Spirit groups to resolve challenges are based on bringing together Tarot involved in the potential challenging aspects in Section 4 that share common Tarot Spirits. Signs grouped by modality and planets involved in T-square or grand square astrological patterns are also included. These are in Section 7 of your *AstroTarot mapping*.
- Positive Manifestation Groups include signs sharing elemental qualities and planets involved in grand trine or Yod astrological patterns. These are in Section 8 of your *AstroTarot mapping*.

Your Basic Personal AstroTarot Circles

There are several circles of Tarot Spirits that can work together as a team. All of these circles are personal for you, based on your unique natal astrological chart and special Tarot Spirits. The basic personal Tarot Spirit circles include:

- Relationship circle: for questions or healing related to love, relationships, and interaction
- Persona circle: for questions or healing related to your image and reputation in the world
- Reflective circle: for questions or healing related to inner truths
- Current circle: for questions or healing related to your current focus and current influences
- Healing circle: a positive supportive group to receive healing, initiation, and empowerment from healing Tarot Spirits and your special Tarot Spirits

AstroTarot Mapping Forms

If you have your *My AstroTarot Report*, find these circles in Section 6. For your own mapping, see the instructions in Appendix H and fill out Section 6 of the blank mapping forms. Most circles include the Tarot Spirit of either your personality, soul, or year card you found in Chapter 7 and listed in Section 1. The circle selections shown below are for the sample chart. Your circles will include different Tarot Spirits. In the sample chart and your chart some Tarot Spirits may be listed twice. Obviously, those appear only once in your actual journey.

Your Relationship Circle

Your relationship circle is a great group to use when exploring advice or healing related to your love life or important personal and work relationships. It includes Mars and Venus, their signs, your soul or personality spirit, your shadow-self, and tarot guide. The sample relationship circle is:

Relationship Circle			For questions of love, relationships and interaction	
Mars & Sign	♂	♈	Tower	Emperor
Venus & Sign	♀	♈	Empress	Emperor
Soul OR Personality T.S.	8	17	Strength	The Star
			Yourself, your Guide & Shadow-self	

Your Persona Circle

Your persona circle is a great group to use when exploring advice, healing, or empowerment related to your reputation or image in the world. It includes your ascendant sign, the Sun, Sun sign, your personality card, your shadow-self, and tarot guide. The sample chart persona circle is:

Persona Circle			For questions about your presentation to the world	
AC sign/Personality T.S.	♐	17	Temperance	The Star
Sun & Sun sign	☉	♓	The Sun	The Moon
			Yourself, your Guide & Shadow-self	

Your Reflective Circle

The reflective circle is a great group to use when exploring advice, healing, or empowerment related to deeper thoughts or life truths. It includes the Moon, her sign, your Soul card, your shadow-self, and tarot guide. The Moon holds the power to access your unconscious, where deeper personal truths are found. The sample chart reflective circle is:

Reflective Circle			For questions of inner truth & emotions	
Moon & Moon sign	☽	♏	High Priestess	Death
Soul / Hidden Factor T.S.	8	17	Strength	The Star
			Yourself, your Guide & Shadow-self	

Your Current Circle

The current circle is a great group to use when exploring advice, healing, or empowerment related to your current life path or current purpose. It includes the rising sign, personality card, the Moon, her sign, the Sun, his sign, your Soul card, year card, your shadow-self, and tarot guide. The current circle for the sample chart is:

Current Circle			For questions of current life focus	
AC sign/Personality T.S.	✗	17	Temperance	The Star
Moon & Moon sign	☽	♏	High Priestess	Death
Sun & Sun sign	☉	♓	The Sun	The Moon
Soul T.S. / Year T.S.	8	7	Strength	Chariot
			Yourself, your Guide & Shadow-self	

Your Healing Circle

Your healing circle is a great group to use when seeking personal healing, healing for others, empowerment, or initiation. Your healing circle includes one or more of the main Tarot Spirit healers. To avoid having too large a group, just pick one or two from the six healers listed. You can also include any other Tarot Spirit you are drawn to as a healer. In addition, include your soul or personality card, your shadow-self, and tarot guide. Request healing for others only when you have their permission. The healing circle for the sample chart is:

Healing Circle			For healing / empowerment / initiation	
Pick a few from	☉	✗	The Sun	Temperance
these six healers	♒	♃	The Star	The Wheel
and special cards	♅♅	♀	The Fool	The Empress
Your Soul or Personality	8	17	Strength	The Star
Your Hidden Factor(s)	17		The Star	
			Yourself, your Guide & Shadow-self	

The Healing Circle can get big. That is OK, because you don't need them all for each session. Think of it like having a sports team. Not all players play together. Many of them are on the bench. So, you have a team with individual players that have different skills and focuses. For a particular healing session, you pick the ones most simpatico with the needs of the healing request. It's like a team manager choosing players for a play. So, the goal of the Healing Circle is to get down on paper a set of

candidates for a very positive group. Then for each use, you put together a working group limited to four to six Tarot Spirits.

From the six mentioned Tarot Spirit healers, pick two of them related to your mission. To transform a situation, include Temperance. For a new venture, include the Fool. The Empress is good for abundance. The Sun provides general healing and positive support. The Star is a powerful general healing force. The High Priestess works well with depression or spiritual/psychological distress.

Tarot Spirit Groups

In addition to the circles just discussed, there are other Tarot Spirit groups. These include groups of Tarot Spirits to help resolve challenges or maintain reconciliation resulting from Pathwork K. There are also groups of Tarot Spirits that can have a positive effect, including providing blessings to life projects or manifestation.

Tarot Spirit Groups to Maintain Challenge Resolution

There are several groups you can work with on a regular basis to maintain resolution of challenges. The initial clearing of conflict from Pathwork K can produce amazing results. For some challenging aspects, a little more maintenance over time may be necessary. You do not need to work with all eight of the groups listed below. You can choose which groups you feel are important for maintenance. Notice if the initial changes from Pathwork K seem to be wearing off. Then revisit the Tarot Spirits involved with a circle of hands. Use one of the variations of Pathwork I and include your guide and shadow-self. Notice which circles or groups have the greatest friction. Regularly, practice the circle of hands pathwork (I1) with a selection of these groups for a smoother life experience. Pick and choose these circles and groups based on what challenges you currently have.

1. Where a tarot key appears multiple times (three or more) in the Section 4 list of potentially challenging aspect pairs, a special challenge group is recommended in Section 7. Bring together in one circle all the challenging aspect Tarot Spirits that share common keys in their pairs. Work all these together as a group after you have done the A/B/C journeys and resolved conflicts for

individual pairs with Pathwork K. Where groups overlap you can experiment with working with a larger inclusive group. Appendix H has examples from the sample chart. Based on the *AstroTarot mapping* below for challenging group 2, you would include the five Tarot Spirits listed along with your guide and shadow-self in the circle of hands pathwork.

Challenging group 2	☿	♂	Magician	Tower
	♄	♅	World	Fool
	♆		Hanged man	

2. Modality sign groups have square and opposition aspect patterns, so they can have challenges. An example of the mutable group is shown below, along with a pattern group discussed under item 6.

Mutable Signs Group	♊	♍	Lovers	Hermit
	♐	♓	Temperance	The Moon
T Cross (Challenge)	♂	♅	Tower	Fool
	♆		Hanged man	

- Cardinal signs: Emperor for Aries, Chariot for Cancer, Justice for Libra, Devil for Capricorn
- Fixed signs: Hierophant for Taurus, Strength for Leo, Death for Scorpio, Star for Aquarius
- Mutable signs: Lovers for Gemini, Hermit for Virgo, Temperance/Fferyllt for Sagittarius, the Moon for Pisces

3. You can expand the modality groups above by adding in the Tarot Spirits for the planets in those signs to each group. This could be an alternative to the groups identified in Section 7 discussed under number 1 above.

4. Revisit the potentially challenging aspect pairs, along with your shadow-self and guide. Focus on Section 4. Section 9 is a much lower priority. Do the pairs regularly that had moderate to high conflict when you did Pathwork K. Or engage a pair when the planetary influences involved relate to life challenges. For example, revisit a pair with Venus when there is a relationship issue.

5. While the Tarot Spirit circles on your *AstroTarot mapping* are generally used for positive intentions, they can also be used to resolve life challenges. Do a circle of hands (Pathwork I1) with the group most associated with a life challenge. If you are looking for advice or healing for a challenging situation, you can use Pathwork H2 or Pathwork J2, discussed later in this chapter.

6. Work with pattern groups in Section 7, based on the planets involved in T-cross or grand square astrological aspect patterns. Not every chart has these patterns. See the pattern discussions in Chapter 12 and Appendix H. For more information on patterns and their meanings search the web for "astrological aspect patterns."

7. Circle the Tarot Spirits for opposing signs and the planets in each opposing sign. The sign oppositions are identified in Section 5. These oppositions are also covered by the modality sign groups in number 2. A single pair of opposing signs might need more attention if there was significant conflict when you originally did Pathwork K with that pair.

8. Work with your shadow-self and your guide. Sometimes it is good to check in with the main players without Tarot Spirits involved.

Several possible groups are listed. To avoid feeling burdened by too many journeys, notice which groups have the most energy or apparent conflict. These are the groups to repeat journeys with regularly.

Positive Manifestation with Circles and Groups

Most of the focus has been on challenging Tarot Spirit pairs and groups. Clearing the friction in those groups provides a significant life improvement by clearing obstacles. Sometimes we need a positive approach. While the Tarot Spirit circles in Section 6 can provide that positive focus, there are other groups that can be engaged. Request the Tarot Spirits in these circles and groups to bless your project or aspiration. Pick and choose these circles and groups based on positive impacts you want to make at any given time.

1. The Tarot Spirit circles in Section 6 of your *AstroTarot mapping* are generally used for positive intentions. Engage with them to

focus on a positive intention in a certain area of life or to give a positive boost to a particular project or manifestation. After requesting assistance from the group for your intention, do a circle of hands (Pathwork I1) to balance power. If you are looking for advice or healing related to the aspiration, you can use Pathwork H2 or Pathwork J2, as discussed later in this chapter.

2. Section 8 of your *AstroTarot mapping* includes some positive groups you can check in with using the circle of hands. These groups are based on signs sharing the same elemental quality and the planets in those signs. The signs are in trine aspect to each other, since they share the same elemental quality. Any planets with a trine aspect by sign will also show up in the groups. Here, rather than balancing challenging power in the circle, you focus positive energy on things you want to manifest using Pathwork I3. As you work with these groups, if you feel any negative qualities from Mars (the Tower) or Saturn (the World), then exclude them from future work with that group. You want this experience to be totally positive. Select the right group for the project based on the elemental quality. Or use the group with the planets related to your issue. Figure 33 shows the Section 8 positive groups for sample chart 1.

3. Other groups in Section 8 are based on planets involved in astrological aspect patterns, including grand trine and Yod. Not every chart has these patterns and the sample chart did not. The patterns are discussed in Chapter 12 and Appendix H.

Sample 1

Mar 5, 1953 2:28 AM

Circle of Hands; Positive Groups

Washington, D.C.   ‹‹== *Birthdate & Time & Location.*

Includes positive groups and grand trine or Yod if applicable

After exercise "A/B/C" and "K," for the groups do "I" & "H2" or "J2"

Circle of Hands

Exclude Mars or Saturn (Tower or World) from group if any negativity.

Positive Fire group	♈	♌	Emperor	Strength
	♐	☿	Temperance	Magician
	♀	♂	Empress	Tower
	♀		Judgement	

Positive Earth group	♉	♍	Hierophant	Hermit
	♑	♃	Devil	Wheel of Fortune

Positive Air group	♊	♎	Lovers	Justice
	♒	♄	The Star	World
	♅		Hanged man	

Positive Water group	♋	♏	Chariot	Death
	♓	☉	The Moon	The Sun
	☽	♅	High Priestess	Fool

Figure 33. Section 8 from the sample *AstroTarot Report* includes signs and planets in positive elemental groups and the representative Tarot Spirits.

Pathwork for Circles and Groups

Once you identify the circles and groups using Appendix G or H, you can move forward to working with these Tarot Spirits. With each group you can use Pathwork I1, as discussed in Chapter 9, for a general power tune-up. You can also use Pathwork H2 for advice, Pathwork J2 for healing, or combine several pathworks into one journey. The process is almost the same as Pathwork H1 and J1, with the only difference that there are multiple Tarot Spirits in the journey who are providing advice or healing. To distinguish from the pathwork with a single Tarot Spirit, we refer to these pathworks as H2 and J2.

If you have not already, do the introductory Pathworks A, B, and C individually with all the Tarot Spirits involved. Clear any challenging natal aspects represented by pairs of involved Tarot Spirits with Pathwork K. Then you can work with any of these circles or groups for self-healing, healing for others, power balance, expressing gratitude, blessing a project, empowerment, or mystery initiation. With each group you can do Pathwork I(1,2,3), J2, H2, or L depending on your focus.

Circle and Group Pathworks

There are four pathworks you can do with a circle or group of Tarot Spirits. Three are extensions of prior pathwork and one is new.

- Pathwork I lets you balance power in a circle of hands in the basic version (I1). It is approached just as outlined in Chapter 9, except you are now working with a larger group. Here we introduce variants: I2 is a gratitude circle and I3 is a blessing circle.
- Pathwork H2 is to receive advice from a group of Tarot Spirits. This pathwork is very similar to Pathwork H1 from Chapter 9, except you are working with a group rather than a single Tarot Spirit.
- Pathwork J2 is to receive healing from a group of Tarot Spirits. This pathwork is very similar to J1 from Chapter 10, except you are working with a healing group rather than a single Tarot Spirit healer.
- Pathwork L, discussed in the next chapter, is a process of learning from a group of Tarot Spirits who merge into a single Spirit Construct. This may look like going to school to receive information in a lesson format. It may look like an instant download of information. It could be an empowerment or initiation related to the information or skills you need. If you use powerful questions, you can be in your own mystery school where the Tarot Spirits are your teachers.

These pathworks may fit any phase of the cycle of becoming: healing, transformation, or initiation. Or these pathworks can be used for practical matters: advice, learning, or planetary improvement. The journey may also fit a combination of these areas that are related.

Pathworks H2, I2, I3, & J2 with Multiple Tarot Spirits

Purpose: Receive healing or advice from the Tarot Spirits. You may wish for healing or advice for yourself, a family member, a friend, the community, the land, or the planet.

The steps are the same as Pathwork H1, I1 or J1 in Chapters 9 and 10. You are just working with a group of Tarot Spirits rather than one Tarot Spirit. It is always beneficial to conclude a healing or advice session with Pathwork I1, the circle of hands from Chapter 9, to rebalance the power in the circle.

Pathwork H2—Advice from a Tarot Spirit Circle

For advice, each individual Tarot Spirit gives advice on your problem or question. Remember that your guide is there to help you interpret or ask for further explanation about any advice or healing provided. You may need help from the guide if you get conflicting advice from different Tarot Spirits. Your shadow-self may also have something to say.

Journey intention: Get aid and advice from a circle or group of Tarot Spirits with Pathwork H2.

1. Formulate your question, then use one of three ways to decide which Tarot Spirits to seek advice from:

    • Give your question/issue to your guide and ask which Tarot Spirits you should take it to.

    • Meet with one of the basic personal circles (relationship, persona, reflective, current, or healing) depending on your topic.

    • Draw tarot cards from a shuffled deck until you get two or three tarot keys (Major Arcana). Take your question with your guide to them. If you are experienced with tarot reading, you might keep in mind the Minor Arcana cards that were turned over, as they may shed some light on your issue.

2. Complete your Tarot Spirit opening steps from Chapter 5. Go with your guide to a neutral meeting place for all the Tarot Spirits involved.

3. Stand in a circle, holding hands with the Tarot Spirits, your guide, and your shadow. Discuss the issue. Request advice, direct intervention, or power from the Tarot Spirits. Ask your guide for clarification whenever needed.

4. Ask for a clearing mantra, phrase or gesture. You can use this later when you work with the answer to the question or if you encounter doubt or concern about it.

5. At this point, complete the circle of hands, Pathwork I1 from Chapter 9. Alternatively, use the gratitude circle (I2) or blessing circle (I3) discussed below.

6. Complete your Tarot Spirit closing steps from Chapter 5.

Pathwork J2—Healing with a Tarot Spirit Circle

You received healing from a single Tarot Spirit in Chapter 10. Now you can expand to receiving healing from multiple Tarot Spirits, with one of the circles or groups discussed earlier in this chapter. When asking for personal healing work, you have a choice. You can receive the healing directly into your body or have a representational object healed. For the representational approach, in your journey visualize an object or form that represents the problem, issue, or disease. See that form in the middle of the circle and watch it being healed by the Tarot Spirits. If you are pursuing healing for another person, remember it is important to get their permission in ordinary reality first.

Journey intention: To receive healing from multiple Tarot Spirits with Pathwork J2.

1. Before you journey,

   • Formulate your healing goal as discussed in Chapter 10: "_____ is the positive outcome I want to receive from this healing."

   • Select several healing Tarot Spirits to work with. Choose from the healing spirits in your healing group discussed earlier in this chapter. Or consult with (journey to) your guide to choose other healing Tarot Spirits aligned with your issue.

2. Complete your Tarot Spirit opening steps from Chapter 5. Go with your guide to a neutral meeting place for all the Tarot Spirits involved.

3. Stand in a circle, holding hands with the Tarot Spirits, your guide, and your shadow-self. Discuss what is out of balance and your desired positive outcome. Request direct intervention or healing

power from the Tarot Spirits. If you are using the symbolic approach, see the object or symbolic manifestation that needs healing in the center of the circle.

4. Receive shamanic healing from the Tarot Spirits, as discussed in Chapter 10. They may work individually in sequence, or take a team approach. They may send healing directly to your spirit body, or to the symbolic object in the circle. You may also experience healing shifts in your physical body during the journey.

5. Ask for a clearing mantra or phrase or gesture. You can use this later if you have a recurrence of symptoms or if you encounter doubt or concern about the healing.

6. At this point, complete the circle of hands. Pathwork I1 from Chapter 9. Alternatively, use the gratitude circle (I2) or blessing circle (I3) discussed below.

7. Complete your Tarot Spirit closing steps from Chapter 5.

8. Pursue post-healing integration as discussed in Chapter 10.

Variations of Pathwork I with Tarot Spirit Circles and Groups

You can do Pathwork I as a separate journey with your Tarot Spirit circle of choice. It is also good to conclude other pathworks (H2, J2, K, or L) with the circle of hands. Once the work in another pathwork is done, simply call for a circle of hands. The circle of hands process allows power to be shared with all participants in the circle. The circle of hands now expands into three variations:

1. The basic **circle of hands** (Pathwork I1) focuses on balancing power and synergy for a larger group of spirits, including your own spirit self, as laid out in Chapter 9.

2. A **gratitude circle** (Pathwork I2) has the intention of sharing what you are grateful for with the circle of spirits, especially those related to the reconciliation and circle work you have completed with them.

3. A **blessing circle** (Pathwork I3) takes the power that is generated by the group or circle of spirits and focuses it on a manifestation intention or project in the real world.

Any of these variations can be done alone as a separate journey or in combination with one of the other pathworks.

Power Balancing (I1) with a larger group of Tarot Spirits

This pathwork is essentially the same as described in Chapter 9. The only difference here is more Tarot Spirits are in the circle of hands.

Journey intention: Balance power and synergy of a group of journey participants.

If this is a separate journey, select a group of Tarot Spirits as in Pathwork H2 or use one of the groups or circles listed earlier in this chapter.

1. For a separate journey, complete your Tarot Spirit opening steps from Chapter 5 and go with your guide to a neutral meeting place for all the Tarot Spirits involved. If following another pathwork in the same journey, proceed to step 2 after the other pathwork is complete.
2. Stand in a circle, holding hands with the Tarot Spirits, your guide, and your shadow. If you or any of the tarot keys are out of balance or alignment, sense how the power should move. Ask the group what you can do or not do in your life to restore balance. In the circle, give permission to balance power with each other and do it. Feel any shifts in your physical body during the balancing process.
3. Complete your Tarot Spirit closing steps from Chapter 5.

Gratitude Circle: Pathwork I2

Being grateful is very powerful. It helps you focus on what is going right and what blessings you are receiving in your life. Furthermore, speaking those gratitudes to your spirit helpers acknowledges the help they are giving you. It encourages them to give you more help. There is scientific evidence that just recounting your blessings improves your mental well-being and increases happiness.[31] [32] So, bringing at least three life events or experiences you are grateful for into your Tarot Spirit

---

[31] fee.org/articles/how-gratitude-can-rewire-your-brain-for-happiness-and-success/

[32] greatergood.berkeley.edu/topic/gratitude/definition#why_practice

balancing sessions can be powerful. Give it a try and notice how your mood or life experience shifts. The things you are grateful for can be small. As Alida Birch points out:

> . . . Acknowledge and celebrate progress, even small progress. As you acknowledge progress, you train your subconscious to recognize movement. When you consistently acknowledge that you are making advances with your goals, you find your intentions are leading you forward, and the subconscious accepts that you are the Predominant Creative Force in your life.[33]

Journey intention: Share things you are grateful for with a group of spirits.

If this is a separate journey, select a group of Tarot Spirits as in Pathwork H2 or one of the groups listed earlier in this chapter.

1. Before the journey, think about at least three things you are grateful for. Search for life changes related to your work with this group of Tarot Spirits.
2. For a separate journey, complete your Tarot Spirit opening steps from Chapter 5 and go with your guide to a neutral meeting place for all the Tarot Spirits involved. If adding on to another pathwork, proceed to step 2 after the other pathwork is complete.
3. Stand in a circle, holding hands with the Tarot Spirits, your guide, and your shadow. Share at least three things in your life you are thankful for. Thank the spirits for their help in maintaining your life path. In the circle, give permission to balance power with each other and do it. Notice any shifts in your physical body during the balancing process.
4. Complete your Tarot Spirit closing steps from Chapter 5.

Blessing Circle: Pathwork 13

When we work with a group of Tarot Spirits it is similar to working with a circle of sincere shamanic practitioners engaged in healing work. We connect as a group with many helping spirits, and bring them into a community healing circle. Often there is residual power available at the

---

[33] From *The Co-Creation Handbook.*, copyright © 2014 by Alida Birch. Luminare Press. Reprinted by permission of author. p 135.

end of the circle's work that can be sent to those in need. You can create a similar result on your own, working with a circle or group of Tarot Spirits. Once you have chosen a worthwhile project or manifestation you want to support—make it something with a positive outcome for yourself and the community—you can engage the Tarot Spirits to support it.

To have a positive result from a blessing circle, keep a few guidelines in mind:

- Make sure your desired manifestation has a clear and positive focus. Have you spent some time thinking about what you want to manifest? Have you gotten clear about what you want and thought about how it could affect the larger community?
- Take time to really call in power before the journey. There are multiple steps outlined in Appendix D around creating sacred space. Make sure you create a special boundary around a blessing journey. Call in power. Call in the directions. Take time with some evocative offerings to set the stage.
- Spend the time doing Pathwork A/B/C/K with the Tarot Spirits you want to support you in this endeavor.

Journey intention: Work with a group of Tarot Spirits to raise power and send it to aid with a project or manifestation.

If this is a separate journey, select a group of Tarot Spirits as in Pathwork H2 or one of the groups listed earlier in this chapter.

1. Before the journey, think about a life change you want, a project you would like to go smoothly, or something you want to manifest.
2. For a separate journey, complete your Tarot Spirit opening steps from Chapter 5 and go with your guide to a neutral meeting place for all the Tarot Spirits involved. If adding on to another pathwork, proceed to step 3 after the other pathwork is complete.
3. Stand in a circle, holding hands with the Tarot Spirits, your guide, and your shadow. In the circle, give permission to balance power with each other and do it. Feel any shifts in your physical body during the balancing process. Let the Tarot Spirits present know what project or manifestation you are seeking a blessing for. Focus

on universal power coming into the circle and going out to bless what you want to manifest. When the blessing is complete, thank the spirits for their help.

4.   Complete your Tarot Spirit closing steps from Chapter 5.

Repeat Circle and Group Pathwork Regularly

Over time, you'll understand which groups of Tarot Spirits are important to engage with regularly. These regular journeys can support the reconciliation you achieved in your paired, circle, and group journeys. Focus on Pathwork I, circle of hands, regularly. You may also do Pathwork H2, J2, or L with the groups.

The "Know" or "Date Cleared" columns at right of your *AstroTarot mapping* gives you a place to verify that you have done Pathwork A/B/C for each individual spirit on that line. Also verify you have done Pathwork K for any challenging pairs before working with the larger group or circle.

There are many circles and groups. You don't need to work with them all. Just pick the ones that are relevant to current issues in your life. Or be creative, and put your own selection of Tarot Spirits together. Regular connection is helpful, so you might want to meet once or twice a week with the Tarot Spirits. Consistent connection on a regular schedule is more important than meeting with every circle and group.

Chapter 14 Recap

In Chapter 14 you learned about Tarot Spirit circles and groups that can be helpful to work with. You expanded beyond meeting one or a pair of Tarot Spirits in your journey to a larger group. Ongoing work with these circles and groups can maintain the positive forward flow in your life.

15: Deeper Mysteries with Tarot Spirit Constructs

Conversation 6: Learning with Tarot Spirit Circles

Isabel hurried to the Middle Eastern restaurant for their special Greek night, wanting to get there just as they opened–they did not take reservations. The table in the front window alcove was her favorite. She was looking forward to the saganaki, a Santorini inspired melted cheese dish. After the host showed her to her favorite table, she ordered a glass of Naousa, a red wine from Macedonia. The new Tarot Spirit work that included circles was on her mind. Each circle had several Tarot Spirits based on her birth chart. The circles worked with questions and issues around relationships, personal image, inner truths, current decisions, or personal healing. After about 10 minutes, she noticed Rachel coming in the door with a big smile on her face. As she joined her at the table in the now crowded restaurant, Rachel said, "Parking is just crazy out there. I had to use the parking garage three blocks away. Thanks for getting our favorite table. How are you?"

"I am feeling pretty good with the Moon in Taurus."

After ordering a glass of wine, Rachel said, "Oh? And what does that mean?"

"Well, I engaged in a mystery training with the Tarot Spirits using my reflective circle. These are several Tarot Spirits that help me look at inner truths, including the High Priestess, Hierophant, and Temperance Tarot Spirits. My question was 'what do the current Moon signs mean for me?' All the Tarot Spirits in the reflective circle merged into one teacher and gave me a lesson. I've done three lessons in journeys so far. I learned that when the Moon is in Taurus, it grounds me by connecting with my birth Moon and activates Venus, who is the ruler of Taurus. The Moon entered Taurus yesterday and, wouldn't you know, the same day at the food co-op, I ran into that guy from the rooftop bar! We started talking and hit it off pretty well. We're going out for dinner on Friday. It's funny. I was not even thinking about romance; I just wanted to understand the spiritual meanings of the Moon signs."

"Sounds like you've got your Venus activated, all right. What about Ron?"

"Yea, what about him? He's gotten more and more cranky—so possessive. I think it's time to move on." She rolled her eyes with a look of frustration on her face. "By the way, it looks like you've got some news to share based on your big smile! Do tell!"

"OK." Rachel grinned from ear to ear. "Yes, definitely some news. You know I've been thinking about my job and finances. Well, I used the Persona Tarot Spirit circle for advice about my work situation. I went into the journey and met with the Hermit, Emperor, Sun, and Lovers. They formed into a single large Spirit being to answer my question about 'how should I improve my work situation?' The teaching Spirit pointed out that I would just never get the respect I deserve from my current firm. I started there as clerical staff, and the partners watched me go to school for my paralegal certificate. The Tarot Spirits suggested that if I wanted to make progress, I would need to look somewhere else and make a fresh start. Remember those two jobs I told you about? Well, I applied for both, had the interviews and they went really well. I got an offer that is a big raise from the first interview. Now I'm just waiting to hear from the second."

"Congratulations! Let's have a special celebration when you decide which offer to accept!"

"Thanks, that would be fun! And hopefully, we will celebrate a new beau for you too!"

The two women laughed quietly together as Isabel reached for Rachel's hand and gave it a squeeze.

"Hmmm," Rachel mused, "Maybe we should invite the spirit helpers to the celebration. What do you think they like to drink?"

A Mystery Focus for Learning or Empowerment

The focus in Pathwork L is usually on learning or empowerment. You use powerful questions or requests, often to explore a mystery. You receive teaching or empowerment from the Tarot Spirits in a new way. You meet them as a single Spirit Construct that is formed from the combined powers of multiple Tarot Spirits from one of the circles. So, you relate to one Spirit Construct rather than multiple Tarot Spirits in a circle.

Powerful Questions

When seeking learning, initiation, empowerment, or transformation, asking the right question can be key. For a question of a single Tarot Spirit or a circle of individual Tarot Spirits, you may use Pathwork H1 or H2, as discussed in Chapters 9 and 14. If you are seeking the combined wisdom of a group of Tarot Spirits, use Pathwork L. Each planet, sign, Tarot Spirit, or other tarot card has a lesson, message, empowerment, or initiation to share. Review these suggested questions to help clarify what you are seeking at this time:

- Who can assist me in **resolving this issue** in my life at present?
- What is the **lesson I need right now** for my greater good from: card / planet / sign / spiritual tradition? For example, use Pathwork H3 to ask the Hermit, "What is the lesson I need right now for my greater good?"
- What is the **mystery** of this card / planet / sign / spiritual tradition? For example, use Pathwork L to ask one of the circles, plus the Temperance Tarot Spirit, "What is the mystery of Temperance?"
- What is the **message I need right now** in my life from card / planet / sign / spiritual tradition? For example, use Pathwork H3 to ask your destiny circle, plus the Empress, "What is the message I need right now in my life from Venus?"
- Please **empower** me from card / planet / sign / spiritual tradition. For example, use Pathwork L to ask your Persona or Reflective circle, plus the Star, "Please empower me with the Power of Aquarius that I need right now in my life."
- Please **initiate** me into the **secrets** of card / planet / sign / spiritual tradition. For example, use Pathwork L to ask your healing circle, plus the Wheel of Fortune "Please initiate me into the mystery of Jupiter that I need right now in my life."

Once you have your request or question clarified, you can select any of the circles you identified in Chapter 14, or any appropriate group of Tarot Spirits to do the journey with.

Mystery Reciprocity

Now, there are many teachings, empowerments, or initiations available from the Otherworld. Know that you may be asked to undertake certain rituals or offerings in exchange. You may be asked to make some changes in your life or in your community to fully realize the potential of what is offered. Prioritize learning for the greater good, not for selfish purposes. That being said, it is OK to empower yourself to be more independent or skillful so you can better offer service to the community. Sometimes you need to bootstrap yourself, letting go of habits or situations that limit your ability to contribute.

Maintain an intention for the greater good in all your Otherworld work. Working selfishly or with any intent to harm others will create a final outcome that is negative for everyone. Negative intentions eventually come back to you. Putting harmful vibes, thoughts, or vibrations out there pollutes the spiritual environment and will eventually impact you personally. We all live in the same spiritual environment. Remember to thank and make offerings or connections to the Tarot Spirits who are helping you.

The Mystery Riff

As you work with powerful questions or requests, you may want to go even deeper. You can learn about the mysteries behind objects, symbols, the questions listed below, or other elements of Western Mystery traditions. Rather than provide a pat answer from mystery literature, going directly to the Spirits for a direct answer can be more effective and more personal.

Let's delve deeper into this mystery concept. You're looking for a powerful question. There are many powerful questions you can ask the Tarot Spirits either individually, working with them as a group of individuals, or working with them as a merged **Spirit Construct**—we will talk about that next. Your mystery question could be about anything. It could be:

- What is the mystery of astrology?
- What is the mystery of the runes?
- What is the mystery of relationships?

- What is the mystery of pink quartz?
- What is the mystery of Water? Fire? Air? Earth?
- What is the mystery of the Chariot tarot card?
- What is the mystery of the herb rosemary?
- What is the mystery of the Chariot Tarot Spirit?
- What is the mystery of the Qabalah?

That provides insight into the variety of topics you might inquire about. Other ways to phrase the question are "tell me about the mystery of [blank]," "show me the mystery of [blank]," "what is the story about the mystery of [blank]," or "what is the mystery story of [blank]?"

Initiations and Empowerments

After you have gotten some information from the spirit about a particular mystery area, move to the next step and ask: "Could I please have an initiation (or empowerment) on the mystery of _____ [fill in the blank]." That may give a deeper result.

Both initiations and empowerments go beyond just receiving information about a mystery topic. In an initiation, you are put on a path to learn how to use one of the mysteries for spiritual or practical purposes. In an empowerment, the Spirits imbue in you the actual power to use a mystery effectively. In many religious or magical organizations, transmission of either an initiation or empowerment typically includes a ceremony led by an authorized person. In shamanic tradition, initiation, or empowerment is often delivered directly from the spirits in non-ordinary reality.

Mysteries have been around for a long time. If we go back to Greek times, we have the mystery schools: Pythagorean Mysteries, Plato's Mysteries, Elysian Mysteries, etc. Typically, a mystery is something that's secret. In a Buddhist community, to be properly empowered to do a particular practice, you need to attend an initiation where there's a direct transmission from a lama. As I developed my practice with shamanism, my preference is to receive direct transmission from a spirit. You have probably heard that shamans need initiation. They may spend years apprenticing under a mentor. Or they may just receive a direct initiation from nature or Otherworld spirits. Stories tell of shamans who are initiated by a tree. Literally, they would sit with the tree and be initiated by a transfer of power. There is a Nordic practice where you gain a power song related to sooth saying by sitting out all night long with your staff until a song is given to you by the spirits.

A path of direct initiation exists from a spirit in the Otherworld. You have an opportunity of working directly with the Tarot Spirits. You have heard of secret societies that have secret initiations. Much of the supposedly secret information has been published. You can read about the knowledge lectures of the Golden Dawn or Qabalah or other mystery schools. Once you absorb the information, move to the next step of initiation. Work with the knowledge in a ritualistic or shamanic way by engaging the spirits directly. It surpasses mere knowledge, bringing about personal comprehension and change.

Another example of the difference between information and experience is the raising earth power exercise from Appendix D. Comments from those who actually follow through and do the exercise is that it was a powerful experience. Well, what is it about connecting to power in the center of the Earth and bringing it up into your body? Until you actually experience that vs. reading or hearing the instructions, it's just an idea. As a thought, it does not mean much. But when you actually experience it, and you feel that power come up into your body, then there's a shift that occurs, a connection that you didn't have before. You had the experience, and something shifted.

Mysteries are about experience and making that connection that is beyond thought. I don't think there's just one mystery out there. I think every Tarot Spirit has some mystery quality to them. Every rune, if you study the runes, has a mystery quality. Each of the elements has multiple mysteries. The planets and signs in astrology have mystery qualities. You can ask about or get engaged with any of these. This means there's much to grasp and absorb experientially. It can be a lifelong path. The further you get into it, the deeper and deeper it will take you.

Exploring any of the mysteries can take a while. I think these deeper mystery questions are important. Connecting with deeper knowledge of different things you work with in the world, especially at a spiritual level, gets you started. Then another level brings additional information to you. This question could pertain to an object. It could be about a concept. It could be about astrology. It could involve tarot or runes. Perhaps it concerns the Qabalah spheres. It could be about archangels, elements, plants, or stones. It could be about the gnostic truth underlying a religious tradition.

Asking about any of those will elicit information from your Tarot Spirit group that you're working with. It's your choice to pick one of these groups, or you can even pull together an ad hoc group of Tarot Spirits you feel would apply to the particular mystery question at hand. If you're asking about relationships, the **relationship circle** would be likely a good choice. The **current circle** is good for issues that are immediate. The **reflective circle** addresses questions of inner truth. Seek answers about your image in the world from the **persona circle**. For questions about healing or for a direct healing experience use the **healing circle**.

Once you have decided on your question or request and selected a group of Tarot Spirits, you can spread your cards out so you can easily scan them at the start of the journey.

Focusing on a Mystery Question or Initiation Request

Remember that you're working shamanically with both practical and esoteric matters. Esoteric work is great for your spiritual development, but it is hard to develop spiritually if your life isn't working practically. It is important to get the practical matters of life working first. If you have a significant practical issue in your life, seek advice or healing for it first.

One thing that is different about the shamanic approach is that instead of just fixing things, problem solving, or patching things together, you can totally transform the situation. You can ask for spiritual help to bring a whole new opportunity into your life.

Once the practical matters and healing requests are complete, you can move on to the mysteries. In this learning pathwork, you will seek the answer to a powerful question. Questions like: "What is the mystery of the Wheel of Fortune card?," or "What is the mystery of a particular stone?"

Let's say you are interested in learning about the pink gem stone thulite. To uncover thulite's mystery, have the physical stone present and embark on a journey of discovery. This direct information from the spirits is more powerful than reading about thulite in a book. You can ask one or all of these questions:

- What is the mystery of thulite?

- What is the message I need right now in my life from thulite?
- What are the healing properties of thulite?

Branching out, you might ask, "What is the message I need right now in my life from Venus" (or Mars, Mercury, or another planet or sign). These are just a few examples of mystery questions. Pursue what interests you.

Pathwork L—Learn from a Spirit Construct

Let's look at the Spirit Construct at the center of Pathwork L. The concept of a Spirit Construct was brought to us by Edwin Steinbrecher.[34] While you are working with the different qualities of multiple Tarot Spirits, their individual essences merge into one Spirit Construct.

What is a Tarot Spirit Construct?

Pathwork L with the Tarot Spirits is like you're going to visit Yoda and get the true download or visit the Guru on top of the mountain. But this teacher is a Spirit Construct that combines the unique essences of multiple Tarot spirits.

We're going to work the mystery question you have using one of the Tarot Spirit circles. You can look at the circles on your *AstroTarot mapping* and choose one, or select a different group of Tarot Spirits that makes sense for your question. Be sure you have already done the A/B/C pathwork with each of them and if there are pairs with potentially challenging natal aspects, do pathwork K with those pairs first. So, you've got a circle of Tarot Spirits to work with for Pathwork L.

In Pathwork L, you work with what's called a Spirit Construct. Rather than asking a group of multiple different Tarot Spirits for help, in this construct approach, you journey and meet them as a group of individual Spirits. Once you introduce yourself to the group and ask your question, you request that all the individual Tarot Spirits merge into one Spirit Construct. That Spirit Construct has the essences of all the individual Tarot Spirits combined into one entity. That Spirit Construct provides the answer to your question.

---

[34] Steinbrecher, E. *The Inner Guide Meditation.* p 227.

Figure 34. A Spirit Construct is a Spirit who combines qualities of multiple Tarot Spirits. The essence of each individual Tarot Spirit merges into one entity or construct. The resulting Spirit Construct can teach you about a topic, or provide you with healing, transformation, or initiation. Graphic *credit: Author using images by DruidCraft Tarot and Mikhail Nilov at Pexels.*

Consider it like attending a class. Usually, you only have one teacher who interacts with you. It is easier to interact with one Spirit Construct instead of getting a committee hearing where you have questions and answers coming at you from all different directions. So, you ask the Spirits to dissolve into their core energy essence and re-form as a single Spirit Construct. The construct typically appears as a humanoid Spirit. And then you ask your question or make your request. Then you will receive your answer. You may also ask if there something you need to do? The Spirit Construct may want you to do a ritual, or some exercise related to the learning. They may want you to spend time with a rock if you're asking about what is the quality of a rock, for instance.

If your question or request is simple, you may have the answer in one session. Alternatively, maybe you will need several sessions. If it is not obvious to you, ask the Spirit Construct if you need a follow-up session later. Maybe you will need a seven or twenty session course with them for a deeper topic.

Once you have your answer, watch the Spirit Construct unmerge back to the individual Tarot spirits and do the circle of hands (Pathwork I1 from Chapters 9 and 14). Then do your closing sequence.

Pathwork L Steps: Multi-Tarot Spirit Learning

Journey Intention: To connect with and learn from or resolve issues with a group of Tarot Spirits by working with their transformed essence as a single construct. Use this exercise with circles, challenge groups, or positive groups. See the discussion on circles and Tarot Spirit group selections in Chapter 14.

1. If you have not already, do exercises B & C first, meeting and getting to know the individual Tarot Spirits from the circle you plan to work with.
2. Get your mystery or learning question ready. You may want to do a separate journey to clarify the question.
3. Complete your Tarot Spirit opening steps from Chapter 5, scanning the cards individually and as a group. Go with your guide to an Otherworld neutral meeting place, temple, or astral classroom.
4. Request a clearing or dismemberment—discussed below—from the assembled Tarot Spirits. For a dismemberment, power animals will also be involved.
5. Ask the guide to bring all the Tarot Spirits in the group to line up in front of you, your shadow-self, and your guide.
6. Ask the Spirits to transform into their core essence and then re-form as a single Spirit Construct that appears as a humanoid spirit.
7. Request the teaching, initiation, or empowerment you are seeking.
8. Ask what you need to do for the mystery, empowerment, skill, or learning to become activated and helpful as part of your essential

being. Alternatively, you can ask one of the "powerful questions" from the list earlier in this chapter.

9. Ask the Spirit Construct if it would set up a classroom so it can teach you, over time, all the mysteries, abilities, and powers you were born with or the deep meaning of the question you asked. You will be mentored and assisted by the Spirit Construct, assisted by your guide and your shadow-self.

10. Review and clarify any necessary life changes needed to realize the benefits of the teachings, healing, or advice.

11. When complete, request that the Spirit Construct return to the individual Tarot Spirits. Stand in a circle, holding hands with the Tarot Spirits and your guide; feel the power flow. Give permission for power to be balanced between all present (see Pathwork I1 in Chapter 9).

12. Complete your Tarot Spirit closing steps from Chapter 5. Note down any agreements and body messages from the interaction in your journal.

Use Pathwork L to meet regularly in the classroom to learn from the Spirit Construct, asking clarifying questions about how to apply the lessons in your life, how to actualize the empowerment or initiation, or to connect more deeply with the mystery.

Clearing and Dismemberment Options

A clearing or dismemberment is an optional beginning to Pathwork L that can provide a deeper, more intense experience. Start the pathwork journey by completing either a clearing or a shamanic dismemberment.

A clearing is similar to a healing from those Tarot Spirits. It's like taking your car to a car wash. If you have fixed ideas or patterns that relate to this mystery question, clearing them out can open your mind to receiving fresh information. Ask the Tarot Spirits present to heal you in a way that clears any obstacles to receiving the mystery knowledge. This healing resembles what you did in Pathwork J2. Once the clearing or healing is complete, continue on with the rest of Pathwork L in the same journey.

Dismemberment goes beyond clearing. It is a shamanic technique that is usually done with your power animals. Tarot Spirits or other Spirits may also be involved. In non-ordinary reality, the power animals tear your spirit body apart to release what is in the way of receiving the teaching. Then the power animals put your spirit body back together in a new way. Admittedly, dismemberment is an advanced shamanic technique. On the other hand, it often occurs spontaneously in journeys of new students. So, it is best to know about dismemberment in case the Spirits decide it is time for you to have one. Michael Harner has taught the shamanic journey to thousands of western students and has this to say about the dismemberment experience:

> As I taught shamanism in workshops beginning in the mid-1970s, I found that students who had never heard of shamanic dismemberment were having spontaneous dismemberment experiences, sometimes even in their first journey . . . their dismemberment experiences would occur unexpectedly at any time and were completely painless. Beyond that the Westerners often reported deep ecstasy in these experiences . . . an ecstatic sense of merging with "everything" and oneness with the universe.[35]

To receive a dismemberment, you just request one from the power animals and open yourself up to being literally opened up in non-ordinary reality. Essentially, your spiritual body will get taken apart into pieces, and then reassembled—or remembered—in a new way. It is optional, so only request it if you want to experience a strong level of change. When you are remembered, you may have crystals or gems placed inside your body. While it may seem like a grisly process, the Spirits are compassionate, and dismemberment is a healing process. Dismemberment brings you transformation and increased resources. You can experience a pretty deep transformation with this process. It's not about tearing down, but tearing apart to let go of unnecessary things.

Again, if you are not ready for dismemberment, you can just request a clearing or cleansing, although sometimes the Spirits will initiate a dismemberment even if you are not sure you are ready. When this happens, the experience is painless and empowering. Either process will take the

[35] From Cave and Cosmos: Shamanic Encounters with Another Reality by Michael Harner, published by North Atlantic Books, copyright © 2013 by the Foundation for Shamanic Studies, Inc. Reprinted by permission of publisher. Chapter 11, which contains more examples of both indigenous and Westerner dismemberment experiences in journeys.

first several minutes of the journey. Then, when you feel you've been put back together, you move on to your teaching or mystery request. All the Tarot Spirits come together into one Spirit Construct as discussed above in Pathwork L, and the Spirit Construct will answer your mystery question or provide teaching on your requested topic. Then, when the training or transmission is complete, move into a circle of hands, sharing the power with the circle of spirits, your guide, and your shadow-self, letting the power balance between all of you around the circle.

Questions about Dismemberment

How do we approach the dismemberment, if that's what we'd like to do? Do we just ask our Tarot Spirits? Do we simply watch and wait? If you want dismemberment, all you do is present yourself to your power animals where you're meeting the Tarot Spirits, who will usually be an audience for this. If you work with particular power animals, then definitely call them. And you just say, "I request a dismemberment." That's it; they'll take care of the rest. Observe and sense the results of the dismemberment. Remember that after a dismemberment you are new in a profound way. You need time to rest and integrate the change. So do spend some down time, relaxing and taking care of yourself.

Reports on Learning from a Spirit Construct

Reports from those who have done this pathwork are included below. Honor the truth of your own experience. Avoid comparing your experience to others.

Renee: The Tarot Spirits said that they were inextricably linked as threshold portals of evolution and the birth of consciousness and the written word. The Major Arcana are the gatekeepers, and they would take you to the mystery teachings of the letters which are connected to each of them: a living temple opening the mystery of existence and the star transmission of understanding. They will show how we came to be formed—humanity was created out of stardust. How does each individual embody their own star map? The Tarot Spirits are living portals to walk through and travel to receive the gifts of the future outside of time—a living library.

Laurie: I had a surprising dismemberment experience. I'm not used to having my power animals tear me apart limb by limb or having six of them eating me and devouring me: all the blood and guts. My Fox just tore off this shoulder here, then another shoulder. And then opened my back where all my arthritis had been and where I've had cancer. So, then they threw it right back together really quick, just like that, and then implanted in my chakras the specific crystals for each chakra: carnelian, citrine, emerald, rose quartz, lapis lazuli. amethyst, and selenite.

Questions about Spirit Constructs

My shamanic journey does not line up with the 10 minute drumming track. Sometimes I'm done before it ends. Other times, I don't have enough time. What do I do? The drumming track is really an arbitrary 10 minutes long. You can use the 20 or 30 minute track to give yourself plenty of time, and then if you're done at 7 minutes, you can come back. No need to wait for the call back. Sometimes, though, waiting a little after you think you are done helps. Some extra information or interaction with the spirits may develop. For Pathwork L journeys, especially if you have a dismemberment request, use a 20 or 30 minute drumming track.

The pre-arranged Tarot Spirit circles don't seem to have the right group for my question. How do I fix that? The circles are just suggestions of groups that might work for you related to particular topics. You can select another group or do a separate pre-journey to your tarot guide to get guidance for which Tarot Spirits are right for your question, healing, or request.

What if I don't get my questions fully answered in one journey session? Your question or topic might be answered in one journey or the Tarot Spirits may want to work with you in an ongoing series of meetings. Many of the deeper mysteries need a step-by-step process to get the full picture.

What if I feel spacey or ungrounded after one of these deep journey sessions? Take a rest if the experience has been powerful. Eating or drinking something nurturing can ground you. Taking a few minutes to get your bearings is helpful. Certainly, wait until you are feeling fully present and back in your body before driving anywhere.

I'm not receiving esoteric information like other people do. Am I doing something wrong? Some people have spent a lot of time researching or experiencing esoteric material and you may hear a lot of embellishment in their sharing. In truth, the purpose of a shamanic journey is to receive the direct truth you need right now in a practical way to produce positive change in your life. Some of the esoteric material is interesting and I love it. It can have deep meaning on a spiritual level. But does it change the way you relate to your friends or neighbors? You can focus on both practical and esoteric aspects in this work.

What do I do if other Tarot Spirits besides the ones I requested show up for the lesson? You can be surprised by what spirits arrive to help your journey and that's OK. In one example, someone thought it was important to work with the Tarot Spirit for the sign of her ascendant as suggested in her persona circle, in this case the Hermit for Virgo. The Magician showed up instead, representing Mercury, who is the ruler of Virgo. Tarot Spirits can enhance astrological aspects beyond your current knowledge. Just go with whoever shows up, and accept the healing, learning or advice from the Tarot Spirits.

Spirit Constructs for Advice and Healing

An alternative approach to receiving either advice or healing from multiple Tarot Spirits is to use a Spirit Construct, just as you did in Pathwork L. The idea is for all the Tarot Spirits to merge into a single Spirit Construct. The only difference is that rather than asking for a lesson, you are asking the Spirit Construct for advice (H3) or healing (J3). You can review the discussion of Pathwork H1 for advice in Chapter 9 and Pathwork J1 for healing in Chapter 10. Also review the Pathwork H2 and J2 discussion in Chapter 14. Just as in Pathwork L, you can choose to include a clearing or dismemberment with either journey.

The Tapping Journey

As you gain more experience with the Tarot Spirits, you may want to check in on something with them when you are short on time. A quicker method of journeying is a tapping journey in bed just before you go to sleep. Just tap with a shamanic rhythm somewhere on your body. You can tap on your collarbone, on your leg, or wherever suits you. That tapping becomes the percussion for the journey. This works better after you have spent some time using drums or rattling for journeying with the Tarot Spirits. Experience with the normal process, means you will be able to visualize their card in your mind's eye rather than scan it. Close your eyes and do a journey requesting healing or advice from the Tarot Spirits.

It's not a replacement for drumming or rattling for important journeys, but it can be valuable. Sometimes you fall asleep and sometimes it leads into your dreams, where the answers come. Often, you get quick answers in the journey or connect to a Tarot Spirit.

Chapter 15 Recap

Chapter 15 was an opportunity to explore work with spiritual mysteries. First powerful questions related to spiritual mysteries helped start the process. Then the concept of a Spirit Construct as a teacher and initiator was developed. Clearing or dismemberment led to a deeper level of healing. This Spirit Construct format can provide deeper learning into the Western Mystery Tradition over time.

Part 4 Recap

You built on the basic engagement in Part 1, the foundational advice and healing in Part 2 with individual Tarot Spirits, and the astrological clearing in Part 3. In Part 4:

- You found your personal Tarot Spirit circles.
- You met Spirit Constructs who provided ongoing healing, learning, or initiatory opportunities.
- Through powerful questions, you were able to receive answers about the mysteries directly from the Tarot Spirits.

Engage with the Tarot Spirits on an ongoing basis through circle of hands to keep your astrological challenges clear. Go deeper into mystery topics with the otherworld connection of Spirit Constructs. Now that you have the methods for learning about the mysteries in place, you can apply them to a wide range of topics.

Conclusion

Congratulations on beginning your work with the Tarot Spirits. This can be a lifelong path. Interacting with these powerful helping beings can improve your life both practically and spiritually. Create a plan for your ongoing work, as discussed in Appendix B. Work with each Major Arcana over time. This Tarot Spirit connection will prove to be a powerful tool to sculpt your life as you wish it to be.

Alternatively, you can work with just the Tarot Spirits that are relevant to your immediate practical, astrological, or spiritual needs. It is valuable to focus on Tarot Spirits related to the potentially challenging aspects in your natal chart. The pathwork you have learned unlocks barriers to the life you want. The work you have done so far can broaden and continue with the other Tarot Spirit work outlined in Appendix B.

Make sure you visit www.reidhart.com/tsh-resources for free tools and updates on other books in the series.

Enjoy this book?
You can make a big difference!

Reviews are the most powerful tool in my arsenal when it comes to getting attention for my books. Much as I'd like to, I don't have the resources of a big publisher. I can't take out full page ads or put posters on the subway.

But I do have something much more powerful and effective than that, and it's something that those publishers would kill to get their hands on.

A committed and loyal bunch of readers and workshop participants.

Honest reviews of my books help get the word out.

If you've enjoyed this book I would be very grateful if you could spend just five minutes leaving a review (it can be as short as you like) on the book's page where you bought it. You can find review links at the book resource page:

www.reidhart.com/tsh-resources

Thank you very much!

APPENDICES

In the *DruidCraft Tarot*, the Wheel image is quite different from the Wheel of Fortune in the *Waite-Smith Tarot*. It depicts the goddess Arianrhod just about to complete a circle of life in the sand.

Appendix A:
Book List and Resources

The following references may be of interest to you if you want to go deeper with certain topics. This list is broad and related to shamanism, tarot, astrology, and the Western Mysteries. It may include topics not covered in this part of the book series. For specific resources, forms, drumming tracks, and free tools that supplement this book, visit: www.reidhart.com/tsh-resources

Recommended Reading

Books on Tarot

Carr-Gomm, Philip and Stephanie Carr-Gomm. Images by Will Worthington. *The DruidCraft Tarot*. Connections Book Publishing, 2004.

This deck is beautiful and follows *Waite-Smith Tarot* symbolism with a touch of Druidry and Wicca. The book is organized well as an introduction to both the Major and Minor Arcana.

Elford, Jaymi. *Tarot Inspired Life: Use the Cards to Enhance your Life*. Llewellyn, 2019.

A worthwhile approach to working with the tarot long term for goals in your life. The process of placing cards for daily viewing is effective in creating manifestation.

Greer, Mary. *Tarot for Yourself: A Workbook for Personal Transformation*. Newcastle, 1984. (35th anniversary Ed. by Weiser, 2019)

The exercises, meditations, rituals, and activities help you connect with the cards in a meaningful way. Check out: marykgreer.com

Payne-Towler, Christine. *The Underground Stream: Esoteric Tarot Revealed*. Noreah Press, 1999.

Christine Payne-Towler provides a deep dive into esoteric tarot history, with a lean toward the continental schools. She documents the various mappings of astrology to tarot. Most of this book is on her website: www.tarot.com/tarot/christine-payne-towler/the-underground-stream

Quinn, Paul. *Tarot for Life: Reading the Cards for Everyday Guidance and Growth*. Quest Books (IL), 2009.

A great introduction to tarot divination based on Waite symbolism. Focused on doing tarot readings.

Renée, Janina. *Tarot Spells*. Llewellyn Publications, 2000.

Tarot Spells is a good introduction to using tarot to create your destiny, although adapting to your own focus and using journey work is recommended. Review all "spells" in this book for conformance with your own personal ethics.

Steinbrecher, Edwin. *The Inner Guide Meditation: A Spiritual Technology for the 21st Century*. Samuel Weiser, Inc., 1988.

Edwin Steinbrecher provides a method for working with an inner guide to contact tarot archetypes through meditation and astrology. The basis is psychological within a Jungian context. While Steinbrecher's approach is a strong influence for the methods here, as presented in this book the approach is shamanic and spiritual. This is distinct from the meditation approach Steinbrecher uses, as discussed in Chapter 1

Books on Astrology

Bloch, Douglas & Demetra George. *Astrology for Yourself: A Workbook for Personal Transformation*. IBIS, 2006.

A great introduction to your own astrological chart if you like a workbook format. Includes the astrological influence of asteroids.

George, Demetra. *Astrology and the Authentic Self: Integrating Traditional and Modern Astrology to Uncover the Essence of the Birth Chart*. IBIS, 2008.

Goes deeper with astrology, incorporating traditional with modern astrological concepts. Good thoughts about doing readings. Intermediate level.

Nichols, Chani. *You Were Born for This: Astrology for Radical Self-Acceptance*. HarperOne, 2020.

Introduces natal astrology for the beginner with a focus on your Sun, Moon, and ascendant. Basis for the Chani app.

Taylor, Carole. *Astrology: Using the Wisdom of the Stars in Your Everyday Life.* DK Pub, 2018.

A broad introduction to astrology with lots of graphics. Focused on modern astrology. Includes case studies. Good for beginners.

Web pages that have good background on astrology:

www.astro.com

This site has many free resources to calculate natal astrological charts using various methods. Includes both modern, traditional, and Hellenistic approaches. Highly recommended.

wiki.astro.com/astrowiki/en/

This site is a reliable source for questions about astrological terms and concepts.

www.astro-seek.com

Many Hellenistic and more esoteric techniques are included here, such as solar returns, progressed lunar cycles, and annual profections. Be sure to include the dash in your search for this site.

There are 10,000+ books on astrology, the ones listed above are good starting points. Your library probably has some good introductory books on astrology as well.

Books on Shamanism

Birch, Alida. *The Co-Creation Handbook: A Shamanic Guide to Manifesting a Better World and a More Joyful Life.* Luminare Press, 2014.

A comprehensive guide to working shamanically with helping spirits to achieve happiness and your goals in life.

Harner, Michael. *The Way of the Shaman.* HarperOne, 1990.

The primary source document for modern core shamanism.

Ingerman, Sandra. *Shamanic Journeying: A Beginner's Guide.* Sounds True, 2008.

A good introduction to effective shamanic journeying.

Resources for Shamanic Healing and Integration

You can check out blogs and information on shamanism and shamanic healing at these websites:

BirchGrove Hearth: www.ReidHart.com www.AlidaBirch.com

Society for Shamanic practice: shamanicpractice.org

Foundation for Shamanic Studies: www.shamanism.org/index.php

Shamanic Teachers: www.sandraingerman.com

You can learn more about shamanic healing and soul retrieval from these books:

Birch, Alida. *The Co-Creation Handbook: A Shamanic Guide to Manifesting a Better World and a More Joyful Life*. Luminare Press. 2014.

Ingerman, Sandra. *Soul Retrieval: Mending the Fragmented Self*. HarperOne, 1991, 2006.

Ingerman, Sandra. *Welcome Home: Following Your Soul's Journey Home*. HarperOne, 1994.

Additional Reading

Arrien, Angeles. *The Tarot handbook: Practical applications of ancient visual symbols*. Jeremy P. Tarcher/Putnam, 1997.

Case, Paul. *The Tarot: A Key to the Wisdom of the Ages*. Penguin. 2006.

Eakins, Pamela. *Tarot of the Spirit*. Weiser Books, 1992.

Eliade, Mircea. *Shamanism: Archaic Techniques of Ecstasy*. Princeton University Press, 1964.

Foxwood, Orion. the Tree of Enchantment: Ancient Wisdom and Magic Practices of the Faery Tradition. Weiser, 2008.

Greer, M. *Tarot Constellations: Patterns of Personal Destiny*. Newcastle, 1987.

Ingerman, Sandra. & Wesselman. Hank. *Awakening to the Spirit World: The Shamanic Path of Direct Revelation*. With: T. Cowan, C. Proudfoot-Edgar, J. Stevens, A Villoldo. Sounds True, 2010.

Kaldera, Raven. *Pagan Astrology: Spell-Casting, Love Magic, and Shamanic Stargazing*. Destiny, 2009.

Matthews, Catlin and John. *Walkers Between the Worlds: The Western Mysteries from Shaman to Magus*. Inner Traditions, 2004.

Poncelet, Claude. *The Shaman Within: A Physicist's Guide to the Deeper Dimensions of Your Life, the Universe, and Everything*. Sounds True, 2014.

Pollack, Rachel. *Seventy-Eight Degrees of Wisdom: A Book of Tarot*. Red Wheel/Weiser, 2009.

Appendix B:
Pathwork Tracking

Overall Tarot Spirit Topics

The following Topics have been included in workshops the author has presented about the Tarot Spirits. Tracking forms have been developed to help capture the results of using shamanic methods to tackle these areas. The first four topics are included in this book:

1. **Meet powerful and loving Tarot Spirits**. Your initial engagement with the Tarot Spirits involves meeting the 22 characters of the tarot Major Arcana as living spiritual entities in the Otherworld.

2. **Your special Tarot Spirits; advice & healing.** Meet and engage with special Tarot Spirits based on your birthdate numerology. You create reciprocity where you receive healing and advice in exchange for recognition of these compassionate and loving spirits.

3. **A shamanic clearing of your natal chart.** You explore the planets and zodiacal signs of your natal chart to learn where challenges lie. You then work with Tarot Spirits as representatives of the planets to resolve challenges and open the way for a smoother and happier life.

4. **Mystery Initiation.** You meet regularly with your personalized Tarot Spirit circles to maintain better balance in your life. Use powerful questions to enter into the Mysteries. Learn from Spirit Constructs in your own mystery school.

Added topics are planned for future books in the *Tarot Spirit* series:

5. **Use a clear and approachable process for personal shadow work and resolve real-world conflicts.** Engaging in Otherworld psychodrama—a dramatic reenactment of shadow conflicts

213

needing resolution—allows deeper discovery of your shadow-self and personal and family dynamics. You work with the tarot court cards as actors in the psychodrama. Following the tradition of "as within, so without" you work in the Otherworld to manifest positive changes in this world.

6. **The places of life—balancing your opportunities**. Two millennia ago, houses were added to astrology to reflect the many facets of life. Working with the Tarot Spirits brings understanding and empowerment, so you can take advantage of the opportunities in your natal chart. The introduction of house planetary rulers expands the Tarot Spirit circles you can work with.

7. **Cycles of time with the Tarot Spirits**. While your life potential is written in your natal chart, different challenges and opportunities unfold over time in your life, based on changing transits and astrological timing techniques. These timing techniques reveal where to focus current efforts for the most personal benefit.

8. **Tarot Spirit healing for others**. Once you have delved into the healing aspects available from the Tarot Spirits in your own life and astrological chart, you can work shamanically on behalf of others to provide access to healing from the Tarot Spirits.

9. **An intersection of Tarot Spirits, shamanism, and the Qabalistic Tree of Life**. Engage with the Tree of Life to connect with age old magic in the Western Mystery tradition. With the Tarot Spirits as your guides, and Celtic cauldrons connecting your body to the Tree, the results are both profound spiritually and helpful practically.

10. **Work magically with Tarot Spirits to manifest your intentions**. Turning the concept of a tarot reading on its head, intentionally create magical tarot card patterns that positively advance manifestation in your world. Engage the power of creation from the Tree of Life in this manifestation process.

11. **Deepen your connection to the Tarot Spirits and become a voice for their wisdom in readings.** Engaging in shamanic readings with the Tarot Spirits provides advice, insight, and spiritual connection for you, your friends, and reading clients.

Pathwork List

There are many exercises or pathwork experiences that you can undertake in this book, future books in the series, or in Tarot Spirit workshops. To keep clear references to the various Pathworks, they are referenced with a letter designator as outlined in the Table below. These pathwork designations are not necessarily introduced in order, but are held consistent across multiple delivery paths, including books, live classes, and video lessons. Each pathwork is used in the Tarot Spirit topics just discussed.

Tarot Spirit Pathwork Index

Ref	Pathwork	Part(s) or Topic(s)
A	Bridge / Message	1
B	Meet / Gift from a Tarot Spirit	1
C	Get to know a Tarot Spirit	1
D	Cauldron / Tree / Temples	9
E	Spheres on the Tree of Life	9
F	Paired Spheres: Hall on the Tree of Life	9
G	Work with Tarot Spirit(s) on Hall/Path	9
H (1,2,3)	Tarot Spirit(s) advice or problem solve	2 / 4
I (1,2,3)	Circle of hands with Tarot Spirits	2 / 4
J (1,2,3)	Healing from Tarot Spirit(s)	2 / 4
J4	Healing your astrological house circle	6
K	Reconcile potentially challenging natal aspects	3
L	Multi- Tarot Spirits-merge Learning	4
M	Resolve interpersonal conflicts	5
N	Meet your shadow-self	2 / 5
O	Shamanic merging with Tarot Spirits	4 / 8 / 11
P	Finding parts of the self	5
Q	Identify the shadow selves	2 / 5
R	Shadow transformation	5
S	Solar return / progressed chart work (K)	7
T	Profection / transit work (K)	7

Only Pathwork for Parts 1, 2, 3, and 4 have instructions in this book.

A Long-Term Plan for the Tarot Spirits

Over time, you will want to work pathworks A, B, and C with each Tarot Spirit, not necessarily on the same day. It is important to finish the Scan (A) before working directly with the Tarot Spirit (Pathwork B then C). For sequencing, choose which Tarot Spirts you are drawn to first or use the group order on the Pathwork A/B/C tracking sheets: Planets I & II, then Signs I, II, III. If you are limited in time, you may want to focus first on those Tarot Spirits that appear often in your *AstroTarot mapping* for potentially challenging aspects. A suggested schedule to work through the different pathworks with all the 22 Tarot Spirits might look like this:

Week or Month:	1	2	3	4	5	6	7
Opening	Wash hands; Call directions or shamanic crossing; Light candle.						
Calling In	Enhanced crossing form, circle of life, or rattling call to directions						
Planets I	Pw. A: Scan	Pw. B: Meet	Pw. C: Know				
Planets II		Pw. A	Pw. B	Pw. C			
Signs I			Pw. A	Pw. B	Pw. C		
Signs II				Pw. A	Pw. B	Pw. C	
Signs III					Pw. A	Pw. B	Pw. C
Other Pathwork	Bridge	Tarot guide	Pw. H: Advice	Pw. I: Circle of Hands *AstroTarot* Pw. K: Reconcile Other Pathwork like Healing (J), Learning (L), & Shadow (N)			
Closing	Thank Spirits; Blow out candle.						

Pw. = Pathwork; See pathwork index table for pathwork reference letters.

Observe that in the suggested schedule you do Pathwork A for a group, then the next week do pathwork B for the same group while doing Pathwork A for a new group, and then the following week, do pathwork C for the original group, adding in B and C for the groups that had A and B the week before. This continues overlaying the groups, starting with A on a new group each week or other period that fits your schedule.

Some of the exercises referred to may not be included in this book of the series (e.g. D through G relate to Qabalah and the Tree of Life and will be covered in a later book in the series as will be Pathworks R, S, and T.)

Everyone takes on spiritual work in their own time and their own way. The above schedule is just a suggestion and fits a 7-week course format and requires 4 to 5 sessions a week. If you do 2 to 3 sessions per week, it would be 7 fortnights or 3 to 4 months. A 7-month option works too.

If your current interest is focused on astrological relationships, then you should focus on the Tarot Spirits representing the traditional seven planets first. Planetary symbols are in the first column of the Pathwork A (scan) worksheet, and include the Sun, Wheel, Magician, High priestess, Tower, Empress, and World. As you learn about different astrological aspects, or groups that are important related to your natal chart, then you can move them up the list to complete the A/B/C pathworks. If you are already aware of potentially challenging aspects in your chart (squares and oppositions) it helps to prioritize the Tarot Spirits related to those planets first. After you have completed A/B/C for the keys needed, you can do the AstroTarot exercises (Pathwork K and others).

An alternative way to order the work is turning over cards randomly until the next tarot key appears. Whichever method is used, using the worksheets or a journal to record your messages, gifts, and requests from the spirits creates an helpful reference. Then you can move on to other exercises or pathwork as appropriate for issues in your personal life.

The key to making progress with the Tarot Spirits is to focus on a brief session of work regularly, rather than trying to complete a marathon session all at once. Once a steady practice of consulting the Tarot Spirits on a regular basis is established, it can continue to be an important ongoing part of your spiritual practice and day-to-day life. You may find that after you have engaged all the Tarot Spirits, you may work with a select group of the Tarot Spirits based on your natal astrology or those that you feel more connected to. You may then consult with the others occasionally when their expertise is required.

Tracking Worksheets

Print out the Tarot Tracking Worksheets—permission to copy them for personal use is granted. You can download them or copy the worksheets on the following pages. These help you to track which Tarot Spirits you have worked with and remember things—like gifts received—long into the future. The worksheets form a good index, but you will probably want to document your journeys in more detail in your journal. The worksheets include:

1. **Pathwork A: Scan the Tarot Spirits**. Summarize the message from each Tarot Spirit in a word or two here. Note that the scans of the royalty and pip cards are optional and intended for someone who is interested in tarot divination. That is discussed further in the Shamanic Tarot Divination mini-course.

2. **Pathwork B: Meet the Tarot Spirits**. You can also note the date you scanned (A) this Tarot Spirit. Summarize the commitment you negotiated and the gift you received in a couple of words.

3. **Pathwork C: Know the Tarot Spirits**. Here you can include impressions of each Tarot Spirit from your follow-on journey(s).

4. **Tarot Spirit Mapping for AstroTarot**. While not a tracking worksheet, this is included here to provide a key to the astrological symbols on the earlier tracking sheets and the Major Arcana Astrological Attributions.. The details of rulerships, houses, and Spheres will be explained in later books. The first column shows the letters you enter for two different astrological symbol fonts: AstroDotBasic and Alchemy.

5. **Tarot Divination Meanings (Major Keys).** Some basic meanings associated with each tarot key are listed here, along with reverse meanings. These are mostly useful if you are doing tarot divination. It is suggested you wait until after you do exercises A/B/C to look at the meanings. This gives you a more direct experience of each Tarot Spirit without preconceived notions.

6. **Tarot Divination Meanings (Minor Arcana).** Some basic meanings associated with the other tarot cards (royalty and pips) are listed here, along with reversed card meanings.

Enjoy your journey into the world of tarot, and may you have great success working with these amazing Tarot Spirits. Remember, there is no rush, and you can meet them all at your own pace.

The tracking worksheets are included on the following pages. If you copy from the book, an enlargement ratio of 130% is suggested. You can also download a pdf version along with other free tools to use with this book at: www.reidhart.com/tsh-resources

Pathwork "A" Scan Tarot Spirits

Tarot Scanning. Light Candle. [Spirit Call. Crossing Form.] Enhanced Crossing Form. Visually scan the card in half inch strips, top to bottom. Close eyes, cross onto the bridge. View the live scene of the card beyond the bridge. Listen or watch for a message. Return. Crossing Form.

Astro	Key #	Scan & Meditate	Date	Message
Planets I	19	Sun		
	3	Empress		
	10	Wheel of Fortune		
	1	Magician		
	2	High Priestess		
Planets II	16	Blasted Tower		
	21	Universe/World		
	0	Fool		
	12	Hanged Man		
	20	Last Judgement		
Signs I	4	Emperor		
	5	Hierophant		
	6	Lovers		
	7	Chariot		
Signs II	11	Strength		
	9	Hermit		
	8	Justice		
	13	Death		
Signs III	14	Temperance		
	15	Guardian/ Devil		
	17	The Star		
	18	Moon		

Discs	Date	Message
K		
Q		
Pr/Kt		
Ps/Pg		

Discs	Date
A	
2	
3	
4	
5	
6	
7	
8	
9	
10	

Cups	Date	Message
K		
Q		
Pr/Kt		
Ps/Pg		

Cups	Date
A	
2	
3	
4	
5	
6	
7	
8	
9	
10	

Wands	Date	Message
K		
Q		
Pr/Kt		
Ps/Pg		

Wands	Date
A	
2	
3	
4	
5	
6	
7	
8	
9	
10	

Swords	Date	Message
K		
Q		
Pr/Kt		
Ps/Pg		

Swords	Date
A	
2	
3	
4	
5	
6	
7	
8	
9	
10	

Traditional seven planets highlighted in ivory. Outer planets share elemental designation highlighted in green. Zodiac signs are not highlighted. Scanning court and numbered cards is optional - a good practice for Tarot Readers.

Pathwork "B" Meet Tarot Spirits

Key #	Name	Astro	Journey Date A. Scan / B. Meet	Tarot Archetype Pathworking with Guide and individual Tarot Spirits "What do you request of me to work together?"	Gift Received: Place in Body
Planets I					
19	Sun	☉			
3	Empress	♀			
10	Wheel of Fortune	♃			
1	Magician	☿			
2	High Priestess	☽			
Planets II					
16	Blasted Tower	♂			
21	Universe/World	♄			
0	Fool	♅ △			
12	Hanged Man	♆ ▽			
20	Last Judgement	♇ △			
Signs I					
4	Emperor	♈			
5	Hierophant	♉			
6	Lovers	♊			
7	Chariot	♋			
Signs II					
11	Strength	♌			
9	Hermit	♍			
8	Justice	♎			
13	Death	♏			
Signs III					
14	Temperance	♐			
15	Guardian/Devil	♑			
17	The Star	♒			
18	Moon	♓			

You may wish to adjust the order to prioritize planets that are involved in "potential challenging aspects."

Pathwork "C" Know Tarot Spirits

Tarot Pathwork. 1. Opening: Light Candle. Crossing Form. 2. Lay out cards and visually scan. 3. Go via bridge **with guide** to Tarot Spirit 4. Hang out and get to know them; like having tea or beer with a friend. 5. Observe their territory, ask clarifying questions.

Astro	Key #	Scan & Meditate	C: Date Know	C: What aspect of my outer reality do you create or sustain?	C: Describe their Territory, their mystery, or answers to other?
☉	19	Sun			
♀	3	Empress			
♃	10	Wheel of Fortune			
☿	1	Magician			
☽	2	High Priestess			
♂	16	Blasted Tower			
♄	21	Universe/World			
♅	0	Fool			
♆	12	Hanged Man			
♇	20	Last Judgement			
♈	4	Emperor			
♉	5	Hierophant/ Innocent			
♊	6	Lovers			
♋	7	Chariot			
♌	11	Strength			
♍	9	Hermit			
♎	8	Justice			
♏	13	Death			
♐	14	Temperance			
♑	15	Guardian/ Devil			
♒	17	The Star			
♓	18	Moon			

Row groups (left margin labels): Planets I (Sun–High Priestess), Planets II (Blasted Tower–Last Judgement), Signs I (Emperor–Chariot), Signs II (Strength–Death), Signs III (Temperance–Moon)

You may wish to adjust the order to prioritize planets that are involved in "potential challenging aspects."

Tarot Spirit Mapping for AstroTarot (Translation Table)

Letter to enter for font AstroDotBasic / Alchemy Houses	Astrology Symbol	Sign of The Zodiac	Sign Element	Sign Quadruplicity	Tarot Key or Archetype	Key #	Key Alternate Names
a / A 1: mask	♈	Aries	Fire	cardinal	The Emperor	4	The Lord
b / B 2: wealth	♉	Taurus	Earth	fixed	The Heirophant	5	The High Priest, Innocent
c / C 3: communication	♊	Gemini	Air	mutable	The Lovers	6	Twins
d / D 4: home	♋	Cancer	Water	cardinal	The Chariot	7	
e / E 5: creative	♌	Leo	Fire	fixed	Strength	8	Fortitude, Lust
f / F 6: growth	♍	Virgo	Earth	mutable	The Hermit	9	
g / G 7: partners	♎	Libra	Air	cardinal	Justice	11	
h / H 8: sex/psychic	♏	Scorpio	Water	fixed	Death	13	Transition
i / I 9: meaning	♐	Sagittarius	Fire	mutable	Temperance	14	The Fferyllt
j / J 10: vocation	♑	Capricorn	Earth	cardinal	The Devil	15	Cernunnos, Guardian
k / K 11: social	♒	Aquarius	Air	fixed	The Star	17	
l / L 12: transcend	♓	Pisces	Water	mutable	The Moon	18	

Sign ruled by planet to right		Planet	Astrology Symbol	Sphere	Sphere Name	Tarot Key or Archetype	Key #	Key Alternate Names
A / Q	♌	Sun	☉	6	Harmony	The Sun	19	
B / R	♋	Moon	☽	9	Foundation	The High Priestess	2	
C / S	♊ ♍	Mercury	☿	8	Honor	The Magician	1	Magus, Alchemist
D / T	♉ ♎	Venus	♀	7	Victory	The Empress	3	The Lady
E / U	♈ ♏	Mars	♂	5	Justice	The Tower	16	The Blasted Tower
F / V	♐	Jupiter	♃	4	Mercy	Wheel of Fortune	10	The Wheel, Fate
G / W	♑ ♒	Saturn	♄	3	Understanding	The World	21	The Universe
H / X	♒	Air; Uranus	♅	1	Crown	The Fool	0	
I / Y	♓	Water; Neptune	♆	2	Wisdom	The Hanged man	12	
J / Z	♏	Fire; Pluto	♇	11	Knowledge	Judgement	20	Rebirth, Last Judgement
M / : Modern Rulerships		Earth	⊕	10	Kingdom			

Tarot Divination Meanings

Tarot Divination. Light Candle. Shuffle. Cut. Lay out cards. Listen or watch for a message while rattling. Return. Crossing Form.

Key	Scan & Medit Meaning	Reversed	Group	Astro
0	Fool	Innocence, Trust, Play	Naivety, Over-Cautious	Severe	♅ ♎
1	Magician	Vision, Empowerment, Will-power, Action	Blocked flow/will, Abuse of power, confusion	Astral	☿
2	High Priestess	Depth, Wisdom, Soul, Depth, Dreams	Repress memories, delusion	Astral	☽
3	Empress	Abundance, Sensuality, Mothering, Creativity, Passion	Repressed feelings, Infertility, Poverty, Blocks	Merciful	♀
4	Emperor	Order, Leadership, Stability, Protection, Competent	Lose control, Indecision, Power struggles, Weak	Merciful	♈
5	Hierophant	Tradition, Conscience, Education, Conformity, Initiation	Rebel, break vow, Unsound advice, flaunt norms	Spirit	♉
6	Lovers	Attraction, Union, Surrender, Trust, Win-win, Passion, Love	Jealousy, Separation, Mistrust, sexual rejection	Higher Self	♊
7	Chariot	Triumph, Will, Brave, Overcome, Fame, Unstoppable	Delay, Adrift, Failure, Unmerited success.	Higher Self	♋
8	Strength	Courage, Faith, Unconditional love, Discipline, Wild	Fear, Lust, weak, depression, lost hope, torment	Higher Self	♌
9	Hermit	Meditation, Studious, Alone, Retreat, Guidance	Fear solitude, Isolated, Imprudence, Distracted	Spirit	♍
10	Wheel of Fortune	Reap rewards, cycles, Karma, Synchronicity, Progress	Stuck, break pattern, false start, difficult time	Astral	♃
11	Justice	Balance, Discerning, fair, Honest, Precise, Clarity, Decision	Imbalance, bias, unfairness, dishonesty, Unjust	Higher Self	♎
12	Hanged Man	Patience, Sacrifice, Reversal, Deepening, Humble, Surrender	Refuse surrender, victimhood, denial, back on feet	Severe	♆ ▽
13	Death	Clear old, Dissolution, Transition, Pre-transform, divesting	Stagnation, Fear of change, Can't move on, deny loss	Severe	♏
14	Temperance	Harmony, Alchemy, Transformation, Mix opposites, Magic	Extremes, wasteful, Fragment, Quarrels.	Merciful	♐
15	Guardian/ Devil	Master life-force, Obsession / Fear, Shame, Shadow, Desire	Abuse Power, Succumb temptation /Liberation	Severe	♑
16	Tower	Revelation, Upheaval, Release, Shaken, Fall from security	Imprisoned, Avoidance, Keep the lid on,	Higher Self	♂
17	The Star	Optimism, Openness, Cooperative, Healing, Ideal, Forgive	Lost innocence or inspiration, Artist block, Waste	Spirit	♒
18	Moon	Dreams, Psychic awakening, Imagination, Withdrawal	Ignore instinct, Confusion, Addiction, Rational	Astral	♓
19	Sun	Happiness, Radiant, Wonder, Freedom, Expression, Clarity	Lack clarity, Failure, Disappointment, Burnout	Astral	☉
20	Last Judgement	Rebirth, Renewal, Decision, Follow a calling, New direction	Deny inner, procrastinate, Complacency,	Spirit	♇ △
21	Universe/ World	Completion, Wholeness, Fulfillment, Euphoric, Top of World	Stasis, Delay, Incomplete, Overfocus on parts	Merciful	♄

Tarot Divination Meanings

Cups is the suit of water, the heart, and emotion.

Swords is the suit of air, mental acuity.

Discs, coins or Pentagrams is the suit of the earth, physical manifestation.

Wands or rods represent fire, the suit of the will.

Cups	Meaning	Rev
K	Composure, sensitive	Emotional spontaneity
Q	Heart, emotional	Numbness
Pr/Kt	Romance	Halt courtship
Ps/Pg	Sensitivity	Distrust

Swords	Meaning	Rev
K	Judicious	Biased
Q	Discernment	Ambivalent
Pr/Kt	Assertion	Stuff it
Ps/Pg	Investigation	Bored

Discs	Meaning	Rev
K	Security	$ Loss
Q	Domestic	Stingy
Pr/Kt	Duty	Shirk
Ps/Pg	Studious	Uninterested

Wands	Meaning	Rev
K	Vision	Arrogance
Q	Faith	Domineering
Pr/Kt	Eagerness	Uncommitted
Ps/Pg	Vigor	Reluctance

Cups	Meaning	Rev
A	Root of Water, Blessing.	Empty soul
2	Love	Separation
3	Abundance	Thwarted
4	Luxury/Discontent	Seek true desires
5	Disappoint-ment/Loss	Moving on
6	Pleasure	Rejection
7	Debauchery	Down to earth
8	Indolence	Persistence
9	Happiness	Lack
10	Satiety	Distrust

Swords	Meaning	Rev
A	Root of Air, Intellect.	Irrational
2	Peace, Indecision	Choose
3	Sorrow	Let go or numb pain
4	Truce	Reengage
5	Overthrow	Win-win
6	Science, Recovery	cancel trip
7	Futility, Evasion	Candor
8	Interference, Restriction	Clarity
9	Cruelty, Anxiety	Calm/Numb
10	Ruin, Defeat	Struggle on

Discs	Meaning	Rev
A	Root of Earth, Prosperity	Risky
2	Change, Juggling	Drop ball
3	Work, Synergy	Inefficiency
4	Power	Hoarding
5	Worry	Recovery
6	Success	Pmt Denied
7	Failure	Change plans
8	Prudence	Disruption
9	Gain	Property issues
10	Wealth	Disinherit

Wands	Meaning	Rev
A	Root of Fire	Premature
2	Dominion	Complacent
3	Virtue	Doubt
4	Completion	Incomplete
5	Strife	Cooperate
6	Victory	Fall short
7	Velour	Defensive
8	Swiftness	Delay
9	Strength	Give up
10	Oppression	Drop load

Appendix C:
Tarot History—
More Than a Pack of Cards

The earliest surviving tarot cards date from Italy in the mid-15th century; however, there are earlier references to many tarot symbols from the Vita Merlini [36] (the life of Merlin), a 12th-century Celtic-sourced manuscript. There is evidence that the key images of the Major Arcana parallel Egyptian images used in the hall of the neophytes for temple initiation. [37] In the 19th and 20th centuries, the symbolism of the tarot was further expanded and the connection with ancient Western Mysteries was documented. The tarot also connects with astrology and the Qabalah, two other cornerstones of the Western Mysteries. Carl Jung [38] commented on the tarot as an archetypal window into our individual and group unconscious.

Origins of the Major Arcana in the Tarot

While tarot cards appeared in Italy in the mid-15th century—often with different key cards than what we see today—most of the modern occult interpretation of the tarot sources from developments in the 18th and 20th centuries. Here is an abbreviated chronology:

- In 1650, the Marseilles Tarot deck was published with key cards mostly matching the names and structure we are familiar with today.
- In 1781, Antoine Court de Gebelin published an essay on tarot. Here we have the first assignment of the key cards to letters in the Hebrew alphabet. Gebelin also postulates an Egyptian source for

---

[36] en.wikipedia.org/wiki/Vita_Merlini
[37] Keizer, L and C. Payne-Towler. *The Underground Stream.*
[38] marykgreer.com/2008/03/31/carl-jung-and-Tarot/

the tarot images just before Napoleon's invasion of Egypt and the discovery of the Rosetta Stone launched the era of modern Egyptology.

- In 1790, Etteilla[39] founded a "new school of magic," although his cartography books on working with cards not related to tarot preceded this, starting in 1770. His teachings paralleled Pythagorean astro-alphanumeric correspondences from the Greek alphabet reforms of 600 BCE.[40] His Egyptian influenced deck had many different keys than the Marseilles deck that later became the standard for tarot decks.

- In the 1850s Éliphas Lévi[41] brought tarot into his magical systems and created a basis for later magical interpretation of the tarot including the Golden Dawn and other magical systems. He went deeper into the connection of Hebrew letters to the major keys and brought forward the images of the Marseilles deck.

- In 1909 the *Waite-Smith Tarot Deck* was published with a shift in symbolism from the Continental to English magical systems. While there were some variations in symbolism from the Marseilles deck, the general structure is similar. The major innovation that Arthur Edward Waite and Pamela Smith brought to this deck was having images on the pip or numbered cards, rather than just the requisite number of suit related items. It should be noted that the earlier Sola Busca Tarot[42] also had imagery on the pip cards and was seen by Waite and Smith as black and white images before they made their famous deck.

- Waite was in and out of various permutations of the Golden Dawn as was Aleister Crowley. They were strong rivals. Crowley eventually created the *Thoth Tarot* deck with the artist Lady Frieda Harris, with posthumous publication in 1969.

---

[39] en.wikipedia.org/wiki/Etteilla
[40] Payne-Towler, C. and L. Keizer. *The Underground Stream: Esoteric Tarot Revealed.* p 127.
[41] Lévi, Éliphas. *The Kabalistic and Occult Tarot of Éliphas Lévi.*
books.google.com/books?id=4znuBgAAQBAJ&printsec=frontcover#v=onepage&q&f=false
[42] en.wikipedia.org/wiki/Sola_Busca_tarot

So, there is a question then of ancient sources for the tarot card images and occult meanings. There has been much back and forth on this matter in the last few decades:

- In 1996, Drummett, Decker, and Depaulis published *A Wicked Pack of Cards: Origins of the Occult Tarot* that strongly debunked the Egyptian symbol origination theory.
- In 1999, Christine Payne-Towler published *The Underground Stream: Esoteric Tarot Revealed*[43] which included an essay by Lewis Keizer: "The Esoteric Origins of Tarot: More than a Wicked Pack of Cards." This essay references web postings by Michael Poe[44] referencing Bernard Bromage's descriptions of Serapis temples in Naples Italy that were unfortunately destroyed in World War II.
- This description of the tarot images at Serapis was attacked by Michael Hurst, using a "you've got no real evidence" approach.[45]
- Mary Greer gives us an interesting overview of the origins that shy away from an Egyptian source; yet refer to the mysteries. She gives an interesting conclusion:

It is said that history tells us outer truth and inner lies, while myths tell us outer lies and inner truth, and so this myth of tarot's Egyptian origin recounts an inner truth about a higher purpose and meaning to our lives.[46]

While a solid historical source can only be clearly traced to the appearance of the tarot cards in Italy in the mid-15th century, the allegorical and archetypal meaning behind the cards likely harkens back to earlier eras. In the AstroTarot process, your own personal experience of each Tarot Spirit is more important than pinning down an exact historical lineage for the Major Arcana. You can honor the factual history of the cards, while you also honor the ancient mystery source of the symbols and archetypes of the Major Arcana.

---

[43] Payne-Towler, C. and L. Keizer. *The Underground Stream: Esoteric Tarot Revealed*. pp 9-16. See: www.tarot.com/tarot/christine-payne-towler/esoteric-origins

[44] www.sacred-texts.com/bos/bos446.htm

[45] www.luxlapis.co.za/at/serapis_02.htm

[46] From *Mary K. Greer's Tarot Blog – Egypt, Tarot and Mystery School Initiations*, copyright © 2007 by Mary K. Greer. marykgreer.com/events/egypt-Tarot-and-mystery-school-initiations Reprinted by permission of the author.

Celtic Origins

One interesting northern document that references many tarot symbols is the *Vita Merlini*[47] (the life of Merlin), a 12th-century Celtic-sourced manuscript. RJ Stewart has explored this source, pointing out that many of the tarot Major Arcana images and symbols are referenced in this historical document. He incorporated many of these in his *Merlin Tarot*.[48]

A Mithraic Source?

An interesting theory is that the origin of tarot images is more likely Persian. Stephen Flowers presents work[49] based on scholarship by Sigurd Agrell in the 1930s. This theory postulates that the Mithraic mysteries provided a means to spread a basic mystery path of initiation with both a connection to astrology and ancient mythology. Supporting this theory is the fact that the Mithraic cult of the magus was open to absorbing outside ideas. It had a reach into Alexandria, multiple Greek territories, Rome, and as far north as the Rhine. The spread of Mithraism occurred over a period from the 2nd century BCE to at least the 4th century CE, parallel in both time and place with the development of Hellenistic astrology.

There are also thousands of archeological Mithraic initiatory sites and a verified location that had frescos in central Italy, relatively close to where the Tarot emerged after the dark ages.[50] Guity Novin, a graphic designer and artist, recounts[51] how the Mithraic process is initiatory as depicted on the frescoes at Capua, Italy and parallel to the initiatory path of the fool in the Major Arcana of the tarot. Its strong planetary focus supports a more ancient connection between Tarot imagery and astrology rather than some manufactured correspondences developed in the 17th century and applied to a pack of cards.

Alternative Tarot Key Names

Many tarot Decks have different names for some cards in the Major Arcana. Several are listed here, although those included are not exhaustive.

[47] en.wikipedia.org/wiki/Vita_Merlini
[48] Stewart, R.J. *The Merlin Tarot.* Aquarian Press.
[49] Flowers, Stephen. *The Magian Taork.* Inner Traditions.
[50] ibid. p 40.
[51] Novin, Guity. 2014. *Mithraism and the Medieval Introduction of Tarot Cards.* brewminate.com/mithraism-and-the-medieval-introduction-of-tarot-cards/

Marseilles names are included only where the English translation of the French name differs from the Waite-Smith name. The decks included in this comparison to the *Waite-Smith Tarot Deck* are Toth (same names as Deck of Ceremonial Magic), DruidCraft, Marseilles (which also has all the names in French), Mother Peace, and Merlin. Again, there are hundreds of tarot decks that may have different names assigned to Major Arcana cards.

Key #	Waite-Smith Name	Alternate Deck	Alternative Name (where different)
1	The Magician	Toth/Spirit	The Magus (3 versions in Toth)
		Marseilles	The Juggler (Le Bateleur)
		Wildwood	The Shaman
2	The High Priestess	Toth	The Priestess
		Marseilles	The Popess (La Papesse)
		Wildwood	The Seer
3	The Empress	DruidCraft	The Lady
		Wildwood	The Green Woman
4	The Emperor	DruidCraft	The Lord
		Wildwood	The Green Man
5	The Hierophant	DruidCraft	The High Priest
		Marseilles	The Pope (Le Pape)
		Wildwood	The Ancestor
6	The Lovers	Wildwood	The Forest Lovers
7	The Chariot	Wildwood	The Archer
8*	Strength	Toth	(11) Lust
		Wildwood	The Stag
9	The Hermit	Mother peace	The Crone
		Wildwood	The Hooded Man
10	The Wheel of Fortune	Toth	Fortune
		DruidCraft	The Wheel
		Wildwood	The Wheel
11*	Justice	Toth	(8) Adjustment
		T. of the Spirit	Karma
		Wildwood	The Woodward
12	The Hanged Man	Mother peace	The Hanged One
		Wildwood	The Mirror
13	Death	DruidCraft	Death
		Wildwood	The Journey
14	Temperance	Toth	Art
		DruidCraft	Fferyllt
		Wildwood	Balance

Key #	Waite-Smith Name	Alternate Deck	Alternative Name (where different)
15	The Devil	DruidCraft Wildwood	Cernunnos The Guardian
16	The Tower	Marseilles Wildwood	The House of God (Le Maison Dieu) The Blasted oak
17	The Star	Wildwood	The Pole Star
18	The Moon	Wildwood	The Moon on the Water
19	The Sun	Wildwood	The Sun of Life
20	Judgement	Toth T. of the Spirit DruidCraft Wildwood	The Aeon Resurrection Rebirth The Great Bear
(0)**	The Fool	Wildwood	The Wanderer
21	The World	Toth/Spirit Wildwood	The Universe The World Tree

* In the *Thoth Tarot* and derivative decks, Justice becomes "Adjustment" at position 8 and Strength becomes "Lust" at position 11.
** The Fool, unnumbered, is placed between 20 and 21 after Lévi and Waite. Other decks usually place The Fool first, with some placing it last.

Which Tarot Deck Should I Use?

What tarot deck do I need to work with the pathwork journeys in this book? Let's look at different tarot decks that are appropriate for shamanic use in this exploration of the Tarot Spirits. First, there are a lot of decks out there, at least 2000 catalogued at Aeclectic Tarot. How do you select one that makes sense to use in this engagement with the Tarot Spirits?

A good place for beginners to start is with a deck that is based on the *Waite-Smith Tarot Deck*, as the English Western Mystery tradition is aligned with the symbolism on cards in that deck. This deck is also referred to as the *Rider-Waite[52] Tarot Deck*, as Rider was the publisher, Waite was the occultist or the symbologist who decided what symbols should go on each card. Pamela Coleman Smith was the artist.

The *DruidCraft Tarot*, shown in this book, is a good alternative. The symbolism is quite similar to the *Waite-Smith Tarot*. To review the imagery of various decks to see which appeals to you, just search for images online or go to reviews at the website Aeclectic Tarot (www.aeclectic.net/tarot/cards/list.shtml). There is also a video reviewing

---

[52] Rider-Waite® is a registered trademark of U.S. Games, Inc.

several tarot decks available at www.reidhart.com/tsh-resources. In the end, the deck you use is your choice.

Waite-Smith Alignment

The Magician is shown below from the *DruidCraft Tarot* deck by Philip and Stephanie Carr-Gomm with artist Will Worthington. The *DruidCraft Tarot Deck* follows the symbology of the *Waite-Smith Tarot Deck* while incorporating druidic, Celtic, and wiccan themes. The gesturing and magical tools match. It adds Celtic symbolism here with Cerridwen in the background, represented as a black hen with a red crown.

The Magician from the *DruidCraft Tarot* is quite similar in gesture and symbolism to the *Waite-Smith Tarot*.

If you are already very familiar with the Waite-Smith symbolism, you may want to branch out into another deck, and several possible groups follow. Each of the following decks are likely one of many in certain categories.

Celtic, Nordic, Egyptian, and Greek Variants

For those with a Celtic world view or that of another pantheon, there are decks that focus more on that heritage than the *Waite-Smith Tarot Deck*. And there are many other decks out there covering a Nordic or Egyptian approach. Decks to consider include:

- *Merlin Tarot* by RJ Stewart is based on the Merlin legend.
- *Wild Wood Tarot* by Ryan and Matthews has strong Druidic leanings.
- Egyptian decks in print include Brotherhood of Light *Egyptian Tarot* by C.C. Zain, The Eternal Tarot, and Lo Scarboro's *Egyptian Tarot Deck*.
- Tarot decks in print with a Nordic theme include *The Giants Tarot* and *Vikings Tarot*.
- Greek mythology is the basis for (*The New*) *Mythic Tarot*.

Continental Variants

Marseilles Tarot or Spanish variants may be worth exploring if your focus is not on the English magical tradition. If so, you will find *The Underground Stream* by Christine Payne-Towler listed in Appendix A worth exploring.

Magical Alignment

While all tarot decks can relate to magical work, four decks that are aligned with tarot magic or alchemy include:

- The *Thoth Tarot* deck by Aleister Crowley
- Lon DuQuette's *Tarot of Ceremonial Magic* deck
- The *Tarot of Holy Light* by Christine Payne-Towler
- *Tarot of the Golden Dawn* by Chic Cicero and Sandra Tabatha

There are certainly many more magical decks out there, but these represent a good starting place.

Visually Invoking Decks

Some decks have more abstract imagery that can provide more intuitive evocation of meaning for the reader. Looking at the deck can invoke multiple personal meanings. Two decks in this category are:

- *Tarot of the Spirit* by Pamela Eakins has a strong connection with the Qabalah.
- The *Voyager Tarot* by James Wanless is a collage-based deck that is well suited to those who wish to look into the card and have a vision arise to provide meaning.

Feminist Decks

In the early 1980s several feminist oriented decks or more feminine interpretations of the *Waite-Smith Tarot Deck* appeared. Notable round feminist decks include the *Daughters of the Moon* and *Motherpeace Tarot*. If you search Aeclectic Tarot for "feminine tarot," 31 tarot decks are listed. The book *A Feminist Tarot* includes non-patriarchal interpretations of the *Waite-Smith Tarot Deck*.

Experiment with Decks of Your Choice

Of course, you can use any deck you're drawn to. You want to feel some sort of connection with that deck, but beware that many decks change the names or numbers of the keys. They usually all have 22 Major Arcana, but there are many different names assigned to some of the particular keys. You will have to trace those names back to the original *Waite-Smith Tarot* to verify the *AstroTarot mapping*.

There are several books on tarot in Appendix A and of course, there are many, many more books on tarot. Unfortunately, many interesting decks are out of print. You can review many different tarot decks online at Aeclectic Tarot: www.aeclectic.net/tarot/cards/list.shtml

An additional resource for reviewing ten leading decks suitable for use with this book is an online video presentation by Reid Hart. This presentation is free for readers of this book here:

www.reidhart.com/tsh-resources

Appendix D:
Creating Sacred Space

As you work with the Tarot Spirits it is important to create sacred or ceremonial space. This entails putting up the "do not disturb" sign. In other words, put your phone on airplane mode and silence your computer. Let other occupants in your space know you don't want to be disturbed. Then drum or rattle a bit and create a brief induction connecting you with the directions, earth and sky, calling power into your body.

Sonic Drive

As discussed with the Shamanic Journey instructions in Chapter 2, drumming or rattling moves you into an altered state of consciousness. Just rattling or drumming for a few minutes creates a shift in your brain waves. You can combine this with some spontaneous body movement if you like, or simply lie down.

Opening Space for Your Spiritual Work

Creating sacred space[53] has broad use throughout native and Western spiritual and magical traditions. It is using a brief ritual to connect to spiritual power. Often, there is a component that brings power from the earth into your body, enlivening power spots in the body and filling you with energy. It often also involves connecting to power above and to the four directions.

We are all aware of power spots where this earth power flows. Stonehenge, standing stone circles, and even less famous natural sites are places where we can feel palpable earth energy if we are quiet and pay attention.

I was once working in Germany and after reviewing the *Michelin Guide* for the day's route, I found a Paleolithic site listed. Not publicized

---

[53] See resource book list in Appendix A and discussion in this appendix.

beyond the guide, the site was accessed through a farmer's field. It consisted of two rows of very large boulders. I remember that walking into the site I was literally bowled over by a strong feeling of palpable power that vibrated in the place. I have felt similar power at Stonehenge, standing stone circles like Avebury, passage tombs in Ireland, Native American cliff dwellings, and areas of old growth forest in the Pacific Northwest. However, the power at the German Paleolithic site was quite strong. In the spiritual work I do today, I will often link up to that site from a distance to connect to the earth power that is present there.

Paleolithic site located 49 km ESE from Bremen, Germany. The author felt very strong earth power here in the mid-1980's. *Photo by author.*

So, you can enhance the power of your experience by thinking of a place you have noticed such power. Keep that feeling in mind as you connect to earth power.

The Three Suns and Seven Directions

Working with the three Suns is one way to connect earth and sky. If you go back to the formation of the earth, there is a molten core that originally came from a star. You can acknowledge that as the Sun in the center of the earth. Then you have the Sun of our solar system, which is the source of energy for life on our planet. Beyond our solar system there are many stars in the universe. So, star stuff is all around us, and in fact you are made of star stuff. This third Sun energy is in the stars overhead.

As you center yourself in sacred space, you have two orientations: horizontal and vertical. The four cardinal horizontal directions added to the three vertical directions make seven. Acknowledging the seven directions places you at the center of both the physical and spiritual universe.

Vertically you are between above and below, inhabiting a middle place. Vertically there are three directions: above, below, and center. In your place, you are located between the shamanic upper world above and the lower world below. You purposely reach into those worlds, drawing power into the middle world where you are located. That creates a vertical axis.

You are also connected horizontally to the directions surrounding us, each direction focusing on one of the four elements and containing power animals, sacred plant spirits, and spiritual beings. While differing traditions have different assignments to the cardinal directions, a common set of assignments is as follows:

- The East is aligned with the element air, the rising Sun, the tarot suit of swords, thought, mental faculties and flying power animals. Spirit teachers or deities that bring the dawn reside here.

- The South is aligned with the element fire, the Sun at noon, the suit of wands, intentionality, fighting spirit, and land power animals. Spirit teachers or deities that have working knowledge reside here.

- The West is aligned with the element water, the setting Sun, the suit of cups, emotions, and water-based power animals. Spirit teachers or deities that have deep magic or provide emotional clearing reside here.

- The North is aligned with the element earth, the suit of coins or pentacles, ancestor connection, and mythical, reptile, and nocturnal power animals. Spirit teachers or deities with creation and life cycle traits reside here.

The assignments listed above are a starting place and as you receive more information from the spirits or work with a particular tradition, some of these attributes will shift. For example, some traditions will place particular power animals or types of animals in each of the four cardinal directions. In my experience, the location of particular power animals or plant spirits is determined by information I get from that particular power animal or Spirit. As an example, many traditions place "flyers" or birds in the east, yet my personal relationship with crow is in the South.

You can define the vertical connection through the three Suns: the star in the center of the earth, the Sun at the center of our solar system, and the many stars above our heads. You can also acknowledge the Moon as being part of the mix, reflecting the light from the Sun and highlighting the many cycles you experience in life. The three Suns also align with the vertical axis and represent the Tree of Life that you will engage with in a later book in the series.

As you work intentionally with these lights, a burning candle provides an offering and a focus for the work. You can look into the candle flame and make a visual connection to the three Suns.

The Awen and the Rays

At the conclusion of various parts of your setting sacred space you can use the power of voice to seal or focus your calling of power. While there are many chants you can use—and if you are strongly invested or initiated into a particular word of power use it—the word Awen is a good choice. "Awen" is a great keyword from the Druid revival[54] in the late 18th century and is used today by the Order of Bards, Ovates, and Druids along with other Druidic orders.

Chanting the Awen has three syllables that are traditionally vibrated or pronounced with a low tone and elongated syllables: "Aaaaah-oooooo-ennnn." The first syllable represents the sky and power from above, the second brings up the power of the earth, while the third stands for ourselves, the human standing between earth and sky.

---

[54] Greer, John Michael. The Druid Magic Handbook, pp 122. Also: aoda.org/publications/articles-on-druidry/druidrevival/

The Druidic Awen symbol or symbol of 3 rays.
Credit: en.wikipedia.org, public domain.

The Awen can be represented by three rays of light, each starting from one of three points above the rays. In the druidic tradition the first ray on the left represents knowledge, the second on the right represents power, and the third in the center represents peace and balance. The rays can be held in the body by holding the arms out to the sides a bit like an upside-down V, with the center ray represented by the body. The outer rays are linked to each Solstice while the center ray is linked to both equinoxes.

Connect to Earth And Sky

The actual process of connecting with the power in the earth and sky is quite centering. It not only opens you up to the Otherworld, but it brings power into your body that can improve vitality and health. You may already have different minor rituals you are familiar with that you can weave into the experience. If you do not have a personal ritual that serves this connection, you can consider one of the following:

- The shamanic crossing ritual as detailed in the next section.
- Opening the faery well, as taught by Orion Foxwood in *The Tree of Enchantment*.
- The rising light form, as taught by RJ Stewart in *The Miracle Tree*.
- Invoking the gates of the elements and the circulation of light, as taught by John Michael Greer in *The Druid Magic Handbook*.

- Shamanically calling the powers and spirits of the directions, as taught by several shamanic teachers, whose books are referenced in Appendix A.
- Casting a circle of power, as taught in many Pagan and Wiccan communities.

The point is that there are multiple ways to create sacred space in which to do your Tarot Spirit journey work. Try a few out and see what puts you in a good place to do the work.

As you work with any of these exercises, modify it so it feels right for you. You can slow it down by taking three or nine breaths between each step. Or you can speed it up when needed. You might want to do it silently. Try it with your eyes open or closed, with or without gestures, with or without words, or speaking out load or subvocalizing internally. See what works for you. The important thing is to connect regularly with positive spiritual power, especially just before a Tarot Spirit journey.

Focus Areas in the Body

You are likely familiar with the chakras, an Eastern system of energy foci in the body. In the Western Celtic tradition, we have the three cauldrons as power centers in the body:

- The first cauldron of warming or incubation is located in the area of the pelvis, belly, womb, and loins. It governs physical health, physical movement, prosperity, and life force.
- The second cauldron of vocation, motion, or yearning is located in the area of the heart. It governs vocational truth, poetry, myth, and social connections. The cauldron is matured through the process of emotional growth experiences.
- The third cauldron of knowing, wisdom, or inspiration is located in the head and includes the third eye. It is associated with the "fire in the head." Advanced poetry, wisdom, divine connection, and prophecy are the rewards for its cultivation.

The three cauldrons are all supported by a fourth area, the feet, that connect us with earth. Working with the cauldrons and the earth connection, we can connect with the four elements, three Suns and the

Moon that is a reflection of the Sun. From bottom to top, these areas of the body have these associations:

1. The feet connect with the earth, the Sun in the center of the earth, and ordinary reality.
2. The belly connects with water, the Moon, and the astral plane.
3. The heart connects with fire, the Sun, and the mental plane.
4. The head connects with air, the stars, and the divine plane.

An additional area we consider is the solar plexus, located between the belly and heart. There we can focus energy or power that is mixed from above and below. At this point we are just introducing the Celtic cauldrons and the idea of a Western alternative to the Eastern chakras. We will do more with the cauldrons in a future book. Compared to chakras, these Western oriented body focus areas may be more suitable for Westerners as a way to connect earth and sky power to the body.

Power of the Universe

As we bring in power from the earth and sky and extend it out to the four directions, it is important to recognize that our body is a conduit that is just transferring power. We are not taking stored up personal power from our body and expending it to extend to the universe, like a battery delivering energy. We are bringing in the inexhaustible power of the universe and letting it flow through our body. In this process, we do not deplete our own power, but instead make that universal connection, and in the process we get filled with power, replenishing our body, mind, and emotional needs. When the process is done properly, the experience is of being filled up and not one of giving or depletion. There is a strong sense of connection to the universe as a whole.

Shamanic Crossing

In the shamanic crossing you raise earth power into your body and bring sky power down into your body to connect with it. The Shamanic Crossing is a concise approach that calls on earth and sky energies.

Work with this practice and integrate it into your own routine. You will want to read through the steps below. What do you say at each step? What are you thinking about? What are you visualizing? What's the intention of each step? You can work with the steps to get the flow of the practice. Once you have the flow, make modifications if needed to make it more personalized. You can call in the archangels, angels, helping spirits, or the deities of a pantheon you work with. You might do this practice just before you journey, do a magical working, or do a reading.

Let's walk through the steps of the shamanic crossing as follows:

1. This practice is best done standing on the balls of your feet. It can also be done sitting. Take a breath and relax. Let your jaw drop. Feel a wave of relaxation going down through your body.

2. Then you raise your right hand up and say: "as above." Then put your left palm facing down and say: "so below."

3. Now you move that left hand to connect with the earth fire of the star in the center of the molten earth. Really feel a ray of power come all the way from the center of the earth to just below your feet. As you raise the hand, guide the ray of earth power up through your body, up through your feet and through your loins. Your hand stops at your solar plexus, but that power keeps going up and through your heart and head and out the top. So, it comes up from the Earth's center and it connects earth power to your entire body.

4. Then with your right hand that's raised up, just move the hand a little bit and connect that hand to a ray of power from a spot directly above you, in the center of the universe. Draw star and sky power down to the crown of your head. As your hand moves down, this power comes in through the crown of your head, merging with the power from the earth, continuing to your heart, merging more, continuing past your solar plexus, where your hand stops on your belly. The sky power continues down to the loin area, merging there, and continues all the way to your feet.

5. So now you've got both earth and sky power connected. The power is focused on those four areas. You can optionally say: "The earth is in my feet. The Moon is in my loins. The Sun is in my heart. The stars are about my head."

6. You let this power come together, flowing in from outside your body, both above and below. It's inexhaustible power of the

universe, and you're letting it build into a ball of power in your solar plexus, as well as activating those four areas in your body.

7. When you feel that the ball in your solar plexus has built to the point where you're ready to expand it out, you say "as within, so without." Simultaneously, move both your arms out to the sides. Visualize the power coming in from the bottom and in from the top into your solar plexus, then going out to the four horizontal directions of the universe: in front of you, behind you, to your right, and to your left. So, you are in the center, like a transformer having this infinite power run through you and out connecting you to the ends of the world—to the ends of the universe.

8. Then you call on something related to the Tree of Life. Once you're connected to the ends of the directions, bring your hands back down to your sides. Say "between justice," bringing your right hand to your left shoulder. Say "and mercy," bringing your left hand to your right shoulder. Let the power continue to flow. Feel the opposites of mercy and justice balanced in your center at a place of harmony. Take a large breath.

9. Then drop your hands into an upside-down V shape. You say "I am that I am." Let the power continue to flow. Feel yourself at the balanced center of the universe channeling infinite power. Take a deep breath at this point.

10. Now recite three Awens. And as you do, your hands and body form an upside-down druidic ray shape. Your arms out to the sides represent the summer and winter solstice, while the center of your body represents the equinoxes. In reciting the Awens, resonate "ahh" with your left arm, "ooo" with your right arm, and then "enn" with the center of your body. Just repeat that three times. Acknowledge the seasonal cycles of the year as you do.

11. Finally, take a deep breath and completely relax and feel empowered. Open your eyes. Take a moment to observe how you are different from when you started the exercise. Now you can go about your day, go about whatever part of work you want. You may want to journal about any insights you had from the experience or notice how you changed as a result of the exercise.

So that's the basic shamanic crossing form. The crossing form is often associated with the Sun. You can do it once a day, four times a day, or just when you feel the need. The four times a day version in the Western Mystery tradition is as follows:

- Do it when you first get up in the morning facing East, greeting the Sun rising.
- Then do it around noon while facing south, acknowledging the Sun reaching the apex or high point in the sky.
- Then you can do it around Sunset, facing to the West, acknowledging the Sun setting and opening the way to night.
- The final daily practice is theoretically at midnight, but just before going to bed is fine. This is done facing to the North, acknowledging the Sun at the lowest point of its path, hidden by the earth. A connection or prayer to the ancestors is appropriate at this time.

You can follow the Sun's daily cycle with that action by repeating this four times a day. Now you probably don't want to do this every day of your life, but you might want to try it every day for a week and just notice if there's a shift. Is there more of a connection to the Sun and to the movement of the Sun throughout the day? And you don't necessarily need to see the Sun. Many of us live where it's cloudy. You can always just think about where the Sun is located as you're doing it, rather than facing the physical direction.

Symbolism in Shamanic Crossing

There are several symbolic or mystical elements in the Shamanic Crossing that can be briefly mentioned and are worthy of further journey work or meditation. These aspects are introduced here and there is much more literature on them in the book list. It is just helpful to know that they are incorporated into the practice and the long mystery tradition of these elements will form a connection with the body, even if they are not explicitly studied intellectually. You may want to first do the exercise naively, without reflection on these more intellectual concepts. Pay attention to changes in your body or messages you receive first. Then, over time, you can incorporate some of these traditional themes into the focus of your practice.

In the Western mystical tradition, there are similar crossing forms—like the Kabalistic Cross—that traditionally use Hebrew phrases to call on the directions or powers. The shamanic crossing incorporates those concepts but uses English words, as they are more meaningful to English speakers. If you work with other languages or systems, you can substitute such declarations to suit your language.

As discussed above, there are two major vectors of connection—vertical and horizontal. Bringing up earth power is quite grounding and important in making a solid connection to physical reality, the power of mother earth, and the lower world of non-ordinary reality. Bringing down sky power connects you with higher planes, the Tree of Life, divine realms, planets, stars, and the upper world of non-ordinary reality. The second vector of horizontal connection is to the four directions and makes a connection to the middle world of non-ordinary reality. The directions are also associated with the elemental powers, the cycle of the day and year, as well as power animals, plant spirits, spiritual teachers, and deities that you associate with each direction.

The duality of the microcosm and macrocosm is invoked with "as above, so below." This important mystery concept is reported in the Emerald Tablet.[55] While most people say the key phrase as quoted in the prior sentence, in most translations of the Emerald Tablet, the phrase is actually "as below, so above." There is a two-way street here, with not just influence from higher planes to our plane, but the reverse. Actions you take on our plane influence what is manifested on the higher planes. While the spoken phrase in the steps above goes from above to below, the actual gestures and bringing in of the power are reversed. You pull up from earth first, then bring down the sky power. So there is a recognition of the flow of power and manifestation in both directions. This area of the directions of manifestation power flow is worthy of deep journeys or meditation. Bringing this concept from duality into a triad invokes "the All" or

---

[55] The Emerald Tablet is attributed to Thoth or Hermes Trismegistus. More info: The Emerald Tablet of Hermes and the Kybalion. Edited by Jane Ma'ati Smith.
www.kybalion.org/TheKybalion.pdf en.wikipedia.org/wiki/Emerald_Tablet

unifying principle and allows personal identification not only with "below," but also "above" and "the All" that includes both.

Reports on Shamanic Crossing Experience

Reports from those who have done this pathwork are included below for texture. Again, honor the truth of your own experience, rather than comparing to others.

> *Tina:* This was both relaxing and energizing. Immediately on dropping my jaw, I could feel the energy move down me as though grounding with earth. Once the cross was completed, I was relaxed and refreshed. What a wonderful grounding, cleansing, protective, and filling ritual. I can certainly see how this is a great way to start a journey with the Tarot Spirits and others.

> *Billie:* Amazing how a few words and gestures can move so much energy.

> *Cara:* WOAH WOWZA a complete collapse of time and space. It was like I was transported through a wormhole and was in a wooden covering within a sacred circle. I was in a woolen cloak tied with a ribbon of green silk. I felt like I was in a coven with the Lady of the Lake and Merlin. I am not familiar with this "old religion," yet I felt I was associated with it in another life. A strange familiarity. Truth is in the goosebumps. It is my hope that the wisdom of my memory returns to the now.

Recommended Sacred Space Resources:

Brief video lessons on the Shamanic Crossing are available to readers of this book at www.reidhart.com/tsh-resources

Appendix E:
Find Your Special Tarot Spirits

Find your Personality and Soul Spirits

If you have your *My AstroTarot Report* (see Appendix G), it lists your special Tarot Spirits. The following instructions are for those who wish to do their own calculation. Copy the worksheet below or download the forms at www.reidhart.com/tsh-resources. Then review the samples and follow the instructions on the following pages.

Your birthdate:				
Month as a number 1 to 12				
Day				
Year				
Add all 3 vertically to get "A"		= Month + Day + Year		
Separate the result "A" into individual digits				
Add the individual digits to get "R"		*If R = 19 see instructions		
If "R" is more than 22 or =19*, add digits again, if not copy "R" as "P"		This is your **personality spirit** number (P)		
If "P" is double digits, add digits again, if not copy down "P" as "S"		This is your **soul spirit** number (S)		

Spirit Numbers	Number	Key Tarot Spirit Name
Personality Spirit (Number "P")		
Soul Spirit (Number "S")		
Hidden Factor Spirit(s) (Shadow Teacher)		
Year spirit for _____ ("Y")		

Find your Soul and Personality Tarot Spirits:[56]

1. Add together the month day and year of your birthday to get "A."
2. Take that 4-digit sum (A), split it into four individual single digits, then add the digits together to get the result "R." (e.g., If A is 1961, "R" = 1+9+6+1 = 17)
3. If the result (R) is more than 22 add individual digits together to get your personality spirit number "P." Check for these special cases if R is 19 or 22:

   - If the number (R) is 22 your personality spirit (P) is 4 (the Emperor) and your soul spirit (S) is 0 (The Fool) *[per Greer; per Arrien Personality=0, Soul=4]*
   - If the number (P) is 19, you work with 19 (the Sun), 1 (the Magician), and 10 (the Wheel) as a team to fill the roles of both personality and soul spirits.

4. If the number (P) is 9 or less, it is both your soul (S) and personality (P) spirit number.
5. If the number (P) is a double digit, but not 22 or 19 [see step 3], then:

   - "P" is your personality spirit number.
   - Add the digits in "P" together if more than 9 to get "S" and that is your soul spirit.

6. You can find your personality and soul spirits based on their assigned Major Arcana number in your favorite deck. Note them on your worksheet.

Deck Numbering Variation: If you are using the *Thoth Tarot* deck (or derivative) or another deck with a different numbering system for the Major Arcana, then use the card that matches the numbers generated in this numerological process. In the *Thoth Tarot* deck if you received 8 for one of the special cards then the Adjustment (Justice equivalent) Spirit

---

[56] Angeles Arrien developed the birth card concept in the 1980s and Mary Greer popularized it in her book *Tarot for Yourself*. Mary Greer expanded the concept to include the hidden factor cards and tarot constellations.

would fulfill that role rather than Strength; if you received 11, then the Lust (Strength equivalent) Spirit would fulfill that role rather than Justice. If your deck has no numbering system, then you might want to use the Waite-Smith numbering based on equivalent card meanings.

Review this example calculation:

To make sure you have the process down, do the sample calculation yourself on a blank worksheet. An excel file that reproduces the calculation is available for download at: www.reidhart.com/tsh-resources

Your birthdate:	March 4, 2010			
Month as a number 1 to 12	3			
Day	4			
Year	2010			
Add all 3 vertically to get "A"	2017	= 3 + 4 + 2010		
Separate the result "A" into individual digits	2	0	1	7
Add the individual digits to get "R"	10	= 2 + 0 + 1 + 7		
If "R" is more than 22 or =19*, add digits again, if not copy "R" as "P"	10	This is your **personality spirit** number (P)		
If "P" is double digits, add digits again, if not copy down "P" as "S"	1+0 = 1	This is your **soul spirit** number (S)		

For this example: the Personality spirit is **the Wheel of Fortune** (10) and the Soul spirit is **the Magician** (1). The birthdate differs from Sample 1 used elsewhere to show a case with unique personality, soul, and hidden factor Tarot Spirits.

Your Year Spirit

Each year, from your birthday to the next birthday (or the calendar year your birthday is in), you have a Tarot Spirit who can guide you for specifics in the year. You can choose to apply your year card from Jan 1st to the next "new years." Or you can follow a more traditional year, like the Celtic year from Samhain (Oct. 31) to the next Samhain. Others choose to apply the year card from one birthday to the next and the truly creative apply both a birthday to birthday card and a traditional year card so there is overlap.

This Tarot Spirit is discovered as follows: Use the same worksheet and instructions as you did for finding your personality and soul cards, except you use your current **birthday** instead of your birthdate. So, if your birthdate was March 5, 1953 and you are looking at the year after your birthday in 1991, you would enter March 5, 1991 in the same worksheet. (A different birthdate with the birthday in 1991 are used here to illustrate the full numerological process.)

Your Year Tarot Spirit would be the (P) personality spirit number from the worksheet. If you get 22, that is the Emperor (4), if more than 22, add the numbers together. If you get 19 that is the Sun. The Fool (0) or Magician (1) are never Year Spirits.

Example Year Spirit Calculation:

Your last birthday:		March 5, 1991			
Month	3				
Day	5				
Year	1991				
Add all 3 vertically to get "A"	1999	= 3 + 5 + 1991			
Separate the result "A" into individual digits	1	9	9	9	
Add the individual digits to get "R"	28	= 1 + 9 + 9 + 9			
If more than 22, add digits again to get "Y"	10	2+8= 10, Your **year** spirit (Y)			

Hidden Factor Tarot Spirits

The hidden-factor Tarot Spirit provides additional insight for you and can also teach you about your shadow aspects. If your personality Spirit is numbered 14 through 18, the personality spirit does double duty as the hidden-factor card, as there are actually no "hidden" related cards in those constellations of cards. The hidden-factor is related to a tarot constellation of cards that all share the same single digit root number numerologically. In most cases the hidden factor is not either the personality or soul card. Look for your personality spirit key number at the left in the first column of the table below. Then find the hidden-factor spirit(s) in the third and fourth columns.

To find your personal hidden-factor teaching Tarot Spirit, start with your personality Tarot Spirit in the table below. Then use the hidden-factor Tarot Spirit(s) listed at right. As noted above, some personality Spirits double as hidden-factor Spirits. Also, where the Personality and Soul Spirits are the same, there may be two hidden factor Spirits.

Table of Hidden Factor Spirits

Personality Key #	Personality Key Name	Hidden Factor Key #	Hidden Factor Key Name
1	The Magician	10 & 19**	The Magician & The Sun
2	The High Priestess	11 & 20**	Justice & Judgement
3	The Empress	12 & 21**	The Hanged Man & The World
4	The Emperor	13 & 22**	Death & The Fool
5	The Hierophant	14	Temperance
6	The Lovers	15	The Devil
7	The Chariot	16	The Tower
8***	Strength	17	The Star
9	The Hermit	18	The Moon
10	Wheel of Fortune	19	The Sun
11***	Justice	20	Judgement
12	The Hanged Man	21	The World
13	Death	(0)	The Fool
14	Temperance	14*	Temperance
15	The Devil	15*	The Devil
16	The Tower	16*	The Tower
17	The Star	17*	The Star
18	The Moon	18*	The Moon
19-10-1	Sun/Wheel/Magus	10	Wheel of Fortune
20	Judgement	11***	Justice
22, (0)	The Fool	13	Death
21	The World	12	The Hanged Man

* Where the personality Spirit is Key 14 to 18, that key also serves as the hidden-factor teacher.
** Where a pair of cards is the hidden-factor Spirit, they team teach or teach as a merged construct.
***For the *Thoth Tarot* deck and other decks with a different or no numbering system, see the earlier discussion on deck numbering variation.

Appendix F:
A Brief History of Astrology

A very brief history of Western astrology through the ages with a focus on horoscopic astrology is provided here as background information. This is followed by a deeper look at the innovations of Hellenistic astrology and the Hellenistic revival. Those with deeper interest in the famous astrologers and more detailed history will find *A History of Horoscopic Astrology* by James Holden a good source. Note that there are also astrological traditions in China, India, South America, and other cultures that are not covered here.

Astrology through the Ages

We trace human interaction with the stars from prehistoric times, through Babylon and Egypt to the development of Hellenistic astrology. Then we follow the thread through Persia into the renaissance and into modern times.

Prehistoric Astronomy and Astrology

There are cave paintings and etchings recording lunar cycles and star movements that are 40,000 years old.[57] In Mesopotamia, the Sumerians noted the movements of the planets and related omens starting around 6000 BCE and produced the first astrological written text, the *Enuma Anu Enlil*. The lunar cycle is engraved in stone at Newgrange in Ireland about 3200 BCE.[58] Around 2500 BCE, we have the construction of both Stonehenge in England and the great pyramids at Giza in Egypt, with their astronomical alignments.

---

[57] earthsky.org/human-world/prehistoric-cave-art-suggests-ancient-use-complex-astronomy/
[58] mythicalireland.com/blogs/ancient-sites/knowth-the-calendar-stone

Babylon and Egypt

From 2400 to 331 BCE, the Babylonians (aka, Chaldeans) invent the first well recorded astrological system. While the focus was more on mundane (societal) astrology, they developed the zodiac wheel and tables of planetary positions by date. The Babylonians believed that the movement of the planets provided omens or messages from the gods and goddesses about the path of human events. The Egyptians focused on the rising times of fixed stars for time keeping at night and developed the Decans or Faces aligned with each 10 degrees of the zodiac wheel. Their calendar was the first with 365 days, and the rising stars became the basis of the Ascendant and eventually the houses.

Hellenistic Astrology

While discussed in more detail later, the rise of Hellenistic astrology can be traced to the founding of Alexandria in 331 BCE and included many innovations, including the importance of the ascendant or rising sign, houses or places, planets with an enhanced Greek mythic meaning as well as sects (day or night birth) and polarity, rulerships, lots, and a reimagining of the Decan subdivisions of signs.[59] The introduction of the tropical zodiac by Ptolemy was also important, aligning the zodiac with the seasons rather than drifting with the Earth axis precession like the fixed or sidereal zodiac.

Saved by the Persians and Arabs

With the fall of the Roman empire around 400 CE and the rise of Christianity, astrology fell by the wayside in the West. Fortunately, Persian and Arab scholars translated many of the Greek astrological texts and expanded the astrological tradition, improving the mathematical precision of planetary position prediction. There were also influences from Hindu (Vedic) astrology into the Arabic writings.

Transition to Renaissance Astrology

After the dark ages in the West, astrology came back to life in the 12th century when the Arabic texts were translated into Latin. With the invention of the printing press in the mid-15th century, astrological texts

---

[59] George, *AATP1*, p 13

and ephemerides were more available and there was a surge of interest in astrology. In the later part of the 16th century, there was a decline of astrology on the European continent due to Catholic suppression. In England there was a later rise in astrology spearheaded by William Lilly's works that reconciled Christianity and astrology.

Modern Astrology

As astrology evolved in the 18th through 20th centuries, there was greater focus on the individual and their natal chart. Psychology was paired with astrology for a deeper personal interpretation. Carl Jung added credence to the use of astrology for personal development. Three new planets were added to the repertoire. The impact of asteroids and hypothetical points in the sky were added to astrological interpretation. The astrological column in the daily paper with Sun sign predictions became ubiquitous. Computerized chart calculations and the internet made astrology much more generally accessible. The computerized calculations allowed for more complex approaches like harmonic horoscopes. Evolutionary astrology emphasized the soul's evolution through reincarnation.

The Hellenistic Astrology Revival

There has been a traditional astrological tradition carried forward in parallel with the modern astrological evolution. Much of Hellenistic astrological theory was captured in the Arabic texts and translated into Latin, forming the basis of medieval and modern astrology.

In the last three decades there has been a Hellenistic revival, bringing into modern translation Greek texts that had been inaccessible to the general public for two millennia. The original Greek astrological texts became more widely available starting in the early 1990s when Project Hindsight[60] retrieved and translated astrological texts for use in modern times. This resulted in an infusion of lost methods into astrological practice in the early 21st century that continues today.

---

[60] www.astro.com/astrowiki/en/Project_Hindsight

Alexandria: Crossroad of Civilizations

Hellenistic astrology was born in Alexandria, a crossroad of civilizations. Babylonian, Egyptian, and Greek influences of astrology and philosophy combined to create something new. Hellenistic astrology brought into play many innovations that transformed astrology for future generations.

Alexander the Great founded Alexandria near the delta of the Nile in Egypt sometime shortly after 332 BCE. Under the Ptolemaic dynasty, Greek culture flourished. Alexandria came to be regarded as a scholastic center, with the library at Alexandria likely built in the 2nd century BCE under Ptolemy II.[61] Three branches of astrological and sky knowledge merged here to form the basis of Hellenistic astrology, which was influenced by astrological traditions from the Babylonians, the Egyptians, and the Greeks.

Babylonian influence. Dating back to the 16th century BCE, [62] Babylonian omen astrology focused on questions of state or mundane astrology, rather than personal questions answered by natal astrology. The Babylonians brought us the constellations—based on third millennium Sumerian roots. At first irregular, the signs of the zodiac were made uniform in the 4th century BCE with 30-degree scopes in a 360-degree circle.[63] This allowed standardized calculation methods to be adopted, moving from a theory that celestial events occurred at the whim of the gods to recognition that there was order and predictability in celestial events. Sometime between the 7th and 4th century BCE, the idea of natal astrology was developed, obviously reserved for the nobility or wealthy; however, there was no use of the ascendant, angles, or houses. The use of cuneiform and clay tablets means that we have horoscopes and ephemeris tables preserved from the 3rd century and possibly the 5th century BCE. The Babylonian priest Berosus established a school of astrology and astronomy on the Mediterranean island of Kos around 280 BCE, likely forming a bridge to interested Greek scholars and astrologers.

---

[61] Wikipedia. en.wikipedia.org/wiki/Library_of_Alexandria
[62] Holden, *HHA*, p 8
[63] Holden, *HHA*, p 3

Egyptian influence. There is open debate [64] whether the early Egyptians had much astronomy and astrology of their own[62] or were originators of astrology. [65] It is clear that they focused on seasonal astronomical events and marked the annual flooding of the Nile by the heliacal rising of Sirius in mid-August. As early as 2400 BCE the Egyptians had identified 36 fixed stars or star groups, later called Decans, located south of the ecliptic that rose about every 10 days.[66] These were used to tell time at night and as a map for the dead on the journey to the Otherworld. The Egyptian system associated each Decan with a fixed star or star group and associated Deity(s), so they were not evenly spaced in time or in the zodiac. When incorporated by the Greeks, the several Egyptian systems of Decans were regularized to 10 degrees with three in each sign and were assigned ruling planets following a Chaldean order. While the Decan rulerships were considered the least important ruler as Hellenistic astrology developed, they did retain importance in medieval astrological talismanic magic under Agrippa.[67] The Decans each carried luck attributes, and by the Ptolemaic age the rising Decan at the time of birth was thought to foretell the character of the native, whether lucky or unlucky.[62] This focus on the time of birth was a shift from the Babylonian horoscope—that was concerned only with the birth day—and developed into the Hellenistic idea of the hour marker or ascendant (*horoskopos* in Greek).

Greek Origins. The Greek world view formed the bedrock for Hellenistic astrological ideas. As Nicholas Campion recounts the ancient astrological history of the 6th century BCE, we learn that Pythagoras, an ancient source for astrology, traveled to Egypt and is rumored to study with the Druids. He also notes that Plato expressed the importance for humans to be in tune with the celestial harmonies.[68]

So, prior to the development of Hellenistic astrology in Alexandria, the Greeks laid a groundwork of mythology, philosophy and science in the 6th to 4th centuries. This brought together the physical and spiritual world.

---

[64] Brennan. *HA*, pp 24-27
[65] Zor. *Stories of Ancient Astrology.*
[66] George. *AATP1*, p 221
[67] Dykes. *The Decans in Astrology.*
[68] Campion. *HWA1*, pp 143-145

The Stoic philosophy developed at the beginning of the 3rd century BCE leans toward determinism, creating tension with a more negotiable view of the future. However, for astrology to have a purpose, there needs to be some reliance on the Platonic idea of a negotiable future.[69]

Celtic Influence. More speculative is the idea of a Celtic influence on the development of Hellenistic Astrology. Earlier we discussed travel by Pythagoras into Celtic areas. Peter Ellis cites the Greek Hippolytus (AD 170-236) reference to the Celts astrological divinations. He further discusses the debate by Greek scholars in the 2nd Century BCE about Greek astrology being influenced by the Celts through Pythagoras.[70]

The Dawn of Hellenistic Astrology

The primary works of Hellenistic astrology are said to have been published around the 1st century BCE and are attributed to Hermes Trismegistus, Asclepius, Nechepso and Petosiris. Unfortunately, intact original texts from these prime sources did not survive, and there exist only paraphrased fragments where the actual authorship may be in question. We rely on quotations and summaries of these early texts captured two to seven centuries later, primarily by authors writing in the Roman empire.[71] Some of the texts took a journey through Sanskrit and Arabic translation before they were rendered into Latin much later. The original and secondary Greek texts lay mostly dormant until a large translation effort in the late 20th century spurred a Hellenistic astrology revival.

Whether invented by an individual, a close group, or viewed more as a collection of individual techniques developed over time, it is clear that in the 1st century CE, prior astrological practice was synthesized into something new. Two examples are (1) the *Thema Mundi* that brings together concepts of sign rulership, sect, planetary polarity, and aspect and (2) the establishment of the places or houses as an important interpretive device. Both innovations represent a significant shift from prior Babylonian and Egyptian astrological practice.[72] The development of

---

[69] Campion. *HWA1*, p 211
[70] Ellis, P. "Early Irish Astrology."
[71] Brennan. Timeline: www.hellenisticastrology.com/articles/timeline-of-ancient-astrologers/
[72] Brennan. *HA*, p 32

Hellenistic astrology carries forward from the 2nd century BCE into the 7th century CE, as the Romans come into power and spread the use of this astrological method.

Innovations of Hellenistic Astrology

With cultural, astrological, and philosophical backgrounds from the Babylonians, Egyptians, and Greeks, the mixing pot of Alexandria created a new astrology with several innovations. These included the importance of an ascendant, houses or places, planets with an enhanced Greek mythic meaning as well as sects (day or night association) and polarity, rulerships, lots, and a reimagining of the Decan subdivisions of signs. [73] The introduction of the tropical rather than fixed or sidereal zodiac was also important. The individual innovations that distinguish Hellenistic astrology from earlier influences are individually discussed.

The places or houses and the ascendant. A unique innovation of Hellenistic astrology is the idea of "places"—referred to as "houses" in later astrological traditions—that form a second diurnal rotation reference overlaid on the annual planetary travels through the signs. Aligning the map of the zodiac to the eastern horizon at the time of birth using the ascendant, drawn from the Egyptian Decans, creates a time-specific orientation of the horoscope with the ascendant or rising sign as the starting place on the left, and the places, aligned with the signs, counting around counter-clockwise. Each of the 12 places was matched in each horoscope with each sign, and each place (*topoi*) had particular topics. In the Hellenistic system, these topics are distinct from the sign meanings, unlike in modern astrological teaching where house meanings have been confounded with sign meanings. Aligning the sign boundaries with the place boundaries results in a stronger interpretative meaning, clarifies planetary aspect relationships, and maintains a stronger interpretative relationship between the signs, ruling planets, and the places or houses.

Planetary sect, polarity. Another innovation without precedent is the assignment of planets to sects—also known as day and night teams.[74] Further, based on Platonic and Aristotelian concepts, planets and signs were assigned polarity, in the sense of directing and receiving, force and

---

[73] George. *AATP1*, p 13
[74] Holden. *HHA*, p 13

form, or yang and yin. Polarity and sect alignments strengthen planetary power, beneficence, and relationships; while contrary situations weaken conditions and lead toward malefic influences.

Planetary qualities. As with earlier ancient astrological approaches, the planets or wandering stars under consideration were all visible to the naked eye. While the Greeks did do their best to align the nature of the gods and goddesses chosen to represent the planets to the prior character of the Babylonian deities, there are subtle differences in the Greek and Roman mythologies behind each character. For example, Ares (Mars) is given the role of war rather than Ninurta (Saturn). The planetary meanings from Valens do align more with the Greek pantheon than the Babylonian pantheon.[75] The Orphic hymns capture the Greek view of the planetary powers in the same timeframe as the development of Hellenistic astrology. The Greeks also brought into play Aristotle's principles of hot, cold, wet, and dry as they related to the elements and planets, as seen in Ptolemy's *Tetrabiblos*.[76] The basic classification of planets as benefic or malefic seems to be taken for granted as Valens often refers to them as malefics or benefics in his *Anthology*, but never really defines the terms except by context. Ptolemy does take on the definition of malefic and benefic planets, using Aristotelian qualities to argue a scientific basis for the assignment.[77]

Sign rulerships. Equal in importance to the places or topics is the innovation of sign rulerships by planets in the Hellenistic tradition.[78] This concept was born fresh in the Alexandrian crucible, not drawn from the Babylonians or Egyptians.[79] The concept of rulerships stems almost directly from the *Thema Mundi*, or birth chart of the cosmos, and was alternatively attributed to Nechepso and Petosiris or Hermes and Asclepius, placing it clearly in the realm of Hellenistic innovation.[80] The Hellenistic astrologers were the first to apply this social construct of hosting and lordly support to the planets and signs in the astrological chart.

---

[75] George. *AATP1*, pp 51-52

[76] Brennan. *HA*, p 102

[77] George. *AATP1*, p 56

[78] One might speculate that the Greek nobility household structure contributed to the idea of hosting and guests as seen in the domicile rulership relationship; however, further review of Babylonian and Egyptian social structures showed similar noble household arrangements to the Greeks.

[79] Holden. *HHA*, p 13

[80] Brennan. *HA*, p 75

Configuration and aspects. Another Hellenistic innovation from the *Thema Mundi* is the idea of configuration or aspects.[79] With a grounding in the Platonic solids, Pythagorean geometry, and Greek optical theories, friendly and hostile aspects between planets and signs are introduced.[81] Aspects and witnessing, along with the planetary qualities and rulerships form the basis of mutual support or denial between the players in a chart and are strong contributors to the concept of planetary condition and its impact on chart interpretation.

Zodiac sign elemental meaning. The original Babylonian and Egyptian association of the triplicities with the winds and four directions was replaced later in the Hellenistic period by an elemental designation sourced from Aristotelian thought and advocated by Valens.[82]

The tropical zodiac. Based on the Greek astronomer Hipparchus' discovery in the 2nd century BCE, Ptolemy advocated four centuries later the use of a Tropical zodiac that aligned the signs with the seasons permanently, reinforcing the quadruplicity meanings.[83] The alternative is using the sidereal zodiac so that the planets are in the actual zodiac signs viewed in real time. When using the tropical zodiac, the original alignment of the signs with the seasons is maintained. As you might imagine, being born in a particular season is more likely to impact personality and the native's life than the actual zodiac constellation a planet is in.

Lots of lots and other innovations. Multiple Lots are secondary points on the chart relative to the ascendant based on the relation of other objects on the chart. Lots were active early in Hellenistic astrology, even though they are now known by the name "Arabic parts" due to the path of the literature from Greek to Arabic translations.[84] Lunar considerations and many timing and profection techniques that are beyond the scope of this book are also contributions from Hellenistic astrology.

Love's Labor Lost

Some Hellenistic innovations have eroded through adoption into medieval and modern astrology. While large contributions such as the

---

[81] Brennan. *HA*, pp 289-317; George, *AATP1*, pp 396-446
[82] George. *AATP1*, pp 161-164; Brennan, *HA*, pp 260-266
[83] George. *AATP1*, pp 122-126 & 154-158; Brennan, *HA*, pp 216-222
[84] Brennan. *HA*, pp 511-534; George. *AATP1*, pp 362-446

importance of the ascendant, houses, configuration or aspects, planet meaning, and rulerships have carried forward, their emphasis has shifted, and some Hellenistic contributions have been abandoned. The shifts can be summarized as follows:

- While the ascendant is an important part of medieval and modern astrology, it has moved to a secondary or tertiary level in chart interpretation, where it was foremost in the Hellenistic eye.
- Houses continue to be used, but their meaning has shifted somewhat. In the modern "12 letter alphabet" teaching house meanings have become conjoined to sign meanings, while in the original Hellenistic implementation they were distinct and provided a clearer structure to the chart meaning. In addition, starting with Porphyry—who developed a system aligned with the chart angles—the houses moved from a whole sign alignment in Hellenistic astrology to more advanced mathematical models that may fit the geographic birthplace location more exactly, but provide less clear house, meaning, and aspect alignment.
- Sign rulership is an important contribution of Hellenistic astrology that continues to this day; however, the symmetry of *Thema Mundi* rulership story has been compromised by stealing sign rulerships for assignment to the newly discovered planets Uranus, Neptune, and Pluto. Modern astrology also focuses on the domicile rulerships, generally ignoring the triplicity lords, bound lords, and Decan lords.
- In planetary meaning and condition, sect is given little weight in modern astrology, and the strong identification of the malefic and benefic impact of planets is lessened in favor of more positive or transformative attributions. Except for retrograde conditions, speed and solar phase are no longer considered. In modern astrology, the planets are on equal footing except for rulership relationships and selection of final dispositors. Furthermore, there are ten planets considered, rather than the visible seven tied strongly to the Greek and Babylonian myths.
- Planetary aspects changed after the Hellenistic era, with a shift from sign aspects to degree aspects and orbs. While degrees are

considered in some of the later Hellenistic developments such as maltreatment and bonification, the primary aspect is by sign with only the major aspects being considered.

Hellenistic Astrology Summary

The fertile Nile delta around Alexandria provided a rich environment for the combination of Babylonian, Egyptian, and Greek philosophy, astrology, and mythology to bring forth a new Hellenistic form of astrology. Many innovations from Hellenistic astrology have carried forward into medieval and modern astrology; however, there is a richness of unique recovered techniques being discovered now in a new Hellenistic astrology revival.

Planetary Association with Deities

In ancient times, the planets were connected to various deities in a pantheon of the local culture. These associations tended to be carried forward from one culture to the next, substituting the earlier culture's assignment with a Deity that has a similar function in the adopting culture. Some associations had to do with the appearance of these wandering stars. Venus was bright and associated with beauty. Mars was red and associated with war. Jupiter was moderately bright and more constant, bringing association with the prime ruler of the heavens. Saturn was dim, therefore associated with coldness and distance from the Sun.

For those working with a cultural pantheon in a ritual way, you can associate the gods and goddesses along with their qualities and myths with the planets in your ritual work. For those just interested in ancient mythology, you can bring the myths of the associated deities into your understanding of the meaning of a planet.

The following table shows Deity associations to the seven ancient planets from several cultures. Of course, you may have deeper knowledge of different cultural deities with different planetary associations. The outer planets—Uranus, Neptune, and Pluto—are not included in this table, as they do not have a strong ancient elemental or deity correspondence, even though they are named for Roman or Greek gods. These names, assigned recently on discovery of these planets, do not have the historical and mythical background of the visible seven planets going back to ancient history including Sumerian, Babylonian, and Egyptian times.

Ancient Planet Deity and Elemental Associations

Planet Astrology Symbol	Planet[a]	Associated God or Goddess				Aristotelian elemental qualities
		Roman *Greek*	Babylonian *Sumerian* [b]	Egyptian [c] *Vedic* [b]	Celtic [d] *Nordic*	
☉	Sun	Sol *Helios*	Shamash *Utu*	Atum, Aten-Ra *Surya*	Belinos, Sulis *Sol*	hot/dry (moderate)
☽	Moon	Luna *Selene*	Sin *Nanna*	Khonsu, Aah, Iah *Chandra*	Belisama, Medb *Mani*	cold/moist (moderate)
☿	Mercury	Mercurius *Hermes*	Nabu *Enki*	Thoth, Seth, Sobek *Budah*	Lugh, Llew, *Odin, Wooden*	varies
♀	Venus	Venus *Aphrodite*	Ishtar *Inanna*	Horus, Isis, Hathor *Shukra*	Uosis, Triple Goddess *Freya*	cold/moist (extreme)
♂	Mars	Martus *Ares*	Nergal *Gugulanna*	Horus-red *Mangala/Kuma*	Ogmios, Ogma, Nodens, Neton *Tyr, Tiw*	hot/dry (extreme)
♃	Jupiter	Jove *Zeus*	Marduk *Enlil*	Amun *Brihaspati*	Taranis, Dagda *Thor*	hot/moist
♄	Saturn	Saturnus *Kronos*	Ninurta *Ninurta*	Horus-bull *Sani*	Samonios. Samhain *Njord, Loki*	cold/dry

[a] Names of planets in multiple languages can be found at en.wiktionary.org/wiki/Appendix:Planets

[b] Babylonian, Sumerian, Egyptian, and Vedic Deity assignments (with variations in spellings) are from www.weasner.com/etx/fun/2008/little/Names_of_the_Planets.htm

[c] Egyptian planets' deity names are based on more modern pantheon use rather than the names used over the many years of Egyptian history, found at: doi.org/10.1093/acrefore/9780190647926.013.61

[d] Celtic Deity assignments are taken primarily from an interpretation of the Gundestrup Cauldrons outer planetary panels[85] There is variation in *Deity* names with seven Celtic languages in play and several other alternative deities could be suggested, some shown in parentheses. Nordic names are based on the Norse/Germanic gods associated with the days of the week in the English language reflected back to Roman weekday planetary attributions. The Nordic god for Saturday is less clear.

---

[85] Boutet, Michel-Gérald. 2017. "On Ancient Celtic Astrology and Naked Eye Astronomy – The Gundestrup Cauldron"

Appendix G:
Your Basic
My AstroTarot Report

You will need *AstroTarot mapping* of your chart to work with the Tarot Spirits. Appendix H contains complete instructions for getting your natal chart and mapping the planets and signs of your natal chart to Tarot Spirits. An alternative approach is to have this mapping done for you. You can obtain a customized *My AstroTarot Report* at the following website:

www.reidhart.com/tsh-resources

As a purchaser of this book, you will receive a discount.

A sample *My AstroTarot Report* is included on the following pages. The report you receive is customized to your birth data, and includes the following sections:

Section	Contents:	Reference Exercises	Pathwork
Cover	Big 3: Sun, Moon, ascendant	Your Astro Keys	
1	Personality, Soul, Hidden Factor & Year Tarot Spirits	Your special cards	H, I, J1
2	Planet & sign mapping	Find your Tarot guide	
2	House locations; astro symbols	Ex. A/B/C each TS	A/B/C
3	Natal (birth) chart	Birth chart; Mapping	
4	Potentially challenging natal planetary aspects	Clear natal conflicts	K
5	Opposing signs (potentially challenging aspects)	Clear Sign Conflicts	K
6	Basic Tarot Spirit circles	Circle of hands	I (H2, J2, L)
7	Circle of hands; potentially challenging aspect groups	Circle of hands	I (H2, J2)
8	Circle of hands; positive groups	Circle of hands	I (H2, J2)
9	Other Tarot Spirit pair aspects	More clearing	K

My AstroTarot Report
Working with the Tarot Spirits

Prepared for:

Sample 1

AstroTarot Spirit Mapping

Optimize your Birth Chart by working with the Tarot Spirits

	Astro symbols:		*Planets and Signs are represented by these Tarot Spirits:*			

Sun in Pisces ☉ ♓

	The Sun	The Moon	19	18

The Sun represents your inner conscious purpose and core sense of identity. Pisces is a water sign that is flexible through mutability and has a receptive character. Your Sun in Pisces indicates a capability to bring forth imaginative gifts or dedication to serving others.

Sect: *Night*

Moon in Scorpio ☽ ♏

	High Priestess	Death	2	13

The Moon represents your emotional and physical needs, along with your feelings and daily habits. Scorpio is a water sign that holds a fixed course and has a receptive character. Your Moon in Scorpio indicates deep and strong emotions and may lead to holding either strong fixed attractions or resentments. Physical action helps temper feelings.

Natal Moon Phase: Disseminating Moon

Sagittarius Rising ✗

Temperance 14

Ascendant ruler: Jupiter ♃

Wheel of Fortune 10

Your ascendant is the sign rising at the time of your birth and represents how you show up in the world-- what you want to be known for. Sagittarius is a fire sign that is flexible through mutability and has an assertive character. Your Sagittarius Ascendant indicates a willingness to enthusiastically put yourself out there, exploring multiple options. Jupiter in Taurus rules your Ascendant, giving importance to how you create opportunities for growth and expansion.

The ascendant accuracy is only as good as the birth time accuracy.

Tarot key numbers and names based on Waite / Smith deck. Other decks may differ.

Welcome to your special personalized report to use in working with the Tarot Spirits.
This report is intended to be used with pathwork or exercise instructions provided in a related course, in separate AstroTarot instructions, or in one of the AstroTarot books.

The report is fairly comprehensive, and includes pairings and circles of Tarot Spirits that not everyone needs to work with, so it is important to prioritize your work and take your time. Section 4, high energy relationships, is the primary focus for most benefit.

Enjoy your work with the Tarot Spirits!   *-Reid Hart*

Shamanic work with the Tarot spirits provides an opportunity to enhance your life.

This mapping shows which Tarot Spirit from the major arcana maps to which planets and signs in your natal astrology or birth chart. Special groups and unique sets of Tarot Spirits to work with based on aspects and configurations in your chart are also included.
Start by engaging with each Tarot Spirit individually through pathworks A/B/C.
Then clear limitations in your life by resolving potential conflicts in your natal or birth chart using Pathwork K.
There are also many groups of Tarot Spirits you can work with using the circle of hands and group techniques:
Pathwork H/I/J. The groups can be used for both clearing obstacles and enhancing projects and destiny in your life.
Deeper work with specific groups uses the construct pathwork (L).
The contents of your personalized Tarot Spirit mapping follows by section n order.
The number of pages may vary for individuals based on their unique natal chart.

Index of Sections in Your Tarot Spirit Report

The following exercises are explained in the chapters and appendices of the book(s) listed below:

Tarot Spirit Healing   (Book 1)   A Shamanic Path to Clear Astrological Challenges

Contents:	Section	Reference Exercises	Find Pathwork Here	Pathwork
Sun, Moon, Ascendant	Cover	Your Astro Keys	Chapters 11 & 12	
Personality, Soul, Hidden, Year TS	1	Your special cards	Chapter 7, 8 & 3, 5, 6	A/B/C, N
Planet & Sign Mapping	2	Find your tarot guide	Chapters 4, 11 ,12	
Planet, Sign, Houses; Astro symbols	2	Scan/Meet/Know each Tarot Spirit	Chapters 3, 5, 6, 11	A/B/C
Natal (Birth) Chart	3	Birth chart; Mapping	Ch. 11-12; Apx. F & H	
Potential Challenging Aspects	4	Clear planet conflicts	Chapter 13	K
Opposing Signs (Challenging)	5	Clear sign conflicts	Chapter 13	K
Basic Tarot Spirit Circles	6	Circle of hands	Chapter 14 & 15	I (H2, J2, L)
Circle of Hands; Challenging Groups	7	Circle of hands	Chapter 14	I (H2, J2)
Circle of Hands; Positive Groups	8	Circle of hands	Chapter 14	I (H2, J2)
Other Tarot Spirit Pair Aspects	9	More planet clearing	Chapter 13	K

Sample 3

Mar 4, 2010 9:54 PM

Your Special Cards

New York, New York

Your AstroTarot Spirits   1

‹‹== Birthdate & Time & Location: printed on 18-Sep-2024

Personality, Soul, Hidden Factor, and Year Tarot Cards

Developed by Angeles Arien and popularized by Mary Greer in the early 1980's, these special cards are based on a numerological reduction of your birthdate. They are not astrological.

The **Personality** Card indicates what lessons are here for you in this life.

The **Soul** Card shows your purpose through all lifetimes.

The **Hidden Factor** Card(s) is a teacher related to personal shadow work.

Working with these cards as Tarot Spirits can be enlightening.

You can meet them individually using the A/B/C journeys, and include them in your Tarot Spirit

Your Birthday

Month	3
Day	4
Year	2010
M + D + Y Total	2017
2 + 0 + 1 + 7 =	10
1 + 0 =	1
1 + 0 =	1

Personality

Soul

Hidden Factor

10	*Personality Card*	**Wheel of Fortune**
1	*Soul Card*	**Magician**
19	*Hidden Factor T.S.*	**The Sun**

Your Year Card

Based on your birthday this year

Your personal **Year** Card represents the tests, lessons and experiences for the year in question. It is best to journey to the Tarot Spirit for that card and ask them what to watch for in the year ahead; or ask what the meaning of events in the current or past year has been.

Month	3
Day	4
Year	2025
Total	2032
2 + 0 + 3 + 2 =	7
7 + 0 =	7
7 + 0 =	7

You can choose to apply your year card from Jan 1st to the next "new years." Or you can follow a more traditional year, like the Celtic year from Samhain (Oct. 31) to the next Samhain.

Others apply the year card from one birthday to the next. And the truly creative apply both a birthday to birthday card and a traditional year card so there is overlap.

2025 Year Card

2025	7	*Year Card*	**Chariot**
2026	8	*Year Card*	**Strength**
2027	9	*Year Card*	**Hermit**
2028	10	*Year Card*	**Wheel of Fortune**
2029	11	*Year Card*	**Justice**
2030	12	*Year Card*	**Hanged man**
2031	13	*Year Card*	**Death**
2032	14	*Year Card*	**Temperance**
2033	6	*Year Card*	**Lovers**
2034	7	*Year Card*	**Chariot**

Note: For Illustrative purposes, the special cards page is based on a different birthdate than the other samples here. This allows unique Personality, Soul, and Hidden Factor cards.

Sample 1
Mar 5, 1953 2:28 AM
Washington, D.C.

Planet & Sign Mapping

Your AstroTarot Spirits **2**
<<=*= Birthdate & Time & Location; printed on 06-Jun-2024*

Note: "AS" = Ascendant; see tables below for symbol definitions.

The Planets in your Natal Chart:		Sign	Planet Tarot	Zodiac Sign Tarot	Whole Sign House	Quadrant Koch House
AS ruler; Sagittarius rising (AS)	♃	♐	Wheel of Fortune	Temperance	1	1
AS is the ascendant or rising sign. The planet associated is the ruler of the ascendant zodiac sign.						
Sun in Pisces	☉	♓	The Sun	The Moon	4	3
Moon in Scorpio	☽	♏	High Priestess	Death	12	10
Mercury in Aries	☿	♈	Magician	Emperor	5	3
Venus in Aries	♀	♈	Empress	Emperor	5	4
Mars in Aries	♂	♈	Tower	Emperor	5	3
Jupiter in Taurus	♃	♉	Wheel of Fortune	Hierophant	6	5
Saturn in Libra	♄	♎	World	Justice	11	10
Uranus in Cancer	♅	♋	Fool	Chariot	8	7
Neptune in Libra	♆	♎	Hanged man	Justice	11	10
Pluto in Leo	♇	♌	Judgement	Strength	9	8

For interpretations of the above planet sign combinations, you can go to the
"astroclick portrait" under "free horoscopes" at www.astro.com

The Alphabet of Astrology; symbols of the planets and zodiacal signs:

Planet Symbols		Zodiac Signs	
☉	Sun	♈	Aries
☽	Moon	♉	Taurus
☿	Mercury	♊	Gemini
♀	Venus	♋	Cancer
♂	Mars	♌	Leo
♃	Jupiter	♍	Virgo
♄	Saturn	♎	Libra
♅	Uranus	♏	Scorpio
♆	Neptune	♐	Sagittarius
♇	Pluto	♑	Capricorn
☊	North Node	♒	Aquarius
As	Ascendant	♓	Pisces
Mc	Midheaven		

Tarot Spirit Pathwork
Now that you know the important Tarot Spirits in your Astrological Chart, you can meet them using the A/B/C journeys.
Your first step is to meet your Tarot guide.
Then, one by one do the A/B/C journeys for each Tarot Spirit.
You might prioritize the Tarot Spirits that show up on the High Energy Relationships in Section 4 of this report.
Instructions on the above are included here:
Astro Tarot Essentials course: (ATE): 1.2, 1.3, 1.4
Tarot Spirits Healing course: (TS1): 1.2, 2.1, 3.1
Tarot Spirits Healing book: (TSH) Chapters 3 to 6

Key to working with pairs or groups of Tarot Spirits (sample data)

Work with some Tarot Spirits in Pairs (when the arrow connects Tarot Spirit names):

				Know
opposition; sign and degree	♀	♄	Empress <= => World	

Work with some Tarot Spirits in Groups (when all are in the same shaded area):

Reflective Circle   For questions of inner truth & Emotions

				Know
Moon & Moon sign	☽	♏	High Priestess	Death	
Soul Card	8		Strength	Self, Shadow, Guide	

In "know" column at right, check off you have done A/B/C pathork with each Tarot Spirit

Your Natal (Birth) Circle Chart:

3

The circle astrological chart has these elements:

1. The circle is oriented as a map of the cosmos at the time you were born:
   a. Left side of the circle (near 9 o'clock at AS) is the east
   b. Top of the circle is the high point of the Sun near noon to the south
   c. The right side of the circle (near 3 o'clock opposite AS) is to the west
   d. The bottom of the circle below the AS line that extends through the center is below the horizon and not visible, the unseen part of the zodiac
2. The signs of the zodiac are shown in the outer ring - see their symbols in Section 2
3. The planets are shown with the degree of their sign - see their symbols in Section 2
4. The whole sign house numbers are the inner ring
5. The major aspects between planets are in the center, red lines are "hard" or challenging aspects and green lines are "easy" or supportive aspects

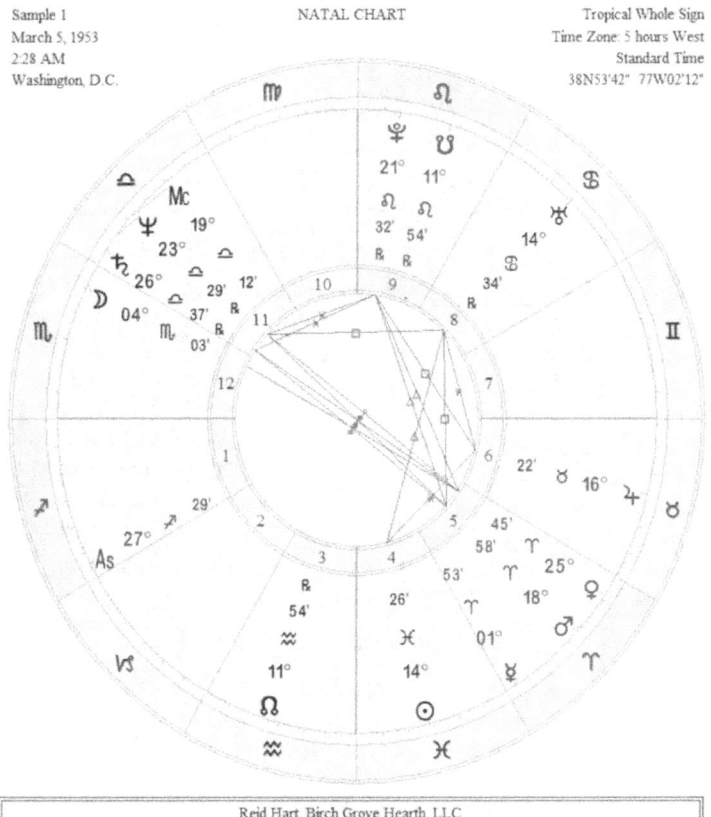

Sample 1
March 5, 1953
2:28 AM
Washington, D.C.

NATAL CHART

Tropical Whole Sign
Time Zone: 5 hours West
Standard Time
38N53'42" 77W02'12"

Reid Hart, Birch Grove Hearth, LLC
POB 21416, Eugene OR 97402 Phone: 541-686-1610 www.reidhart.com

Note: Aspect lines are for degree-based aspects. Sign-only-based aspects are listed on next page.

Sample 1 — *Potential Challenging Aspects* — **Your AstroTarot Spirits** 4

Mar 5, 1953 2:28 AM — Washington, D.C. — *<<== Birthdate & Time & Location; printed on 06-Jun-2024*

Potential Challenging Aspects

Work these challenging aspects in pairs to identify and resolve conflicts. Prioritize traditional planets with aspects by both sign and degree. After exercise "A/B/C" with each separatly, do pathwork "K" with the pair.

Planetary Oppositions and Squares

				Reconcile Date
opposition; sign and degree	♀	♄	Empress <= => World	
opposition; sign and degree	♂	♄	Tower <= => World	
challenging conjunction	☿	♂	Magician <= => Tower	
challenging conjunction	♀	♂	Empress <= => Tower	
opposition by sign	☽	♃	High Priestess <= => Wheel of Fortune	
opposition by sign	☿	♄	Magician <= => World	
opposition by degree	☽	♀	High Priestess <= => Empress	

Classic Planets above (Priority 1 & personal) / Outer Planets Below (Priority 2/generational)

opposition; sign and degree	♀	♆	Empress <= => Hanged man	
opposition; sign and degree	♂	♆	Tower <= => Hanged man	
square by sign and degree	♂	♅	Tower <= => Fool	
square by sign and degree	♃	♇	Wheel of Fortune <= => Judgement	
square by sign and degree	♅	♆	Fool <= => Hanged man	
challenging conjunction	♄	♆	World <= => Hanged man	
opposition by sign	☿	♆	Magician <= => Hanged man	
square by sign	☽	♇	High Priestess <= => Judgement	
square by sign	☿	♅	Magician <= => Fool	
square by sign	♀	♅	Empress <= => Fool	
square by sign	♄	♅	World <= => Fool	

Opposing Signs (Challenging) — Your AstroTarot Spirits 5

Opposing Signs *- Work in pairs with Pathwork "K" (after A/B/C) as potential challenging aspects.*

Prioritize the pair with your ascendant: Sagittarius Rising, represented by Temperance.

				Date	
Signs: Aries vs Libra	♈	♎	Emperor <= => Justice		
Signs: Taurus vs Scorpio	♉	♏	Hierophant <= => Death		
Signs: Gemini vs Sagittarius	♊	♐	Lovers <= => Temperance		ASC
Signs: Cancer vs Capricorn	♋	♑	Chariot <= => Devil		
Signs: Leo vs Aquarius	♌	♒	Strength <= => The Star		
Signs: Virgo vs Pisces	♍	♓	Hermit <= => The Moon		

Sample 1
Mar 5, 1953 2:28 AM

Basic Tarot Spirit Circles
Washington, D.C.

Your AstroTarot Spirits   **6**
‹‹== Birthdate & Time & Location; printed on 06-Jun-2024

These circles are based on your natal astrological chart

Tarot guide & shadow self are in all circles		*Your Tarot Guide*	*Your Shadow*	I

Each group of Tarot Spirit advisors includes your tarot guide & your shadow and after exercises "A/B/C" individually and "K" where needed., can be worked with as a group using exercises "H", "I" & "J";

Relationship Circle
For questions of love, relationships and interaction — Know

Mars & Sign	♂	♈	Tower	Emperor	I
Venus & Sign	♀	♈	Empress	Emperor	I
Soul OR Personality T.S.	8	17	Strength	The Star	I

Yourself, your Guide & Shadow-self

Persona Circle
For questions about your presentation to the world — Know

AC sign/Personality T.S.	♐	17	Temperance	The Star	I
Sun & Sun sign	☉	♓	The Sun	The Moon	I

Yourself, your Guide & Shadow-self

Reflective Circle
For questions of inner truth & emotions — Know

Moon & Moon sign	☽	♏	High Priestess	Death	I
Soul / Hidden Factor T.S.	8	17	Strength	The Star	I

Yourself, your Guide & Shadow-self

Current Circle
For questions of current life focus — Know

AC sign/Personality T.S.	♐	17	Temperance	The Star	I
Moon & Moon sign	☽	♏	High Priestess	Death	I
Sun & Sun sign	☉	♓	The Sun	The Moon	I
Soul T.S. / Year T.S.	8	7	Strength	Chariot	I

Yourself, your Guide & Shadow-self

Healing Circle
For healing / empowerment / initiation — Know

Pick a few from	☉	♐	The Sun	Temperance	I
these six healers	♒	♃	The Star	The Wheel	I
and special cards	♅♄	♀	The Fool	The Empress	I
Your Soul or Personality	8	17	Strength	The Star	I
Your Hidden Factor(s)	17		The Star		

Yourself, your Guide & Shadow-self

Sample 1

Mar 5, 1953 2:28 AM

Circle of Hands; Challenging Groups   7

Washington, D.C.   <<== Birthdate & Time & Location: printed on 06-Jun-2024

Includes challenging groups & grand square or T-cross if applicable

You may combine challenging groups that have almost the same members

Circle of Hands

After exercise "A/B/C" and "K," for the groups do "I" &"H2" or "J2"

				Circle Date
Challenging group 1	☽ ♃	♀ ♀	High Priestess / Wheel of Fortune	Empress / Judgement	
Challenging group 2	☿ ♄ ♆	♂ ♅	Magician / World / Hanged man	Tower / Fool	
Challenging group 3	☽ ♂ ♅	♀ ♄ ♆	High Priestess / Tower / Fool	Empress / World / Hanged man	
Challenging group 4	☿ ♂ ♅	♀ ♄ ♆	Magician / Tower / Fool	Empress / World / Hanged man	
Cardinal Signs Group	♈ ♎	♋ ♑	Emperor / Justice	Chariot / Devil	
Fixed Signs Group	♉ ♏	♌ ♒	Hierophant / Death	Strength / The Star	
Mutable Signs Group	♊ ♐	♍ ♓	Lovers / Temperance	Hermit / The Moon	
T Cross (Challenge)	♂ ♆	♅	Tower / Hanged man	Fool	

Focusing on areas that appear to need maintenance, do pathwork I regulary with circles above, plus:

Any pairs from Section 4 or opposing signs from Section 5 that are not fully reconciled,

Sample 1

Mar 5, 1953 2:28 AM

Circle of Hands; Positive Groups

Washington, D.C.

‹‹== Birthdate & Time & Location; printed on 06-Jun-2024

8

Includes positive groups and grand trine or Yod if applicable
After exercise "A/B/C" and "K," for the groups do "I" & "H2" or "J2"

Circle of Hands

Exclude Mars or Saturn (Tower or World) from group if any negativity.

Circle Date

Circle of Hands				
Positive Fire group	♈ ✕ ♀ ♀	♌ ☿ ♂	Emperor / Temperance / Empress / Judgement	Strength / Magician / Tower
Positive Earth group	♉ ♑	♍ ♃	Hierophant / Devil	Hermit / Wheel of Fortune
Positive Air group	♊ ♒ ♅	♎ ♄	Lovers / The Star / Hanged man	Justice / World
Positive Water group	♋ ♓ ☽	♏ ☉ ♅	Chariot / The Moon / High Priestess	Death / The Sun / Fool

Blessing Circle of Hands:
When working with Tarot Spirit Ccircles or the positive groups, you can engage a special blessing circle of hands.
Begin with Pathwork I, balancing power between all the participants. Then, once the power in the circle is balanced, request all present to send a blessing or positive power toward a project, manifestation, or intention.

Technical notes *for those deeper into astrology:*
This report uses a mix of modern and Hellenistic astrology, which have different approaches to aspects.
The priority is finding potentially unharmonious planetary relationships for Tarot Spirits to clear.
So, when there is a conflict between sign-based and degree-based aspects, then oppositions, squares, or conjunctions are prioritized over quincuxes, trines, or sextiles and semi-sextiles.

For degree based aspects, similar orbs (technically moiety) are used for all planets. The moieties used are: 10 degrees for conjunctions, squares, trines, and oppositions; 6 degrees for sextiles, and 3 degrees for averse configurations, including quincux and semi-sextile. These match the defaults at astro.com.
An exception is a 15 degree moiety for conjunctions with the Sun--representing a planet being "under the suns beams" or invisible. A 15 degree moiety is used for determining constructs with outer planets related to the Sun, Moon, or ascendant.

In Section 2, planetary house locations are shown for both the whole sign and Koch quadrant house systems. For the basic Tarot Spirit work related to this report, the houses and sign rulers are not used.

Sample 1
Mar 5, 1953 2:28 AM

Other Tarot Spirit Pair Aspects
Washington, D.C.

Your AstroTarot Spirits 9
<<== Birthdate & Time & Location; printed on 06-Jun-2024

Other Aspects

Similar to pathwork "K", but asking: "What you can do to help them work in harmony." Priority 4.
Compared to the challenging aspects, these aspects are lower priority to work with, as they are usually positive. However, they may need realignment. First focus on pairs that only have the traditional 7 planets.
For the averse aspects, your goal or question is "What can I do to help you see each other better?" Averse aspects to traditional ruler are in category 4.
Category 5 minor aspects are not all included here.

Verify
Date

Planetary Conjunctions & Sextiles with only traditional planets

conjunction by sign	☿	♀	Magician <= =>Empress	
conjunction by degree	☽	♄	High Priestess <= =>World	
sextile by sign & degree	☉	♃	The Sun <= =>Wheel of Fortune	

Above are major aspects -- You may also want to work the averse aspects below or other minor aspects

Planets Averse to Traditional Ruler (Quincunxes & Semi-Sextiles) with all planets

Date

quincunx by sign	☽	♂	High Priestess <= =>Tower	
quincunx by sign	☉	♀	The Sun <= =>Judgement	
semi-sextile by sign	♀	♃	Empress <= =>Wheel of Fortune	

Planets Averse (Quincunxes & Semi-Sextiles) with only traditional planets

Date

quincunx by sign and degree	☽	☿	High Priestess <= =>Magician	
semi-sextile by sign & degree	♂	♃	Tower <= =>Wheel of Fortune	
quincunx by sign	☉	♄	The Sun <= =>World	
quincunx by sign	♃	♄	Wheel of Fortune <= =>World	
semi-sextile by sign	☉	☿	The Sun <= =>Magician	
semi-sextile by sign	☉	♀	The Sun <= =>Empress	
semi-sextile by sign	☉	♂	The Sun <= =>Tower	
semi-sextile by sign	☿	♃	Magician <= =>Wheel of Fortune	

Planetary Conjunctions & Sextiles including outer planets

Date

conjunction by degree	☽	♆	High Priestess <= =>Hanged man	
sextile by sign & degree	♃	♅	Wheel of Fortune <= =>Fool	
sextile by sign & degree	♄	♀	World <= =>Judgement	
sextile by sign & degree	♆	♀	Hanged man <= =>Judgement	

Above are major aspects -- You may also want to work the averse aspects below or other minor aspects

Planets Averse (Quincunxes & Semi-Sextiles) including outer planets

Date

quincunx by sign	☉	♆	The Sun <= =>Hanged man	
quincunx by sign	♃	♆	Wheel of Fortune <= =>Hanged man	
semi-sextile by sign	♅	♀	Fool <= =>Judgement	

Appendix H:
Get and Map Your
Natal Astrological Chart

If you want to learn how to get your chart and complete the *AstroTarot mapping* rather than obtain the *My AstroTarot Report* discussed in Appendix G, this appendix provides all the details, including blank forms to fill out. There are several steps covered here:

1. Get a copy of your personal natal astrological chart
2. Map the planets to their sign positions and Tarot Spirits
3. Identify and map potentially challenging planetary aspects
4. Map groups of Tarot Spirits for circles
5. Identify challenging groups for circle of hands
6. Identify positive groups for circle of hands
7. Identify other aspects that may need attention

Important Note: If you obtain a copy of the *My AstroTarot Report* discussed in Appendix G, that report will include your chart and all the items listed above that are needed for the different pathwork. If so, you don't need to follow the step-by-step instructions here to map Tarot Spirits to the planets and signs. The instructions are included if you want to learn how. Do review your natal chart and the general astrological background in Chapters 11 and 12. You may wish to look up the Tarot Spirits for a couple of planets in your chart and their associated signs, just to verify you understand the mapping process, but you don't need to do them all if you get the *My AstroTarot Report*.

Get Your Natal Chart

If you already have a copy of your natal chart with major aspect information, then you can use that. If not, the instructions here will help you quickly get the data you need to proceed. We will show instructions for the astro.com website to generate the chart, but you can use whatever source you prefer. This is a straightforward process that will take just a few minutes. Before you start, gather the following information:

- Birth date and time of birth, preferably from a birth certificate
- Birth place: town, state or province, country

If you do not have an accurate birth time from your birth certificate, do the best you can to estimate the birth time. This can be based on some stories from your parents, like the pilot who heard his wife gave birth just as he saw sunrise while flying. As a personal aside, I relied on an estimate of my birth time from my mother for many years, until I finally looked at my birth certificate. That shifted the time 17 minutes earlier, which was enough to make my ascendant sign Sagittarius rather than Capricorn—quite a difference in character, and more truly aligned with how I present myself in the world.

As we discussed in Chapter 11, if you are new to astrology, you might pick one chart type to work with, either modern or Hellenistic. If you are already familiar with modern astrology, it would be a good exercise to create both a modern and a Hellenistic chart and see what the differences are.

The directions here are for the site www.astro.com. Menus and interface may change over time, so we will describe general steps and then provide the details needed at the time of publication. There are many other sites you can use. Here are the steps for astro.com:

1. Go to the website www.astro.com
2. Navigate to **creating a natal chart**. Select either:

    - On the main page [Charts & Calculations] then [Extended Chart Selection]
    - From the drop down menu at the top left of any page [Horoscope Drawings and Data] then [Extended Chart Selection]

3. Select [Enter birth data]
4. Enter your name, birth date, time, and location information.
5. If you don't already have an account at astro.com, you will be asked to create a user profile. This lets you store your birth information, and birth information for your friends and family.
6. Make the following chart selections and display your chart:

   - Under **Zodiac and houses**: House system: [whole signs] (unless you have another preference; Placidus is most popular)
   - Now go to **Display and calculation options**; Under **Aspects** select [only major aspects]
   - Then click [Show the chart]

7. On the chart that appears, verify your birth information is correct, then click on the chart to open a window with just a picture of the chart and get rid of ads.
8. You have multiple choices to save an image of your chart:

   - In windows, right click and [Copy Image]; then you can open a new word or excel file and use "Ctrl-V" to paste the image into a document.
   - Print the chart out if you have a printer attached to your computer.
   - In windows, right click and [Save image as…] and save a PNG format image file to a computer folder for your Tarot Spirit work.
   - In Safari for IOS, [File] [Export as PDF…] and save with your chosen name in a computer folder for your Tarot Spirit work.
   - Use a snipping app or screen capture method to save as a file.

Get a Hellenistic Chart Too

You now have a copy of your modern natal chart stored so you can access it later. You can stop here, but while you are on the site and have put in your birth data, you might as well get a **Hellenistic chart** as well:

1. Click [<- prior page] or [<- Chart Selection] and under **Sections** select the [o Round] tab. If you did not do a modern chart first,

you will need to do steps 1 through 5 above to get your birth data and basic settings in.

2. Under the main "Chart Drawing Style" select [Hellenistic]
3. Under **Zodiac and houses** make sure that for **House System**: [whole Signs] is selected
4. Under **Display and calculation options**, click these boxes:

    •   (Traditional astrology options) [Uranus-Pluto off/on]
    •   (Aspects) [only major aspects]
    •   Optionally, under **Additional objects** you can select other objects (asteroids, etc.) that interest you. Use the [Ctrl] key to select multiple items under **Common elements**. For the Hellenistic chart style, the main lots of Fortune, Spirit, and Eros are automatically included.
    •   Then click [Show the chart >>]
    •   Then either print, copy, or save the image of the Hellenistic chart.

You will use this chart later if you wish to get a Hellenistic view of astrology or to include both modern and Hellenistic aspects in your mapping.

Alternative Chart Sources

An online alternative site for getting a chart that has both modern and Hellenistic options is horoscopes.astro-seek.com/birth-chart-horoscope-online. Don't forget the hyphen in Astro-seek. Again, if you register here, your birth information will be saved. This site provides more accessible interpretations and lays out some of the aspects in a more friendly manner. Once you do your modern chart, a **Traditional Chart** link shows up below it if you want a Hellenistic chart.

Of course, you can purchase and use astrological software like Sirius or Solar Fire to generate your charts. There are a lot of options.

A Tour of Your Natal Chart

Take the tour of your natal chart in Chapter 11, noticing the different elements of your own chart. You can see four versions of the sample chart under "A Tour of Your Natal Chart" in Chapter 11.

Map Your Natal Chart to the Tarot Spirits

Astrology is a large and complex subject. Fortunately, when you use the Tarot Spirits to work with your natal chart, the process becomes quite simple, and you do not need to get into complex interpretation. To proceed here, you should either be familiar with or have reviewed the astrology basics in Chapters 11 and 12 and have a copy of your natal chart as instructed under *Get Your Natal Chart* above. In summary, you should:

- Understand astrology basics: symbols; planets; zodiacal signs; houses
- Have a copy of your natal astrology chart

You will work in the next section to translate or map your natal chart planets and signs to the Tarot Spirits. Before that, let's see what references you will need and get an overview of the general steps you will follow.

Mapping forms

Mapping forms are available as a download and are also included for copying at the end of this appendix.

At www.reidhart.com/tsh-resources you will find the following forms:

- Blank forms in pdf format to print out and fill in by hand
- A sample form filled out for the sample chart used in this book (Use this to compare with your mapping as you go along.)
- A word version of the blank forms. If you want to fill out astrological symbols on your computer then you need to install an astrological font on your computer:

You can search for the "Astro Dot Basic font" and install it on your computer. The symbol cells in the word version are formatted with that font and you can input upper case A-J for planets and lower case a-l for the signs. As with most download sites, you need to be careful what buttons you click on to avoid downloading other programs.

The pathwork process in the chapters of this book, introduces and familiarizes you with the Tarot Spirits. They become advisors, healers, and helping spirits who you reliably access through the shamanic journey. You may also be interested in their relationship to the Qabalah or Tree of Life as mystical teachers, but this is optional and not necessary for AstroTarot.

Once you meet the individual Tarot Spirits, you work with them on your personal astrology and resolve any potential conflicts found in your birth chart. Once you create your personal *AstroTarot mapping* you can engage the pathwork in Chapters 13, 14, and 15.

The Mapping Key for the Tarot Spirits

The Major Arcana (22 key cards) of the tarot exist as Tarot Spirits and can be contacted and worked with using shamanic methods. Each Tarot Spirit represents a major astrological influence, either a planet or a zodiac sign. You will want a copy of the astrology-to-tarot mapping key in front of you as a reference while you do the mapping. The mapping key is repeated in multiple versions and you just need one:

- The English magic school attributions are listed in the two mapping tables in Chapter 12 (Tarot Spirit Mapping to Zodiacal Signs & Tarot Spirit Mapping to Planets), along with the symbols used for the planets and signs of the zodiac.
- Similar mapping key tables are located at the end of the blank AstroTarot mapping form download and blank forms at the end of this Appendix. Sign rulers are included.
- A compact mapping key table is located at the end of the tracking form download and in Appendix B. Sign rulers are included.
- Variations in the tarot-to-astrology correspondences are also discussed in the variants section later in this Appendix. This option is useful if you want to use other than the English magic approach.

The Basic Tarot Spirit Mapping Overview

Tarot Spirit mapping to your natal astrological chart is straightforward. The process is outlined here. Don't start doing the mapping until the next section where detailed instructions and examples are provided. The general flow is listed, followed by a table that lists the *AstroTarot mapping* section and the related chapters and pathwork where mapping in that section is used.

- Complete Sections 1 and 2, special spirits and planet mapping.
- When section 2 is finished, fill out the first cover page with the big three: Sun, Moon, and ascendant.

- Insert your birth chart(s) as Section 3.
- Complete Sections 4 and 5: potentially challenging aspects. Optionally note other potentially challenging aspects in Section 9.
- Complete Sections 6, 7, and 8 for Tarot Spirit circles and groups.
- Optionally complete the planet interpretative paragraphs at the end of this appendix.

The table below shows the name of each section of the *AstroTarot mapping* and what chapters those Tarot Spirits will be used in.

Section	Contents:	Find Pathwork in Chapter	Pathwork
Cover	Big 3: Sun, Moon, Ascendant	11 & 12	Interpretation
1	Personality, Soul, Hidden, and Year Tarot Spirits	7, 8 (& 3, 5, 6)	A/B/C, N
2	Planet, Sign, & ASC Mapping	3, 4, 5, 6, 11,12	A/B/C
3	Natal (Birth) Chart	11 & 12; Appendix F & H	
4	Potential Challenging Aspects	13	K
5	Opposing Signs (Challenging)	13	K
6	Basic Tarot Spirit circles	14 & 15	I, H2, J2, L
7	Circle of Hands; Challenging Groups	14	I1, H2, J2
8	Circle of Hands; Positive Groups	14	I2, I3, H2, J2
9	Other Tarot Spirit Pair Aspects	13	K
10	Interpretation of your planets	Appendix H	Interpretation

For all the *AstroTarot mapping* sections above, the process is the same. Identify which planets or signs are involved in each astrological relationship and substitute the Tarot Spirits representing those planets and signs into the pair or group that needs to work together. You can use the *AstroTarot mapping* forms or simply record your mapping on blank paper. Now let's do the mapping.

Start Here: Your Personal AstroTarot Mapping

Before you work through the mapping forms make sure you have the following easily available for reference:

- Your natal chart with an aspect matrix. It can be modern, Hellenistic, or you can have both.

- Astrology-to-tarot mapping keys for both planets and signs as discussed earlier.
- A copy of the aspect symbol table from the Chapter 12 topic: *Aspect Symbols and Matrix.*
- A blank set of forms to fill out, either hard copy or on the computer. Alternatively, you can simply write down the needed information on blank sheets of paper.

Blank mapping forms are available as a download in either word or pdf format here: www.reidhart.com/tsh-resources

Download a set of blank forms for yourself, or copy them from the set at the end of this Appendix. We will show the filled out sample forms as we walk through the step by step process of filling them out for yourself.

This is an ongoing process, and **you do not need to get it all done right away.** Your basic goal is to list all the signs aligned to the planets in your natal chart and identify the Tarot Spirits assigned to the signs, planets and your ascendent. Then completing Section 4 will prepare you for the important reconciliation work with Pathwork K in Chapter 13.

Hold off on the cover data until you complete Section 2.

Section 1: Your Special Tarot Spirits

Based on the Special Spirits you found in Chapter 7 and Appendix E, fill out Section 1. Here is the form filled out for the sample chart:

Section 1: Your Special Cards

Personal Special Tarot Spirits	Meaning	Key Number	Key Card Name
Personality spirit ("P")	What lessons are here for you in this life?	17	The Star
Soul spirit ("S")	Your purpose through all lifetimes	8	Strength
Hidden Factor Spirit ("H")	Your shadow self or teacher	17	The Star
Year spirit for _2024_ ("Y")	What is my lesson, focus, or opportunity for the year?	7	Chariot

Section 2: Your Natal Chart Map

Look at your natal chart and identify the signs all your planets are in. The sign each planet is in is listed in the Aspect matrix at the bottom. Look closely at the aspect matrix for each chart type. The upper-left part of the aspect matrix is shown below for both modern and Hellenistic charts from astro.com. Note that the astro.com modern chart uses three-letter abbreviations for the signs, while the Hellenistic chart uses symbols. Both matrices list the planet symbol, name and location in what sign by degree, minutes, and seconds.[86]

Modern Planet/Zodiac Sign list

☉ Sun	14 Pis 26' 2"
☽ Moon	4 Sco 3'11"
☿ Mercury	1 Ari 52'57"
♀ Venus	25 Ari 44'43"
♂ Mars	18 Ari 57'58"
♃ Jupiter	16 Tau 22' 8"
♄ Saturn	26 Lib 37'14"r

Hellenistic Planet/Sign list

☉ Sun	♓ 14° 26' 2"
☽ Moon	♏ 4° 3' 11"
☿ Mercury	♈ 1° 52' 57"
♀ Venus	♈ 25° 44' 43"
♂ Mars	♈ 18° 57' 58"
♃ Jupiter	♉ 16° 22' 8"
♄ Saturn	♎ 26° 37' 14"r

Read the first row: The Sun is in Pisces at 14 degrees, 26 minutes, 2 seconds. In the second row: The Moon is in Scorpio at 4 degrees, 3 minutes, 11 seconds. You can see that the location of the planets in the signs is the same for both Modern and Hellenistic astrology, as both systems use the tropical zodiac.[87]

Note the following in Section 2 of your *AstroTarot mapping* forms for each planet:

- Signs in column 2 and symbols for the signs in column 4.
- The Tarot Spirit who represents that sign in column 6

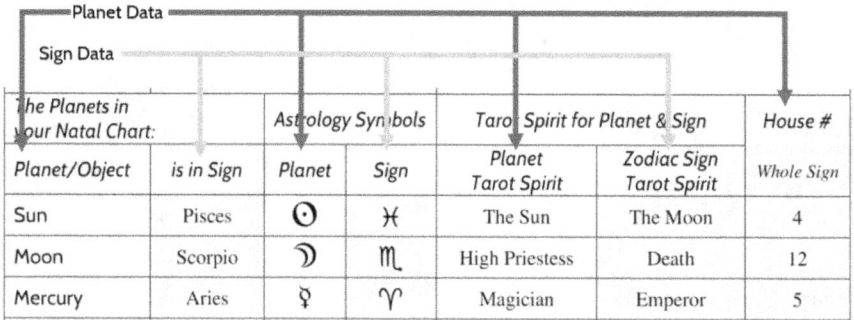

The Planets in your Natal Chart:	is in Sign	Astrology Symbols		Tarot Spirit for Planet & Sign		House #
Planet/Object	is in Sign	Planet	Sign	Planet Tarot Spirit	Zodiac Sign Tarot Spirit	Whole Sign
Sun	Pisces	☉	♓	The Sun	The Moon	4
Moon	Scorpio	☽	♏	High Priestess	Death	12
Mercury	Aries	☿	♈	Magician	Emperor	5

We only show the Sun, Moon, and Mercury here, but fill in the signs and the sign symbol for all planets on the form. Then, you can optionally

---

[86] A degree (°) is divided into 60 minutes (') and a minute is divided into 60 seconds (")
[87] If you are using a Vedic astrology chart that uses the sidereal zodiac, some planets will be located in different signs. Use the signs of your preferred system for Tarot Spirit selection.

record in the seventh column the house each planet is in. Find the house numbers in the center of your circle natal chart. You will evaluate houses in more detail in a later book in the series. If you are looking at both modern and Hellenistic astrology, record both houses where they are different. We only touch lightly on house interpretation here.

Mapping Form Section 2 for the Sample Chart

Once the signs are identified for each planet, notice which Tarot Spirit represents the sign for each planet. Look up the Tarot Spirit for each planet's sign in your reference table(s) of astrology-to-tarot mappings. List the Tarot Spirits in the "Zodiac Sign Tarot Spirit" column. Continue for the rest of the planets on the page. Section 2 of the *AstroTarot mapping* forms would be filled out as follows using the English magic (Waite) recommended Tarot Spirit mapping for the sample chart:

Section 2: Planet and Sign Mapping

Name	Sample Chart 1			AstroTarot Personal Tarot Spirits		
Birthdate	3/5/1953			MM/DD/YYYY		
Birth time	2:28 AM			HH:MM AM/PM		
Birth Location	Washington, DC, USA			City, State/Provence, Country		
The Planets in your Natal Chart:		Astrology Symbols		Tarot Spirit for Planet & Sign		House #
Planet/Object	is in Sign	Planet	Sign	Planet Tarot Spirit	Zodiac Sign Tarot Spirit	Whole Sign
Sun	Pisces	☉	♓	The Sun	The Moon	4
Moon	Scorpio	☽	♏	High Priestess	Death	12
Mercury	Aries	☿	♈	Magician	Emperor	5
Venus	Aries	♀	♈	Empress	Emperor	5
Mars	Aries	♂	♈	Tower	Emperor	5
Jupiter	Taurus	♃	♉	Wheel	Hierophant	6
Saturn	Libra	♄	♎	World	Justice	11
Uranus	Cancer	♅	♋	Fool	Chariot	8
Neptune	Libra	♆	♎	Hanged man	Justice	11
Pluto	Leo	♇	♌	Judgement	Strength	9
AC*Ascendant	Sagittarius		♐		Temperance	1
AC sign Ruler: Jupiter	Ruler sign Taurus	♃	♉	Wheel	Hierophant	6

* "AC" = Ascendant; the eastern horizon at your birth time.

The planet associated with the ascendant is the ruler of the ascendant zodiac sign (optional)

You can skip the ascendent ruler for now. Sign rulers are covered in a later book in the series and are not needed for the pathwork in this book. Of course, if you are familiar with planetary rulerships, you can enter the Tarot Spirit information for the ascendant ruling planet, and the sign that ruling planet is in. Sign rulers are included in the download astrology-to-tarot key tables.

Variants in Tarot-to-Astrology Mapping

Most people will want to use the English magic (Waite) mapping of tarot keys to planets and signs. This approach was discussed in Chapter 12 and is listed in the mapping key tables discussed under *The Mapping Key for the Tarot Spirits* earlier. If you want to pursue other than the English magic mapping method, then review this section.

Whatever method you choose should be consistent after a period of experimentation. There are various historical mappings of the planets and signs to the tarot Major Arcana. Payne-Towler identified eight variations or streams, which generally fall into three main groups.[88] The major differences in astrological assignments are discussed below:

- The continental schools include Lévi, the Old Alexandrian, and Gra streams. Here the Magus represents the Air element, the Star is Mercury, the Emperor is Jupiter (except in Gra the World is Jupiter), and Judgement is Saturn.
- The Marseilles/Spanish schools include Maxwell, Dali and Balbi streams. Here the Magus represents the Sun, the Emperor is Jupiter, the Hierophant is Mercury, and Death is Saturn.
- The English schools include Waite/Case and Crowley. Here the Magus represents Mercury, the Wheel is Jupiter, and the World is Saturn.

All the mapping approaches have their own rationale and none of them is considered the "right" method. Payne-Towler suggests methods to find the stream that is most compatible with your own focus and process.[89] Exploring these subtleties is for the advanced user. If you want to investigate other than the English Magic (Waite) tarot-to-astrological

---

[88] Payne-Towler, C. 1999. *The Underground Stream: Esoteric Tarot Revealed*. pp 118-119.
[89] ibid. pp136-150.

mapping, then I strongly recommend reviewing the options in *The Underground Stream: Esoteric Tarot Revealed* by Payne-Towler. Again, most will want to use the English magic mapping established by Waite and included in the mapping tables in Chapter 12.

Section 3: Your Natal Chart

Keep a copy of your chart(s) with your mapping forms for reference. Print it out if you are filling out the forms by hand. You can insert the chart image in the file if you are filling out the forms on the computer. If you have both modern and Hellenistic charts, include both.

Map Challenging Aspects to the Tarot Spirits

Once you have mapped your Tarot Spirits associated with your birth chart planets and signs in Section 2, you move to mapping the potentially challenging aspects in your natal chart for Section 4. Section 9 includes other planetary aspects that may also be challenging. Working with the spirits involved in these challenging aspects in Chapter 13 is a highly effective way to clear limitations and obstacles in your life. In this section you will:

- Understand how to map the various aspects of planets in astrology based on what you learned about aspects in Chapter 12.
- Identify potentially challenging aspects, both by degree and by sign in your chart of the traditional seven planets and the three outer planets
- Identify and map the Tarot Spirits involved in the potentially challenging aspects in priority groups

Prioritization Method

You may work with a pair of Tarot Spirits on your list of potentially challenging aspects and find that everything is simply fine. In addition, not all aspected planets are that impactful. This is discussed further in Chapter 13. You can prioritize the challenging aspects into 5 groups:

1. Potentially challenging aspects related to the seven traditional planets (excluding Uranus, Neptune, and Pluto). Include all squares and oppositions related to these planets. Also include

conjunctions involving Mars, Saturn, and the Sun (within 15 degrees either way for the Sun).

2. Potentially challenging aspects that include the outer planets: Uranus, Neptune, and Pluto. Include all squares and oppositions related to these planets. Include conjunctions involving Mars and Saturn with the outer planets.

3. The third group in priority includes the signs, rather than planets, that oppose each other.

4. The lowest priority group is for those who want to be quite thorough. These aspects rarely need to be addressed and are called the "Other Aspects." These planetary aspects include conjunctions that were not covered under priorities 1 or 2, and sextiles with the seven visible planets. Conjunctions with Mercury not already covered in priority 1 should be included. Also include averse aspects related to sign rulers or topical situations as discussed under Section 9.

5. Going beyond the lowest priority group are the full range of minor aspects and the aspects in item 4 related to the outer planets. Include averse aspects not included in item 4 as discussed under Section 9. These are rarely going to have problems for resolution and are not included in the *My AstroTarot Report*. The minor aspects include quintile (72°), semi-square (45°), sesquiquadrate (135°), and biquintile(144°).

The identification of potentially challenging aspects gives the map of which Tarot Spirits you should work with. For all of the Tarot Spirit pairs identified, you will use *Pathwork K, reconciling potentially challenging aspects,* that is discussed in Chapter 13.

Identifying the potentially challenging aspects is similar for all the priorities. You will use the *AstroTarot mapping* forms as follows for potentially challenging aspects:

- In Section 4 record the priority 1 and 2 pairs of Tarot Spirits for planets with potentially challenging aspects.
- In Section 5 note which signs have opposing planets for priority 3 pairs of Tarot Spirits.

- In Section 9 record the priority 4 pairs of Tarot Spirits for planets with other aspects. Optionally, you can include priority 5 pairs here too.

Section 4: Your Potential Challenging Planetary Aspects

To indicate which Tarot Spirits to do A/B/C journeys with first, focus on identifying the priority 1 pairs with potentially challenging aspects in Section 4 of your *AstroTarot mapping* forms. A Section 4 form filled out for the sample chart is shown here:

Section 4: My Potential Challenging Aspects - Tarot Spirit Pairs (Priority 1 & 2)

Priority 1: Potential challenging aspects (any oppositions or squares, plus conjunctions with Mars, Saturn, the Sun or Mercury) with **only** the first seven planets involved:

Aspect Type	Priority	First Planet	Second Planet	First Planet Tarot Spirit	Second Planet Tarot Spirit	Date Cleared
Opp, Deg/Sign	1	♀	♄	Empress	World	
Opp, Deg/Sign	1	♂	♄	Tower	World	
Opp, Sign	1	☿	♄	Magician	World	
Conj, Deg/Sign	1	♂	♀	Tower	Empress	
Conj, Sign	1	♂	☿	Tower	Magician	
Opp, Sign	1	☽	♃	High Priestess	Wheel	
Opp, Deg	1	☽	♀	High Priestess	Empress	

Finding Priority 1 Potentially Challenging Planetary Aspects

The major challenging aspects are the square and the opposition. Let's find the potentially challenging aspects by degree according to modern astrology for the first seven planets in this sample chart. Look for the red square and opposition symbols in the aspect matrix. Then you will add conjunctions with Mars, Saturn, and the Sun.

In the example above we noted three aspects that are both **by degree** and **by sign**:

- Saturn opposite Venus
- Saturn opposite Mars
- Mars conjunct Venus

There is also a potentially challenging aspect **by degree** only:

- Moon opposite Venus

There are also three aspects **by sign** only:

- Saturn opposite Mercury
- Mars conjunct Mercury
- Moon opposite Jupiter

For illustration, lets look at the modern aspect matrix and chart to find two aspects:

- Moon opposite Venus
- Mars conjunct Venus

⊙ Sun	♓ 14° 26' 2"
☽ Moon	♏ 4° 3' 11"
☿ Mercury	♈ 1° 52' 57"
♀ Venus	♈ 25° 44' 43"
♂ Mars	♈ 18° 57' 58"
♃ Jupiter	♉ 16° 22' 8"
♄ Saturn	♎ 26° 37' 14"r
♅ Uranus	♋ 14° 34' 20"r
♆ Neptune	♎ 23° 28' 34"r
♇ Pluto	♌ 21° 31' 34"r

You can see how the aspect matrix matches the identified aspects on the wheel chart. In the chart below, identify the same planetary aspects:

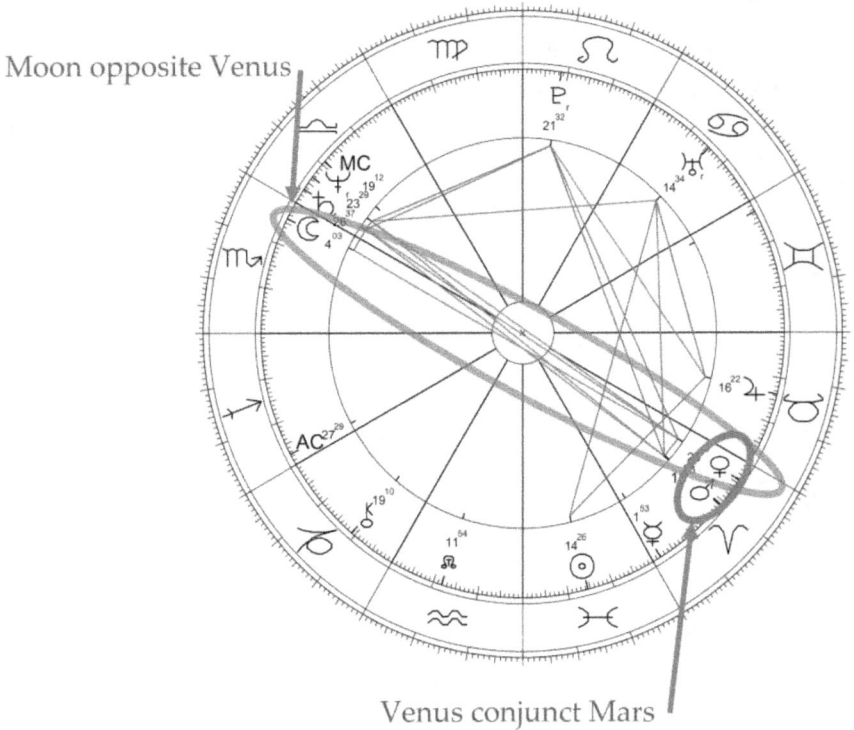

Moon opposite Venus

Venus conjunct Mars

Some red conjunction aspect symbols are not important. Ignore the conjunctions for now unless they include either Mars, Saturn, or the Sun (within 15 degrees either way for the Sun—this did not occur in the sample chart). The potentially challenging aspects above are listed on the sample *AstroTarot mapping* Section 4. They are noted as being "Opp, Deg" meaning opposition **by degree**. You add the "/sign" designation if you also find the opposition by sign in a Hellenistic aspect matrix.

Hellenistic vs. Modern Planet Aspects

If you are only doing either modern or Hellenistic astrology right now, you can skip this and the next two sections. Just use the aspect matrix for the type of chart you choose to work with.

There is a benefit to using the potentially challenging aspects from both systems. You play it safe by including both modern and Hellenistic aspects in your Tarot Spirit work. It is optional, but it is like covering your bases. When you get in conference with the Tarot Spirits, they will let you know if there is a conflict that needs work or clearing. If so, just note that the aspects are deg, sign, or both (deg/sign). We get into the subtle differences between the two, but you can rely on the aspect matrix to point out the potentially challenging aspects for each system.

In Hellenistic astrology, the relationships of the planets are called configurations. For simplicity we will refer to them as aspects. They have similar meanings: a square is challenging, and a trine is positive. The difference is:

- Aspects in Hellenistic astrology are based primarily on the sign each planet is in. In Hellenistic astrology, the square occurs to any planet located three signs away on the wheel, and a trine to any planet located four signs away.
- For aspects in modern astrology, a square is an aspect based on about a 90 degree angle between the two planets involved on the chart, while the trine aspect is 120 degrees. The number of signs between the planets do not matter in modern astrology. So a square aspect can occur in modern astrology, even if the planets are not three signs away from each other.

Each aspect **by degree** counts when the degrees are within an orb of each other. The orbs vary by planet and aspect with larger orbs for the Sun and Moon (between 5 and 9 degrees) to smaller orbs for the transpersonal outer planets (between 2 and 5 degrees). The range indicates a variance by aspect with conjunctions and oppositions the largest, sextiles the smallest and trines and squares in between. Note that the astro.com site accounts for orbs when creating your chart and aspect matrix, so you don't really need to. Here are examples from each system:

In **modern astrology**, the Sun opposite Saturn has an opposition if their degrees in opposite signs are within 10 degrees of each other (half the 20 degree orb) or if within 170 to 190 degrees apart.

- The Sun at 15 degrees Aries **would be in opposition** to Saturn at anywhere between 5 and 25 degrees Libra.
- The Sun at 15 degrees Aries would **not** be in opposition to Saturn at 4 or 26 degrees of Libra.
- The Sun at 29 degrees Aries **is opposite** Saturn at 5 degrees Scorpio, even though their signs are not opposite. The range where Saturn would have a valid opposition is 29 degrees Libra, plus or minus 10 degrees. That is from 19 degrees Libra to 9 degrees Scorpio.

In **Hellenistic astrology**, the aspects are by sign. So, if the signs are opposite each other on the chart, planets in those signs are in opposition **by sign**, even if they are not in opposition **by degree**. We can look at three similar examples in Hellenistic astrology:

- The Sun at 15 degrees Aries is in opposition to Saturn **anywhere in the sign** Libra.
- The Sun at 15 degrees Aries **would be in opposition** to Saturn at 1 or 29 degrees of Libra.
- The Sun at 29 degrees Aries is **not** in opposition Saturn at 1 degree Scorpio, even though the orb (moiety) is only 2 degrees. They have an aspect by degree, but their signs are not opposite. In this situation the potential aspect is called out-of-sign or dissociate. We could say in this case that the Sun and Saturn have a dissociate opposition, but a Hellenistic astrologer would not consider that a valid opposition.

If that discussion had too many numbers and was hard to follow, don't worry. All you need to do is trust the aspect matrix for the type(s) of chart you want to consider, as discussed on the next two pages.

Comparing Modern to Hellenistic Aspects

More description of Hellenistic vs. modern differences follow. Below are two aspect tables from our sample chart. We can look at two sets of planets for a comparison. In the modern chart (aspects by degree) the Aspect Matrix is shown below.

- Mercury has no aspect to Venus, Mars, or Saturn
- Moon opposes Venus (by degree)

☉ Sun	♓ 14° 26' 2"
🌙 Moon	♏ 4° 3' 11"
☿ Mercury	♈ 1° 52' 57"
♀ Venus	♈ 25° 44' 43"
♂ Mars	♈ 18° 57' 58"
♃ Jupiter	♉ 16° 22' 8"
♄ Saturn	♎ 26° 37' 14 "r

In the Hellenistic chart (aspects by sign) Aspect Matrix below.

- Mercury is Conjunct Venus and Mars, as they are in the same sign
- Mercury is Opposite Saturn, as they are in opposite signs
- The Moon does not see Venus, so there is no opposition by sign as the signs Scorpio and Aries are not opposite each other. You might see this more clearly looking at the modern sample chart a few pages back. While the Moon and Venus have an opposition by degree, they are dissociate. Venus would have to be in Taurus rather than Aires to have an opposition by sign with the Moon in Scorpio.

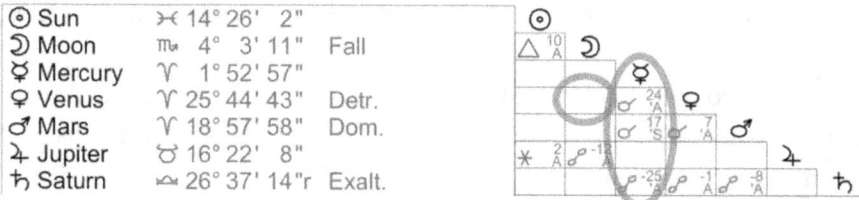

☉ Sun	♓ 14° 26' 2"	
🌙 Moon	♏ 4° 3' 11"	Fall
☿ Mercury	♈ 1° 52' 57"	
♀ Venus	♈ 25° 44' 43"	Detr.
♂ Mars	♈ 18° 57' 58"	Dom.
♃ Jupiter	♉ 16° 22' 8"	
♄ Saturn	♎ 26° 37' 14"r	Exalt.

In the process of adding the mapping of Hellenistic aspects to the personal Tarot Spirit worksheet, look for the squares, conjunctions and oppositions and include them with the potentially challenging aspects. If they already are there by degree, just add the notation "/sign."

Mapping both Hellenistic and Modern Aspects

Here is a partial example mapping both modern and Hellenistic aspects from the aspect matrices of each chart to the table in Section 4:

Modern (by degree):

☉ Sun	♓ 14° 26' 2"
☽ Moon	♏ 4° 3' 11"
☿ Mercury	♈ 1° 52' 57"
♀ Venus	♈ 25° 44' 43"
♂ Mars	♈ 18° 57' 58"

Hellenistic (by sign):

☉ Sun	♓ 14° 26' 2"
☽ Moon	♏ 4° 3' 11"
☿ Mercury	♈ 1° 52' 57"
♀ Venus	♈ 25° 44' 43"
♂ Mars	♈ 18° 57' 58"

Aspect Type	Priority, Astro Type	First Planet	Second Planet	First Planet Tarot Spirit	Second Planet Tarot Spirit	Date Cleared
Conj, Sign	4, Hel	♀	☿	Empress	Magician	
Conj, Sign	1, Hel	♂	☿	Tower	Magician	
Conj, Sign/Deg	1, Both	♂	☿	Tower	Empress	
Opp, Deg	1, Mod	☽	♀	High Priestess	Empress	

Note: the order of the planets does not matter

For illustration, the table above includes the conjunction of Venus and Mercury by sign, even though that is a priority 4 aspect. Conjunctions are priority 1 only when Mars, Saturn, or the Sun is one of the paired planets. While Mercury can bring some challenges, it often does not. So, include Mercury conjunctions in Section 9 of the *AstroTarot mapping*. Also note that we do not include the Sun trine Moon aspect in either Section 4 or 9, as it is always a positive aspect.

Let the software calculate the aspects for you, and note the aspects of interest in the aspect matrix for the system(s) you are interested in. Do not include aspects to objects other than planets in your tables. So, from the aspect matrix, ignore aspects to the ascendant or angles (AC, DC, MC, IC), lots (Fortune, Spirit, Eros), Centaurs and Asteroids (Chiron, Ceres, etc.), or nodes.

To thoroughly understand this process, you can compare Section 4 from the full set of filled out *AstroTarot mapping* forms for the sample chart. You can download the filled-out sample at www.reidhart.com/tsh-resources. The sample forms include both a modern and Hellenistic chart with the aspect matrices above. A copy of the priority 1 portion of Section 4 for the sample chart can also be found just after the heading "Section 4: Your Potential Challenging Planetary Aspects" a few pages back.

Compare Section 4 of the sample forms with both the modern and Hellenistic sample charts and aspect matrices to see if you can find all the potentially challenging aspects. The sample forms have both Hellenistic and modern aspects listed. Those noted as "Deg" are modern interpretations, those noted as "Sign" are Hellenistic, and those noted as "Deg/Sign" are considered challenging natal aspects in both systems.

Outer Planet Challenging Aspects—Priority 2

Now let us expand our search to include the outer planets in the sample chart and find some more potentially challenging aspects. Since these outer planets are slower moving and more societal than personal, they are lower priority potentially challenging aspects. We put these aspects in the forms under priority 2 in Section 4. After noting the planets we map the Tarot Spirits to each pair. The mapping cross reference is included in Chapter 12 or at the end of the blank mapping forms. The sample chart has these pairs:

Priority 2: Potentially challenging aspects with Uranus, Neptune, or Pluto:

Aspect Type	Priority	First Planet	Second Planet	First Planet Tarot Spirit	Second Planet Tarot Spirit	Date Cleared
Square, Deg/Sign	2	♂	♅	Tower <=	=> Fool	
Square, Sign	2	♄	♅	World <=	=> Fool	
Opp, Deg/Sign	2	♂	♆	Tower <=	=> Hanged man	
Conj, Deg/Sign	2	♄	♆	World <=	=> Hanged man	
Square, Sign	2	☿	♅	Magician <=	=> Fool	
Opp, Sign	2	☿	♆	Magician <=	=> Hanged man	
Square, Sign	2	♀	♅	Empress <=	=> Fool	
Opp, Deg/Sign	2	♀	♆	Empress <=	=> Hanged man	
Square, Deg/Sign	2	♅	♆	Fool <=	=> Hanged man	
Square, Sign	2	☽	♇	High Priestess <=	=> Judgement	
Square, Deg/Sign	2	♃	♇	Wheel <=	=> Judgement	

Section 5: Your Potential Challenging Sign Aspects

One additional set of potentially challenging aspects includes the natural oppositions of signs in the zodiac. You will work with these pairs of Tarot Spirits just as you work with planetary challenging aspects. When filling out the table, the signs and Tarot Spirits are already identified, as they are the same for everyone. Just identify your ascendant sign and list planets with opposition aspects on the line for the pair of signs they are located in.

You can optionally note the house numbers associated with each sign in the "Opposite Houses" column. In the Hellenistic system, there is always one-to-one alignment of signs to houses, based on the whole sign house system. In quadrant house systems, you might have the cusp of two houses in a single sign, with some signs having no house cusps. For systems other than whole sign houses, The first cusp of each house, moving counterclockwise, shows what sign the house is associated with.

Here is the Section 5 result for the sample:

Section 5: Opposing Signs (Challenging) (Priority 3)

You can sub-prioritize by starting with the pair containing your ascendent sign.
Then do pairs where there are opposing planets, followed by the rest.

Signs Opposite		Opposition Signs (challenging) Tarot Spirit Pairs	Opposition Planets, ASC	Opposite Houses*		Date Cleared
♈	♎	Emperor <= => Justice	♄ ☿ ♂ ♀ ♆	5	11	
♉	♏	Hierophant <= => Death	☽ ♃	6	12	
♊	♐	Lovers <= => Temperance	♐ASC	7	1	
♋	♑	Chariot <= => Devil		8	2	
♌	♒	Strength <= => Star		9	3	
♍	♓	Hermit <= => The Moon		10	4	

*Identifying Houses is optional for the Basic AstroTarot work.

It is best to just reconcile all six pairs of sign Tarot Spirits. If your journey time is limited, you can prioritize which sign pairs to work in the following order:

- Focus on the pair that includes your rising sign first (house 1).
- Focus on pairs that include opposing planets.
- Focus on pairs where the signs include your Sun or Moon.

Opposition planets are best found from your Hellenistic chart. They need to be "by sign" to match the sign oppositions. When there are opposition planets, the sign reconciliation is higher priority.

Section 9: Other Tarot Spirit Pair Aspects

The last set of Tarot Spirit pairs are other aspects. We address these before the Tarot Spirit circles and groups, as the method is similar to section 4. These aspects include conjunctions unless they were already accounted for in Priority 1 & 2, sextile aspects, and averse aspects. For modern astrology you could also include other minor aspects. These aspects rarely create conflict. So, you can skip them for now and return to them later if you want to be thorough. The sample Section 9 mapping follows:

Section 9: Other Tarot Spirit Pair Aspects (Priority 4 & 5)

Priority 4: Lowest priority are conjunctions and sextile aspects (exclude conjunctions already included in Priority 1 & 2). Priority 5 (not shown) relates to outer planets or minor aspects.

Aspect Type	Priority	First Planet	Second Planet	First Planet Tarot Spirit	Second Planet Tarot Spirit	Date Cleared
Conj, Deg	4	♄	☽	World <=	=>High Priestess	
Sextile, Deg/Sign	4	☉	♃	The Sun <=	=>Wheel	
Conj, Sign	4	☿	♀	Magician <=	=>Empress	
Quincunx, Sign	4	☽	♂	High Priestess <=	=> Tower	
Quincunx, Sign	4	☉	♇	The Sun <=	=> Judgement	
Semi-Sext'l, Sign	4	♃	♀	Wheel <=	=>Empress	

Averse aspects. From a Hellenistic point of view, we can include averse aspects in priority 4. Averse aspects include semi-sextile (30° or 1 sign apart) and quincunx (150° or 5 signs apart), also called inconjunct aspects. Averse aspects lack a regular polygon connection in Hellenistic astrology. This means that the planets cannot see or communicate with each other. In some cases, such as inconjunct rulers of important houses, averse aspects can benefit from reconciliation. Rulership is an advanced topic beyond the scope of this book. Most averse aspects will be priority 5 for modern charts and priority 4 for Hellenistic. For those familiar with rulership and planetary interpretation, there are two cases where modern averse aspects would move up to priority 4:

- Where the planetary ruler of a planet's sign has an averse aspect, reconciliation is likely desirable, as it can help communication between a planet and its sign ruler.
- Where a pair of planets representing a topical life challenge have an averse aspect, reconciliation can likely be helpful. Examples include a life where romantic relationships are difficult and Venus and Mars are aversely aspected or where there are money troubles and Jupiter is aversely aspected to the Sun or Moon.

To find averse aspects, you will need to visually scan [90] your Hellenistic chart. Semi-sextile averse aspects are by sign and the planets

---

[90] An aspect matrix does not help here because averse aspects are not shown on the astro.com Hellenistic style. You can get them on a modern chart, but those aspects are by degree, not sign. Since averse configuration is a Hellenistic concept, you want aspects by sign.

are in adjacent signs. Quincunx averse aspects are also by sign and five signs away in either direction. Find the quincunx for each planet in the sign adjacent on either side of the opposing sign.

Semi-sextile and quincunx (averse) aspects between a planet and its sign ruler are shown in grey. These indicate the inability of one planet to see another, which is important in Hellenistic astrology for sign rulers. For modern charts, these aspects are the very lowest priority and unlikely to create conflict in most cases.

If you are working with a thematic issue related to planetary averse aspect, there can be some benefit to reconciling the planets.

Do not worry about trine aspects, as these are extremely positive and take care of themselves.

Map Tarot Spirit Circles and Groups

Sections 6, 7, and 8 include your Tarot Spirit circles and groups. These are each fairly straightforward to map.

Section 6: Your Basic Tarot Spirit Circles

Many of the Circle Tarot Spirits are already shown on the blank circle mapping forms, generally planets that are part of each circle. You just need to consult Section 2 of your basic *AstroTarot mapping* to match up the signs that go with the planets for your chart and note your special Tarot Spirits from Section 1. In the Current Circle example below, you would indicate the sign of your ascendant (Sagittarius for the sample), the signs for your Moon and Sun, and your special personality, soul, and year tarot key numbers from Section 1 of your *AstroTarot mapping*. Then just bring forward the related Tarot Spirits you already mapped in Sections 1 and 2. Here is the sample mapping for the Current Circle:

Current Circle			For questions of your current focus		Know
AC sign/Personality T.S.	♐	17	Temperance	The Star	I
Moon & sign Moon is in	☽	♏	High Priestess	Death	I
Sun & sign Sun is in	☉	♓	The Sun	The Moon	I
Soul T.S./Year T.S.	8	7	Strength	The Chariot	I
				Your Shadow-self & Guide	

Find the other circle mappings for the sample chart in Chapter 14.

Section 7: Your Circle of Hands Challenging Groups

These groups are mostly challenging. There are three types:

- Challenging aspect groups that share common Tarot Spirits
- Set groups of signs with common modality characteristics
- Groups based on astrological aspect patterns- discussed separately after the Section 8 positive groups

Challenging Aspect Groups

Challenging aspect groups occur when any planet has three or more challenging natal aspect pairs in Section 4. Include all Tarot Spirits that are paired with that planet in the group. You may combine challenging groups that have almost the same members.

The easiest approach to find the challenging aspect groups is to review Section 4 for both priorities 1 and 2. Note any planets that show up on 3 or more rows. Let's look at some samples from the sample chart.

The Moon shows up three times, associated with Venus, Jupiter, and Pluto. This is the first challenging group in the sample chart, and the mapping forms are filled out like this:

Challenging Group 1	Spirits from multiple challenging pairs			Know
Sharing:	☽	♀	High Priestess	Empress	I
The Moon (High Priestess)	♃	♇	Wheel of Fortune	Judgement	I
					I
			Your Guide	Your Shadow	

In the sample chart, Mars shows up five times in Section 4, combined with Mercury, Venus, Saturn, Neptune, Uranus, and Pluto. You also see a separate group where Mercury shows up four times, paired with all the same planets except Venus. See the exception note that the Venus and Mercury do not have challenging aspects. You could either make separate similar challenging groups or combine them into one. The combined group looks like this:

Challenging Group 2	Spirits from multiple challenging pairs			Know
Sharing:	☿ ♂	Magician	Tower	I
Mars (Tower)	♄ ♅	World	Fool	I
Mercury (Magician)	♆ ♀	Hanged Man	Empress	I
Exception not: ♀ to ☿		Your Guide	Your Shadow	

The next group you find has Venus four times, paired with the Moon, Mars, Saturn, Neptune and Uranus. Here are the sample mapping forms for that group:

Challenging Group 3	Spirits from multiple challenging pairs			Know
Sharing:	☽ ♀	High Priestess	Empress	I
Venus (Empress)	♂ ♄	Tower	World	I
	♅ ♆	Fool	Hanged Man	I
		Your Guide	Your Shadow	

Challenging Sign Groups by Modality

The set groups of signs that represent both opposition and square sign aspects would be listed in Section 7 for the signs in the chart. These are grouped by sign modality:

- Cardinal signs: Emperor for Aries, Chariot for Cancer, Justice for Libra, Devil for Capricorn
- Fixed signs: Hierophant for Taurus, Strength for Leo, Death for Scorpio, Star for Aquarius
- Mutable signs: Lovers for Gemini, Hermit for Virgo, Temperance for Sagittarius, the Moon for Pisces

You can optionally expand those three modality groups by adding the planets in those signs. This could become a substitute for the challenging aspect groups discussed next.

Section 8: Your Circle of Hands Positive Groups

The positive groups include elemental sign groups with their planets and groups based on two of the astrological patterns. Most of the focus has been on challenging Tarot Spirit pairs and groups. Clearing the friction in those groups provides a significant life improvement by clearing obstacles. Sometimes we need a positive approach. While the Tarot Spirit circles in Section 6 can provide that positive focus, there are four groups of signs that are elementally aligned. Signs with the same element have a trine aspect to each other. Any planets in those signs have a trine aspect by sign and should be added to the groups.

Here is the Positive Fire Group for the sample chart:

Positive Fire Group		Spirits from fire signs and their planets		Know
♈	♌	Emperor	Strength	I
♐	☉	Temperance	Sun	I
☿	♀	Magician	Empress	I
♂	♇	Tower	Judgement	
		Your Guide	Your Shadow	

You can see that the signs and their Tarot Spirits are already filled out on the forms, since they are the same for everyone. A special note about Mars and Saturn in these groups. If there is any negativity from their Tarot Spirit representatives when doing the circle of hands, then exclude them from the group. You want this experience to be totally positive.

Astrological Aspect Patterns

Let's focus on recognizing groups with the special patterns discussed in Chapter 12. There are four chart patterns to consider for AstroTarot. T-square and grand cross are listed in Section 7, while the grand trine and Yod are listed in Section 8. Not every chart has these patterns. When looking for these, use aspects by degree, not by sign.

The T-square pattern has two planets in opposition, with a third planet squaring both of the opposed planets. The sample chart T-cross is highlighted in the chart at left below with Mars and Neptune in opposition—each squared by Uranus.

A grand trine is formed when three trines combine to form a triangle with shared planets. Two grand trines from another chart are shown at right above. The Moon and Mercury are common to both grand trines, with Jupiter and Uranus unique to each separate grand trine.

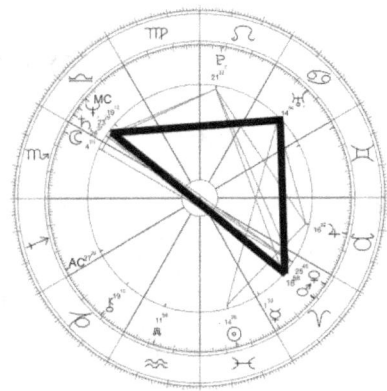

T-square pattern.
Credit: www.astro.com

Two grand trine patterns.
Credit: www.astro.com

The *AstroTarot mapping* in Section 7 for the sample 1 chart T-square pattern group is as follows:

T-cross or Grand Square			Spirits from planets in patterns		Know
T Cross (Challenge)	♅	♆	Fool	Hanged Man	I
	♂		Tower		I
			Your Guide	Your Shadow-self	

For the grand trine mapping, you could create two groups with three planets each and their Tarot Spirits, or one group with all four planets. Fill out the mapping form similar to the T-square. The trine patterns are not challenging.—in fact quite positive—so include in Section 8.

A grand square or grand cross starts with a T-cross and adds a fourth planet opposite the squaring planet. A grand square pattern is highlighted in Conan O'Brien's chart at left below. There is a double grand square, with Mars, Mercury, and Uranus common to both grand squares and the Moon and Saturn unique. Again, you could map all five to one group, or have two overlapping groups in Section 7 with four Tarot Spirits each.

A Yod or Finger of God pattern is shown in Pablo Picasso's chart at right. The Yod has a sextile aspect as the base of a triangle, with two quincunx aspects from the base planets to a single planet opposite the base. In Pablo Picasso's chart, the base planets are Venus and the Moon which both have separate quincunx aspects to Saturn.

Two Grand-square (cross) patterns.
(Conan O'Brien) *Credit: www.astro.com*

Yod or Finger of God pattern.
(Pablo Picasso) *Credit: www.astro.com*

Finding the Yod is a bit more challenging than the other patterns. You can look for sextiles and find the midpoint between the planets with the sextile aspect. Then, see if there is a planet in opposition to the midpoint. Those three planets have a Yod pattern. Alternatively, turn off [major aspects only] in a new modern chart to see the quincunxes in the aspect matrix. Any quincunxes that share a planet will have a sextile between the other two planets, forming the Yod. Map any Yods in Section 8.

These four main patterns are worth looking for and including in your AstroTarot work. Remember that many charts do not have any of these patterns. Interpretation of these patterns is discussed in Chapter 12. There are several other astrological aspect patterns if you want to go further. Search for "astrological aspect patterns" on the internet if you are interested. The sites you find will also give you some background on interpretation of these patterns.

AstroTarot Mapping Blank Forms

Blank mapping forms and filled out sample forms can be downloaded in 8.5" x 11" pdf format here: www.reidhart.com/tsh-resources

Blank forms are included on the following pages. To enlarge the blank book forms to A4 or 8.5" x 11" size just use a magnification of 1.30 or 130% on your copy machine or all-in-one printer. You are given permission to copy these forms for your own use.

My AstroTarot Spirit Mapping for _____
The Big Three: Sun, Moon & Ascendant

Add notes about your Sun sign, Moon sign, and Ascendant. See Section 2 instructions to map these.

Chart Item	Meaning	Symbol	Key Number	Tarot Spirit	Notes
Sun and	The Sun represents your inner conscious purpose and core sense of identity.	☉	19	The Sun	
Sun Sign					
Moon and	The Moon represents your emotional and physical needs, along with your feelings and daily habits.	☽	2	High Priestess	
Moon Sign					
Ascendant Sign and	Your ascendant is the sign rising at the time of your birth and represents how you show up in the world--what you want to be known for.				
Ruling Planet					

Shamanic work with the Tarot spirits provides an opportunity to enhance your life.

This mapping shows which Tarot Spirit from the major arcana maps to which planets and signs in your natal astrology or birth chart. Special groups and unique sets of Tarot Spirits to work with based on aspects and configurations in your chart are also included. See Appendix H of *Tarot Spirit Healing* for mapping instructions.

- Start by engaging with each Tarot Spirit individually through pathworks A/B/C.
- Then clear limitations in your life by resolving potential conflicts in your natal or birth chart using Pathwork K.
- There are also many groups of Tarot Spirits you can work with using the circle of hands and group techniques: Pathwork H/I/J. The groups can be used for both clearing obstacles and enhancing projects and destiny in your life.
- Deeper work with specific groups uses the construct pathwork (L).

Section 1: Your Special Cards

Personal Special Tarot Spirits	Meaning	Key Number	Key Card Name
Personality Spirit ("P")	What lessons are here for you in this life?		
Soul Spirit ("S")	Your purpose through all lifetimes		
Hidden Factor Spirit ("H")	Your shadow teacher		
Year spirit for _____ ("Y")	What is my lesson, focus, or opportunity for the year?		

Section 2: Planet and Sign Mapping

Name		AstroTarot Personal Tarot Spirits			
Birthdate		MM/DD/YYYY			
Birth time		HH:MM AM/PM			
Birth Location		City, State/Provence, Country			
The Planets in your Natal Chart:		*Astrology Symbols*		*Tarot Spirit for Planet & Sign*	*House #*
Planet/AC	*is in Sign*	*Planet*	*Sign*	*Planet Tarot Spirit* / *Zodiac Sign Tarot Spirit*	
Sun		☉		The Sun	
Moon		☽		High Priestess	
Mercury		☿		Magician	
Venus		♀		Empress	
Mars		♂		Tower	
Jupiter		♃		Wheel	
Saturn		♄		World	
Uranus		♅		Fool	
Neptune		♆		Hanged man	
Pluto		♇		Judgement	
AC*Ascendant					1
AC sign Ruler:	*Ruler sign*				

* "AC" = Ascendant; Where the sun rises on the eastern horizon at your birth time.
The planet associated with the ascendant is the ruler of the ascendant zodiac sign (optional)
*Sign rulers are not covered in **Tarot Spirit Healing or AstroTarot Essentials**.*
See symbol and mapping key tables for signs and planets at the end of the forms.

Section 3: Insert your Natal Chart(s) here

Section 4: Potential Challenging Aspects - Tarot Spirit Pairs (Priority 1 & 2)

Priority 1: Potential challenging aspects (any oppositions or squares, plus conjunctions with Mars, Saturn, the Sun or Mercury) with **only** the first seven planets involved:

Aspect Type	Priority	First Planet	Second Planet	First Planet Tarot Spirit	Second Planet Tarot Spirit	Date Cleared

Priority 2: Potential challenging aspects with Uranus, Neptune, or Pluto:

Aspect Type	Priority	First Planet	Second Planet	First Planet Tarot Spirit	Second Planet Tarot Spirit	Date Cleared

Section 4: Additional Potential Challenging Aspects - (Priority 1 & 2)

Priority 1 or 2: Additional space for any potential challenging aspect pairs:

Aspect Type	Priority	First Planet	Second Planet	First Planet Tarot Spirit	Second Planet Tarot Spirit	Date Cleared

Section 5: Opposing Signs (Challenging) (Priority 3)

You can sub-prioritize by starting with the pair containing your ascendent sign.
Then do pairs where there are opposing planets, followed by the rest.

Signs Opposite		Opposition Signs (challenging) Tarot Spirit Pairs	Opposition Planets, ASC	Opposite Houses*	Date Cleared
♈	♎	Emperor <= => Justice			
♉	♏	Hierophant <= => Death			
♊	♐	Lovers <= => Temperance			
♋	♑	Chariot <= => Devil			
♌	♒	Strength <= => Star			
♍	♓	Hermit <= => The Moon			

*Identifying Houses is optional for the Basic AstroTarot work.

Section 6: Basic Tarot Spirit Circles

Work with these basic circles for questions on relevant topics. After you complete Pathwork A/B/C with each involved Tarot Spirit individually they can be worked with as a group using Pathwork H2, I, J2 and L. Where two Tarot Spirits in the same group have potential challenging aspects, you should also do Pathwork K with that pair beforehand. These are just suggestions, and you can bring together other Tarot Spirits your Guide suggests, or you think are relevant to a particular question or inquiry.

Relationship Circle

		For questions of love, relationships and interaction		Know
Mars & Sign Mars is in	♂	Tower		I
Venus & Sign Venus is in	♀	Empress		I
Your Soul (or Personality)			Your Shadow-self & Guide	

Persona Circle

		For questions about your image in the world		Know
AC sign/Personality T.S.				I
Sun & sign Sun is in	☉	The Sun		I
			Your Shadow-self & Guide	

Reflective Circle

		For questions of inner truth	Know
Moon & sign Moon is in	☽	High Priestess	I
Soul / Hidden Factor T. S.			I
		Your Shadow-self & Guide	

Current Circle

		For questions of your current focus		Know
AC sign/Personality T.S.				I
Moon & sign Moon is in	☽	High Priestess		I
Sun & sign Sun is in	☉	The Sun		I
Soul T.S./Year T.S.				I
			Your Shadow-self & Guide	

Healing Circle

			For direct healing from Tarot Spirits		Know
Pick 2 or 3 from	☉	♐	The Sun	Temperance	I
these six healing	♒	♃	The Star	The Wheel	I
Tarot Spirits	♅	♀	The Fool	The Empress	I
Soul, Personality, H.F. T.S.					I
				Your Shadow-self & Guide	

Section 7: Circle of Hands; Challenging Groups

Challenging aspect groups occur when any planet has three or more challenging natal aspects (See Section 4). Include all Tarot Spirits that are paired with that planet.

- You may combine challenging groups that have almost the same members.
- Do pathwork A/B/C and K for any pairs before working with the group.
- Focus on Pathwork I, circle of hands, regularly.

Challenging Group 1	*Tarot Spirits from multiple challenging pairs*			Know
				I
				I
				I
		Your Guide	Your Shadow-self	

Challenging Group 2	*Tarot Spirits from multiple challenging pairs*			Know
				I
				I
				I
		Your Guide	Your Shadow-self	

Challenging Group 3	*Tarot Spirits from multiple challenging pairs*			Know
				I
				I
				I
		Your Guide	Your Shadow-self	

Challenging Group 4	*Tarot Spirits from multiple challenging pairs*			Know
				I
				I
				I
		Your Guide	Your Shadow-self	

Section 7 (continued): Circle of Hands; Challenging Groups

Also include Planets in astrological aspect patterns T-cross or grand square. Not every chart has these patterns.

T-cross or Grand Square		Tarot Spirits from planets in patterns		Know
				I
				I
		Your Guide	Your Shadow-self	

T-cross or Grand Square		Tarot Spirits from planets in patterns		Know
				I
				I
		Your Guide	Your Shadow-self	

You can work with each group of four signs grouped by modality below. These include Cardinal, Fixed, or Mutable modalities. These signs are in an opposition or square aspect relationship. An optional approach would be to combine the previously identified challenging planet group(s) with the signs those planets are in. That larger group would substitute for the separate planet and sign challenging groups.

Challenging Cardinal Group		Tarot Spirits from cardinal signs		Know
♈	♋	Emperor	Chariot	I
♎	♑	Justice	Devil	I
		Your Guide	Your Shadow-self	

Challenging Fixed Group		Tarot Spirits from fixed signs		Know
♉	♌	Hierophant	Strength	I
♏	♒	Death	Star	I
		Your Guide	Your Shadow-self	

Challenging Mutable Group		Tarot Spirits from mutable signs		Know
♊	♍	Lovers	Hermit	I
♐	♓	Temperance	the Moon	I
		Your Guide	Your Shadow-self	

You can also do circle of hands with any of the challenging aspect pairs that you do not feel are resolved. These are found in Section 4. Include your shadow-self and guide.

Section 8: Circle of Hands; Positive Groups

Positive elemental groups share the signs with the same elemental quality, plus the planets in those signs. Include all Tarot Spirits that are mapped to those signs and planets.

- Do pathwork A/B/C for each Tarot Spirit and K for and Section 4 pairs in the group.
- Focus on Pathwork I, circle of hands, regularly.
- You may also do Pathwork H2 or J2 with the groups.
- If there is any negativity from Mars (Tower), Saturn (World), or Pluto (Judgement), exclude them.

Positive Fire Group

		Tarot Spirits from fire signs and their planets		Know
♈	♌	Emperor	Strength	I
♐		Temperance		I
				I
		Your Guide	Your Shadow	

Positive Earth Group

		Tarot Spirits from earth signs and their planets		Know
♉	♍	Hierophant	Hermit	I
♑		Devil		I
				I
		Your Guide	Your Shadow	

Positive Air Group

		Tarot Spirits from air signs and their planets		Know
♊	♎	Lovers	Justice	I
♒		Star		I
				I
		Your Guide	Your Shadow	

Positive Water Group

		Tarot Spirits from water signs and their planets		Know
♋	♏	Chariot	Death	I
♓		the Moon		I
				I
		Your Guide	Your Shadow	

Section 8 (continued): Circle of Hands: Positive Patterns

Also work with Planets in astrological aspect patterns including grand trine and Yod. Not every chart has these patterns.

Grand Trine or Yod			Tarot Spirits from positive patterns		Know
					I
					I
		Your Guide		Your Shadow	

Grand Trine or Yod			Tarot Spirits from positive patterns		Know
					I
					I
		Your Guide		Your Shadow	

Section 9: My Other Tarot Spirit Pairs (Priority 4 & 5)

Priority 4: Lowest priority are conjunctions (exclude conjunctions already included in Priority 1 & 2) , averse aspects, and sextile aspects. Priority 5 relates to outer planets or minor aspects.

Aspect Type	Priority	First Planet	Second Planet	First Planet Tarot Spirit	Second Planet Tarot Spirit	Date Cleared

Use interpretation fill in the blank text at the end of Appendix H for Section 10.

Tarot Spirit English Magical Mapping to Zodiacal Signs

Astrology Symbol	Sign of the zodiac	Tarot Spirit or Key (Major Arcana)	Tarot Key #	Sign Ruler**	Astro *** Font Input
♈	Aries	The Emperor	4	♂	a
♉	Taurus	The Hierophant	5	♀	b
♊	Gemini	The Lovers	6	☿	c
♋	Cancer	The Chariot	7	☽	d
♌	Leo	Strength	8*	☉	e
♍	Virgo	The Hermit	9	☿	f
♎	Libra	Justice	11*	♀	g
♏	Scorpio	Death	13	♂ (♇)	h
♐	Sagittarius	Temperance	14	♃	i
♑	Capricorn	The Devil	15	♄	j
♒	Aquarius	The Star	17	♄ (♅)	k
♓	Pisces	The Moon	18	♃ (♆)	l

* In the Thoth and derivative decks, Justice is 8 and Strength becomes "Lust" at position 11. The signs map to the Tarot keys by name rather than number.

** The traditional sign domicile ruling planets are shown for reference. Modern rulerships are shown in parentheses where different. Rulerships are not used in *Tarot Spirit Healing*.

Tarot Spirit English Magical Mapping to Planets

Astrology Symbol	Planet	Tarot Spirit or Key (Major Arcana)	Tarot Key #	Astro *** Font Input
☉	Sun	The Sun	19	A
☽	Moon	The High Priestess	2	B
☿	Mercury	The Magician	1	C
♀	Venus	The Empress	3	D
♂	Mars	The Tower	16	E
♃	Jupiter	The Wheel of Fortune	10	F
♄	Saturn	The World	21	G
♅	Uranus	The Fool	0	H
♆	Neptune	The Hanged man	12	I
♇ ♇	Pluto	Judgement	20	J

*** To locate fonts for astrological symbols, search the web for "AstroDotBasic." At the time of publication, this font was found at: https://www.fontspace.com/search?q=astrodotbasic
Alternative fonts with similar coding are "Astro Gadget" and "Astro Ganza".
Other astrological fonts with different coding are "Alchemy", "Astro", "Astronomicon", and "Enigma".

Natal Chart Interpretation

OK, you've got your natal Chart [See Appendix E1 or F]. We work directly with the Tarot Spirits in this book to resolve conflicts or get healing or advice. While the pairs and groups of Tarot Spirits you work with are based on your natal astrology, because you work shamanically, you don't really need to do detailed astrological interpretation.

But of course, you are curious. So while astrological interpretation is not a focus here, there are some resources available for you. Start by reviewing the first few pages of your *My AstroTarot Report* if you have one.

For modern astrological interpretation, go to:

www.astro.com/cgi/aclch.cgi?btyp=ack&lang=e

With the "AstroClick Portrait," you just click on the various planets on your chart and you will get an independent interpretation for that planet/sign, aspect, or planet/house situation. While not an overall combined interpretation, it does give you a lot of information. There are also other "free" interpretations you can view at astro.com.

Another site that has astrological interpretations is:

horoscopes.astro-seek.com/birth-chart-horoscope-online

First, focus on the Sun, Moon, and ascendant interpretations. They are the most important. Skip the ascendant if your birth time is questionable.

Have fun learning about what the stars have to say about you!

Deeper into Natal Chart Interpretation

You can go deeper with your astrological interpretations. Get a copy of your chart and one of the basic texts on astrology. You can use one of the three from the reading list (Carole Taylor's *Astrology: Using the Wisdom of The Stars in Your Everyday Life*, Demetra George's *Astrology for Yourself*, Chani Nichols *You Were Born for This: Astrology for Radical Self-Acceptance*, or any other basic book on astrology.) Alternatively, get an introductory book on astrology from your library.

For individual planet considerations, the basic grammar of astrology[91] goes like this:

In my birth chart **[planet]** shows how I will **[planetary influence]** as expressed through the **[zodiac sign significations]** of **[sign]** in the **[house number]** house of **[house significations]** in my life.

Here is an example of how this might be said for each planet in a particular chart (see Sample chart 1 in Chapter 11):

In my birth chart the **Sun** represents my true path, will, inner authority and creative power, as expressed through the idealistic, poetic, and mystical qualities of **Pisces** in the **4th** house of establishing roots and foundations through connection to the land in my life.

In my birth chart the **Moon** demonstrates my emotional response, feelings, rhythms, self-nurturing, and security needs, as expressed through the occult, transforming, and cathartic qualities of **Scorpio** in the **12th** house of transcendence with inner searching and freedom from past restrictions in my life.

In my birth chart **Mercury** governs how I think, communicate, learn, and make connections, as expressed through the competitive, energetic, and inspiring qualities of **Aries** in the **5th** house of creative expression through teaching, children, and hobbies in my life.

In my birth chart **Venus** indicates my appreciation of aesthetics and capacity for attracting love, enjoyment, and pleasure, as expressed through the energetic, assertive, and enthusiastic qualities of **Aries** in the **5th** house of creative expression through theatre and recreation in my life.

In my birth chart **Mars** brings forward my assertiveness, drive, and actions based on personal desire, as expressed through the energetic, assertive, and enthusiastic qualities of **Aries** in the **5th** house of creative expression through theatre and recreation in my life.

In my birth chart **Jupiter** holds the key to my good fortune, meaning, ethics, and confidence, as expressed through the practical, reliable, and persistent qualities of **Taurus** in the **6th** house of self-improvement through analytical introspection and a strong work ethic in my life.

---

[91] More extensive examples of the grammar of astrology can be found in *Astrology for Yourself* by D. Bloch & D. George.

In my birth chart **Saturn** channels my ability to create structure, have discipline, honor tradition, and working within limits, as expressed through the thoughtful, assertive, and social qualities of **Libra** in the **11th** house of community service, social ties, and friends in my life.

In my birth chart **Uranus** channels rebelliousness, abrupt change, uniqueness, and individuality, as expressed through the emotional, stubborn, safety seeking, family oriented, intuitive, caring, shy, tenacious qualities of **Cancer** in the **8th** house of inner values, sexual attraction, and psychic abilities in my life.

In my birth chart **Neptune** opens me to dreams, transcendence, ideals, illusions, and fantasies, as expressed through the thoughtful, assertive, and social qualities of **Libra** in the **11th** house of community service, social ties, and friends in my life.

In my birth chart **Pluto** represents how I regenerate, relate to mortality, and welcome transformation, as expressed through the Leaderlike, glamourous, generous, prideful, organized, and expressive qualities of **Leo** in the **9th** house of personal meaning, travel, religion, and spirituality in my life.

Following the example above and using the basic sign and house vocabulary in one of the basic astrological texts or the sign and house tables in Chapter 11, complete the basic planetary interpretations for your chart by filling in the blanks on the next 2 pages with the following steps:

- For each planet, note the sign the planet is in
- For each planet, note the house the planet is in
- Using the sign table in Chapter 11, fill in a selection of the relevant words for the general qualities or meaning of the sign
- Using the house table in Chapter 11, fill in a selection of the relevant words for the life areas impacted by the house

The fill in the blank interpretation is included with the blank mapping forms download here: www.reidhart.com/tsh-resources

Alternatively, fill in the blank interpretation is included on the following pages. To enlarge the blank book forms to A4 or 8.5" x 11" size just use a magnification of 1.30 or 130% on your copy machine or all-in-one printer. You are given permission to copy these forms for your own use.

Natal Chart Interpretation for _____

In my birth chart the Sun represents my true path, will, inner authority and creative power, as expressed through the _____
_____ qualities of
_____ [sign] in the _____ house of _____
_____ in my life.

In my birth chart the Moon demonstrates my emotional response, feelings, rhythms, self-nurturing, and security needs, as expressed through the _____
_____ qualities of
_____ [sign] in the _____ house of _____
_____ in my life.

In my birth chart Mercury governs how I think, communicate, learn, and make connections, as expressed through the _____
_____ qualities
of _____ [sign] in the _____ house of _____
_____ in my life.

In my birth chart Venus indicates my appreciation of aesthetics and capacity for attracting love, enjoyment, and pleasure, as expressed through the _____
_____ qualities of _____ [sign] in
the _____ house of _____
_____ in my life.

In my birth chart Mars brings forward my assertiveness, drive, and actions based on personal desire, as expressed through the
_____
_____ qualities of _____
[sign] in the _____ house of _____
_____ in my life.

In my birth chart Jupiter holds the key to my good fortune, meaning, ethics, and confidence, as expressed through the _____

_____ qualities of

_____ [sign] in the _____ house of _____

_____ in my life.

In my birth chart Saturn channels my ability to create structure, have discipline, honor tradition, and work within limits, as expressed through the _____

_____ qualities of _____

[sign] in the _____ house of _____

_____ in my life.

In my birth chart Uranus channels rebelliousness, abrupt change, uniqueness, and individuality, as expressed through the _____

_____ qualities

of_____ [sign] in the _____ house of

_____ in

my life.

In my birth chart Neptune opens me to dreams, transcendence, ideals, illusions, and fantasies, as expressed through the

_____

qualities of_____ [sign] in the _____ house of

_____ in my life.

In my birth chart Pluto represents how I regenerate, relate to mortality, and welcome transformation, as expressed through the

_____

__ _____qualities of_____

[sign] in the _____ house of _____

_____ in my life.

Bibliography, Permissions, and Credits

References for works cited throughout the book are included here. There are additional or duplicate works included in *Appendix A: Book List and Resources* with more information about their content.

Bibliography for Chapters

Arrien, Angeles. *The Tarot Handbook: Practical Applications of Ancient Visual Symbols*. Arcus, 1987.

Birch, Alida. *The Co-Creation Handbook: A Shamanic Guide to Manifesting a Better World and a More Joyful Life*. Luminare Press, 2014. Quotes are used with permission.

Bloch, Douglas & Demetra George. *Astrology for Yourself: A Workbook for Personal Transformation*. IBIS, 2006.

Case, Paul F. *The Tarot: A Key to the Wisdom of the Ages*. 2006. Penguin.

Castaneda, Carlos. *Journey to Ixtlan*. Simon & Schuster, 1972.

Flowers, Stephen. *The Magian Taork: the Origins of the Tarot in the Mithraic and Hermetic Traditions*. Inner Traditions, 2019.

Gearhart, Sally and Susan Rennie. *A Feminist Tarot*. Persephone Press, 1981.

Greer, Mary. *Tarot for Yourself: A Workbook for Personal Transformation*. Newcastle, 1984.

Harner, Michael. *Cave and Cosmos: Shamanic Encounters with Another Reality*. North Atlantic Books, 2013.

Hickey, Isabel. *Astrology: A Cosmic Science*. CRCS Publications, 1992.

Jung, Carl. *The Archetypes and the Collective Unconscious*. Routledge, 1991.

Keizer, Lewis and Christine Payne-Towler. "The Esoteric Origins of Tarot" in *The Underground Stream: Esoteric Tarot Revealed*. Noreah, 1999.

Steinbrecher, Edwin. *The Inner Guide Meditation: A Spiritual Technology for the 21st Century*. Samuel Weiser, Inc., 1988.

Stewart, R. J. *The Miracle Tree: Demystifying the Qabalah*. Career Press, 2003.

Bibliography for Appendices

Some chapter references may apply to appendices also.

Boutet, Michel-Gérald. 2017. "On Ancient Celtic Astrology and Naked Eye Astronomy – The Gundestrup Cauldron"

Brennan, Chris. *(HA) Hellenistic Astrology: The Study of Fate and Fortune*. Amor Fati, 2017.

Brennan, Chris. 2017. "Timeline of Ancient Astrologers" www.hellenisticastrology.com/articles/timeline-of-ancient-astrologers/

Campion, Nicholas. *(HWA1) A History of Western Astrology; Volume 1: The Ancient World*. Bloomsbury Academic, 2008.

Dykes, Benjamin. "The Decans in Astrology." 2004. www.daneel.franken.de/Tarot/libert/libertdeck/THE%20DECANS%20IN%20ASTROLOGY.html

Ellis, Peter. "Early Irish Astrology: An Historical Argument." *Réalta* (vol 3. n. 3, 1996), *The journal of The Irish Astrological Association*, 1996. cura.free.fr/xv/11ellis1.html

George, Demetra. *(AATP1) Ancient Astrology in Theory and Practice: A Manual of Traditional Techniques; Volume 1: Assessing Planetary Condition*. Rubedo Press, 2019.

Greer, John Michael. *The Druid Magic Handbook: Ritual Magic Rooted in the Living Earth*. Red Wheel / Weiser, 2007.

Greer, Mary K. *Tarot for Yourself*. Weiser, 2019.

Holden, James Herschel. *(HHA) A History of Horoscopic Astrology*. American Federation of Astrologers, 1996.

Payne-Towler, Christine. *The Underground Stream: Esoteric Tarot Revealed*. Eugene, Oregon: Noreah Press, 1999.

Lévi, Éliphas. *The Kabalistic and Occult Tarot of Éliphas Lévi*. Lulu.com, 2013.

Smith, Jane Ma'ati Editor. *The Emerald Tablet of Hermes and the Kybalion*. www.kybalion.org/TheKybalion.pdf en.wikipedia.org/wiki/Emerald_Tablet

Stewart, R.J. *The Merlin Tarot: Images, insight and wisdom from the age of Merlin*. Aquarian Press, 1988.

Taylor, Carole. *Astrology: Using the Wisdom of the Stars in Your Everyday Life*. DK Pub, 2018.

Wikipedia. "Library of Alexandria." 2020. en.wikipedia.org/wiki/Library_of_Alexandria

Zor, Karni. *Stories of Ancient Astrology*. CreateSpace, 2018.

Permissions and Image Credits

The Permissions and Image Credit section is an extension of the copyright page. All quotes and images are used by permission, license, or are in the public domain.

Quotes in Chapters 2 and 14: *The Co-Creation Handbook*, copyright © 2014 by Alida Birch. Luminare Press. Reprinted by permission of author.

Quotes for reports on pathwork experience in Chapters 4-6, 8-10, 13, and 15. These reports are direct transcriptions of actual workshop participants' reactions to each pathwork. All reports are included by permission of the participant. Only the first name is included for anonymity.

Quote in Chapter 15: From *Cave and Cosmos: Shamanic Encounters with Another Reality* by Michael Harner, published by North Atlantic Books, copyright © 2013 by the Foundation for Shamanic Studies, Inc. Reprinted by permission of publisher.

Quote in Appendix C: From *Mary K. Greer's Tarot Blog – Egypt, Tarot and Mystery School Initiations*, copyright © 2007 by Mary K. Greer. marykgreer.com/events/egypt-Tarot-and-mystery-school-initiations Reprinted by permission of author.

Cover: Graphic design by MiblArt, Ukraine (miblart.com) licensed for commercial use.
Sun Cover art adapted, with permission, from a Sun Face image copyright © 2013 by Deborah Koff-Chapin (touchdrawing.com).

Figures 1, 2, 5, 7, 8, 9, 12, 14, 31, 32: Appendix intro, Magus in Appendix C: From *DruidCraft Tarot Deck* copyright © 2004 by Will Worthington, Card images reprinted by permission of the artist.

Figure 3: Bridge image from public domain pictures at Pixabay.

Figure 4: Figure by author using background image from *DruidCraft Tarot Deck* copyright © 2004 by Will Worthington, card image adapted by permission of artist.

Figures 6: Receiving hand photo credit: Peter Herrmann (Tama66@pixabay), licensed for commercial use.

Figures 10, 23, 29, 30, 33, other uncaptioned excerpts, including those in Appendix G: *AstroTarot Report* © by BirchGrove Hearth, LLC. Image reprinted by permission of publisher. Some include tarot card images from *the DruidCraft Tarot Deck*, copyright © 2004 by Will Worthington, Card images reprinted by permission of artist.

Figure 11, Figure by author using background image by Emmie Norfolk at Pixabay, licensed for commercial use.

Figure 13, Photo credit: Graham H. at Pixabay, licensed for commercial use.

Figures 15, 18, 19, 20, 27, 28, Appendix H patterns: Figures by author using astrological charts generated at astro.com. Chart images reprinted by permission from Astrodienst AG in accordance with website terms.

Figures 16, 17, 26: Details from astrological charts generated at astro.com. Chart images reprinted by permission from Astrodienst AG in accordance with website terms.

Figure 21: Traditional square Hellenistic chart generated with Valens software, open source under GNU general public license. sites.google.com/site/astrovalens/

Figure 22: Zodiac ceiling relief from Hathor Temple at Denderah, public domain (picryl, Wikimedia Commons).1809.

Figures 24, 25: From *Ancient Astrology in Theory and Practice Volume One* by Demetra George, p 397. Copyright © 2019. Rubedo Press. Diagram reprinted by permission from Demetra George.

Figure 34: Figure by author with images of Chakra being by ChakMikhail Nilov at Pexels, licensed for commercial use and images of *DruidCraft Tarot Deck* Cards copyright © 2004 by Will Worthington, card images reprinted by permission of artist.

Awen image in Appendix D: en.wikipedia.org, public domain.

Trademarks

Rider-Waite® is a registered trademark of U.S. Games, Inc.

Glossary

Arcana/Arcane: A mystery or secret knowledge known only by a few.

Arcana, Major: The major mystery in the first 22 cards in a tarot deck that have archetypical images. These are also known as the "keys" or "trumps" of the tarot deck. These 22 cards are numbered from 0 to 21, with each assigned the name and image of the archetype of the card. In this work, each card is considered the image of a Tarot Spirit. Some decks may have a few additional or deleted cards in the Major Arcana. Some decks have multiple versions of the same card. (e.g., the *Thoth Tarot* deck has three versions of the Magus card.)

Arcana, Minor: The minor mystery in the tarot. These 56 cards are divided into four suits, just like modern playing cards. The suits include swords representing the element air, wands representing fire, cups representing water, and coins or pentacles representing earth. Some decks use different names for the suits. The Minor Arcana cards can be divided into court (or royalty) cards, with 4 in each suit and number cards or "pips" with 10 in each suit. The pips are numbered from 1 (Ace) to 10. So there are 40 pips and 16 court cards. The 4 court cards in each suit have names representing gender and maturity, like King, Queen, Knight, Page; Father, Mother, Brother, Sister; King, Queen, Woman, Warrior; or other variations.

Archetype: An image representing a recurrent symbol or characteristic entity in mythology or literature. In a Jungian psychological context, an archetype represents a primitive or core mental image that comes to us from ancient human ancestors and is present in the collective unconscious. In general, the keys of the tarot Major Arcana represent archetypes.

Asteroid: See Celestial objects.

Astrological chart, natal: See: Natal astrological chart

Astrology: The study and practice of the relationship of planetary positions among the stars and the impacts of those positions on human lives.

AstroTarot: A process where tarot cards represent the planets and signs in a natal astrological chart. In that process, the spirits of those representative cards can work with each other to aid the native whose chart it is.

Aspect: An angular relationship, measured from earth, between two planetary positions in the zodiac.

Birth astrological chart: See: Natal Astrological Chart

Bounds: The bounds are unequal divisions of each sign into five segments. Also called "terms," the bounds are each assigned a planet, called the bound lord or term lord. There are four schemes for these assignments, called Egyptian terms, Chaldean terms and two versions of Ptolemaean terms. See: Dignity.

Cabala/Cabalism/Cabalistic: A body of esoteric Hebrew spiritual practice or study with a Christian focus related to the Tree of Life. See also: Tree of Life, Kabbalah, and Qabalah.

Celestial objects: There are multiple celestial objects referenced by astrology, generally referred to as planets and asteroids. The "planets" include the luminaries: the Sun that is actually a star and the Moon that is actually a satellite. Pluto is now considered a dwarf planet. Recently asteroids have entered the astrological lexicon, the main one being Chiron that is actually a centaur—a combination of asteroid and comet or rock and ice.

Celtic cauldrons: Three otherworld cauldrons within the human body. In the womb and stomach area is the cauldron of warming. In the heart area is the cauldron of yearning. In the head area is the cauldron of knowing.

Centaur: See Celestial objects.

Circle of hands: A process (or pathwork) where multiple spirits exchange energy with others in the circle with the intention of balancing power. See: Chapter 9.

Clearing, Clear: Removing obstacles or barriers to optimum health and achievement, primarily at the spiritual level.

Court cards. See: Arcana, Minor.

Crossing, Shamanic crossing: An intentional exercise or pathwork intended to connect the practitioner with the four horizontal directions and the earth, sky, and center.

Decans: Also called "faces," the decans cover each 10 degrees of the zodiac. There are three decans per zodiac sign. Each decan has a planetary sub-ruler or decan lord assignments There are three schemes for these assignments, called traditional, Manilius, and Chaldean decans. See: Dignity.

Dignity: Dignity of a planet contributes to determining planetary condition, or how effective a planet is in an astrological chart. **Essential dignity** of a planet is determined primarily by the planet's sign or degree location within a sign of the zodiac. Essential dignities by sign include domicile, exaltation, detriment, fall, and triplicity. Location within the sign connects the planet to bound (or term) lords and decan (or face) lords. **Accidental dignities** involve relationships or aspects with other planets, fixed stars, or houses, as well as planetary speed. See also: Decans and Bounds.

Eastern esoteric methods: Methods originating in Asia, such as meditation, asceticism, or yoga that are often focused on reducing the impact of ego and detachment from physical sensation. Such methods often have a mystic or occult quality where they cannot be understood logically, but only through the experience of the method employed.

Ecliptic: The plane the Sun and planets appear to move in when viewed from Earth.

Emerald Tablet: The *Emerald Tablet* is attributed to the Egyptian god Thoth or Hermes Trismegistus. A cornerstone text of the Western Mysteries, the Emerald Tablet is the source of the phrase "As Below, so Above."

Ephemeris: A book or generated table that shows where planets and other astronomical objects like asteroids are located in the zodiac at various times, usually daily at midnight or noon.

Face: See: Decans.

Guide: See: Tarot guide.

Hellenistic: Relating to the culture, language, philosophy, and history of the Greeks and early Romans from the death of Alexander the Great around 323 BCE to the defeat of Cleopatra and Mark Antony by Octavian in 31 BCE. During this period, Greek culture centered on Alexandria in Egypt and spread through the Mediterranean and into the Near East and Asia.

Hellenistic astrology found its roots in the Hellenistic period starting in the 3rd century BCE, but continued to evolve through the 7th century CE. The astrology was a merger of Babylonian and Egyptian astrology and introduced the concept of the ascendant and houses related to the time of birth.

House, astrological: One of twelve places on your natal chart based on the time and location of your birth. Houses are different from the zodiac signs. Each house relates to a specific area of your life, like reputation and career, home, finances, partnerships, etc.

Journey, Shamanic journey: An intentional movement into an altered mental state using percussion—usually drumming or rattling—to induce a shamanic state of consciousness. Sometimes psychoactive drugs are used to create a similar altered state. In the journey, the journeyer has perceptions of non-ordinary reality or the Otherworld where they meet spirit helpers who may provide information, advice, healing, initiation, or empowerment to the journeyer or a client of the journeyer.

Kabbalah/Kabbalism/Kabbalistic: A body of esoteric Hebrew spiritual practice or study based on a symbolic interpretation of the Torah (Old Testament) related to the Tree of Life. See also: Tree of Life, Cabala, and Qabalah.

Key: A tarot card in the Major Arcana. See: Arcana, Major.

Law of three-fold return: Related to the *Witch's or Wiccan Rede*, which cautions against sending out harmful intent or magic. The caution is an amplification of the golden rule: if you use magic to send out influences to others it will come back to you as harm or good three times amplified.

Lord: See ruler, bounds, and dignity.

Lower world, Shamanic lower world: One of the three worlds in the Otherworld or non-ordinary reality. One goes down to journey to the lower world. Typically Spirits met here include power animals, ancestors, plant spirits, teachers and other Spirits. In core shamanic thinking, the Spirits encountered here are compassionate and loving. The lower world often is perceived as multiple levels of landscapes similar to an earth experience, but inhabited by Spirits rather than ordinary reality people, plants, and animals. Not to be confused with the underworld or land of the dead (Hades) in classical mythology, although the land of the dead may be accessed from the lower world. See also: Middle World, Upper World.

Magic: There are multiple definitions from different sources:
- Alister Crowley: "the science and art of causing change to occur in conformity with will."
- Dion Fortune: "the science and art of causing change in consciousness to occur in conformity with will."
- Don Emberto (Q'ero Elder, Peru): "A spiritual process where you recognize that what you want already exists."
- Reid Hart: "In Shamanic Magic, the shaman journeys to the spirits in the Otherworld and requests an intervention. Many cultures have a spirit tradition. In core shamanism, the Spirits are more open and

mixed—not necessarily based on cultural tradition, but based on experience, not belief. Effective magic results in practical changes in ordinary reality, or spiritual changes in oneself."

Major Arcana: See: Arcana, Major

Middle world, Shamanic middle world: One of the three levels in the Otherworld or non-ordinary reality. One goes out horizontally to journey to the middle world. Not to be confused with the actual ordinary reality, the shamanic middle world is more like the hidden spiritual essence that exists behind ordinary reality. Typically Spirits met here include spiritual forms of living ordinary reality creatures, landscape elements, plants, ancestors, ghosts, confused spirits who have not moved on to the light, and other Spirits. In core shamanic thinking, the Spirits encountered here are mostly compassionate and loving, although ghosts and similar spirits can be confused about their location and cause attachments (possession) or mischief (poltergeists). The middle world often is perceived as parallel to ordinary reality but inhabited by Spirits of people (living and dead), plants, mountains (*Apus*), faery folk, and animals. Some spirits are of a meta nature, like the oak spirit, that represents all oak trees rather than individual trees, or the horse spirit that relates more to all herds of horses rather than individual animals. See also: Lower World, Upper World.

Minor Arcana: See: Arcana, Minor

Moiety: See: Orb

Natal astrological chart: A two-dimensional representation of the position of the luminaries (Sun and Moon), planets, and possibly asteroids or other theoretical astronomical points as viewed from Earth at the date, time, and location of birth of an individual, sometimes referred to as the "native."

Orb: Generally, the range of accuracy for which an aspect between planets is considered valid. In modern astrology the orb is measured plus or minus the degree from the exact aspect angle from the first planet to the second. If the orb was 7°, a square (theoretically 90°) would count if the angle between planets was anywhere between 83° and 97°. A traditional or Hellenistic astrologer would refer to that as a "moiety" of plus or minus 7° and would call the "orb" 14° or the entire arc that made a valid aspect. The allowed orbs vary by tradition and usually by planet. An allowed aspect usually has larger orbs for the Sun and Moon (between 5 and 9 degrees) to smaller orbs for the transpersonal outer planets (between 2 and 5 degrees). The range of orbs may also vary by aspect with conjunctions and oppositions the largest, sextiles the smallest, and trines and squares in between (or sometimes the same as the conjunction).

Otherworld: A sensed area or landscape outside of what we call ordinary reality, normal reality, or consensus reality. In this place you can meet spirits, who are non-ordinary entities you can communicate with. It is also called non-ordinary reality in the core shamanic tradition.

Path: An Otherworld area for exploration, specifically a path connecting two Sephirot or spheres on the tree of life. Also "halls." See also: Tree of Life.

Pathwork is a shamanic journey to work with the Spirits. The term comes from a Western Mystery tradition of connecting with particular parts of the Otherworld to build an initiate's understanding and power. A specific example is working the paths of the Tree of Life in Qabalah. Pathwork can be performed in a meditation, guided visualization, trance, or shamanic journey. Pathwork can be synonymous with exercise or process. Multiple pathworks related to Tarot Spirits are presented in this book and other educational contexts. See Appendix C for a list of the various Tarot Spirit pathworks.

Pip: See: Arcana, Minor.

Power animal: Also Animal Spirit guide or Shamanic power animal. A spirit that appears in animal form in the Otherworld. Power animals often represent power, luck, or ability to avoid accidents. Mostly found in the lower world, although they can appear in the upper world as well.

Qabalah/Qabalism/Qabalistic: A body of esoteric Western Mystery spiritual practice or study related to the Tree of Life. See also: Tree of Life, Kabbalah, and Cabbalah.

Royalty cards. See: Arcana, Minor.

Ruler, Rulership: Ruling planets can also be referred to as "lords." The planet that rules a particular zodiac sign and is considered in its home or domicile when in that sign. The Hellenistic rulership scheme is based on the ancient seven planets with The Sun ruling Leo, Moon ruling Cancer, Mercury ruling Gemini and Virgo, Venus ruling Taurus and Libra, Mars ruling Aries and Scorpio, Jupiter ruling Pisces and Sagittarius, and Saturn ruling Capricorn and Aquarius. In modern astrology, the primary rulers of three signs were switched to accommodate the three newly discovered planets, with Uranus ruling Aquarius, Neptune ruling Pisces, and Pluto ruling Scorpio. These three signs are considered as having both primary and traditional rulers. See also: Bounds and Decans.

Sect: Planets are assigned to two teams or sects. The day team is the Sun, Jupiter, and Saturn. The night team is the Moon, Venus, and Mars. Mercury is on the Day team if a morning star and the night team otherwise. If you are born in the daytime, your chart is a day chart. If at night, a night chart. In Hellenistic astrology, sect plays into the determination of planetary condition and the relative weight given to the helpful (benefic) and hindering (malefic) planets.

Shadow: A personal psychological tendency that is either hidden or repressed. It can include negative tendencies that are generally not accepted by society, but could also include areas of life that could be viewed as positive but that we did not pursue. There is often shame or regret tied up with these shadow tendencies. In many cases, we may be unconscious of them.

Shadow-self: A spiritual entity in the Otherworld that represents and can help express our personal shadow material.

Shadow work: Working with your personal shadow to bring into consciousness shadow tendencies or shadow parts. The goal is to resolve the shadow parts or at least bring them into consciousness and release the energy drain of keeping them hidden.

Shamanic journey: See: Journey.

Shamanic lower, middle, and upper worlds: See: lower world, middle world, and upper world.

Shamanism: A spiritual practice that involves a practitioner interacting with the spirit world through altered states of consciousness for the purpose of divination, healing, or community aid in the ordinary world.

Spheres, Sephirot *(pl. Hebrew)***:** The ten emanations of "the all." Also called spheres, emanations, vessels, or attributes of the divine. Sephirah *(singular Hebrew).*

Spirit: An entity in the otherworld such as a power animal, teacher, or guide that a shamanic practitioner interacts with while in an altered state of consciousness.

Stoic, Stoicism refers to a school of Hellenistic philosophy that flourished in Ancient Greece and Rome. The Stoics believed that the practice of virtue is enough to achieve a well-lived life. They assumed that much of life was fated, and the best approach was preparing oneself to handle the challenges that fate would bring you.

Tarot: Of or relating to a 78-card deck of images that have been assigned esoteric meanings in the Western Mystery Tradition. Includes the esoteric archetypal meanings of the cards. See also: Arcana, Major and Arcana, Minor.

Tarot Spirits: Otherworld Spirits connected with the 22 tarot "Major Arcana" or "key" cards in the tarot deck. See: Arcana, Major.

Tarot court cards, Royalty cards: See: Arcana, Minor.

Tarot guide: A spirit entity in the Otherworld who works with a human to meet the Tarot Spirits and work with them for spiritual and practical purposes. In this context, a tarot guide is an Otherworld being who personally guides you to meet and work with the Tarot Spirits.

Tarot Spirit healing: The process of receiving shamanic healing from a Tarot Spirit or group of Tarot Spirits.

Terms: See: Bounds.

Transit: An astrological occurrence when a planet's (or other object's) current position in the zodiac relates through an aspect or angle to a planetary position in a natal astrological chart.

Tree of Life: A map of part of the Otherworld based on Qabalah (or Kabbalah or Cabbalah) where there are 10 spheres or emanations of "the All" or "divine truth" with 22 pathways, occupied by the Tarot Spirits, interconnecting them.

Trump: A tarot card in the Major Arcana. See: Arcana, Major and Key.

Upper world, Shamanic upper world: One of the three levels in the Otherworld or non-ordinary reality. One goes up to journey to the upper world, often breaking through a membrane to get there. Typically Spirits met here include Spirit teachers, deities of various pantheons, archangels, daimons, and other Spirits. In core shamanic thinking, the Spirits encountered here are compassionate and loving. The upper world often is perceived as multiple levels of more abstract places inhabited by spirits rather than people, plants, and animals. Not to be confused with heaven in religion, although the celestial spheres may be accessed from the upper world. See also: Middle World, Lower World.

Western Mysteries, Western Mystery Tradition: A collection of pathworks or methods of approaching spiritual power, occultism and esotericism. Includes a wide range of loosely related ideas and movements related to the occult (or hidden knowledge) that developed within Western society.

Index of Headings

The index of headings lists all levels of headings in the book.

Acknowledgements

Foremost, I thank my wife, Alida, who inspired me with her own book writing experience and supported me patiently in the process of developing this book over the last few years. Our life together has been one of exploring the shamanic path, and this book is a result of that.

The next group essential to the progress of the work were my beta readers who provided valuable feedback on the initial drafts. Thanks to Faye Schrater, Terry Moore, Steven Kauder, Bob Hiland, Gary Rayor, Alida Birch, and Colette Babson. Their comments helped me focus on where structural and clarifying improvements were necessary. The next group that helped was my advanced readers circle, who gave helpful feedback on the final draft.

Essential to the development were the many participants in workshops and online courses over the last dozen years, as I developed the pathworks, lectures, tracking forms, and other materials that helped people delve into this material. Their questions and sharing was a big part of creating this work. Special thanks goes to those willing to have their journey sharing included in the book. Hearing what others have discovered opens the possibility of growth for readers and lets one know what this AstroTarot path is all about.

The teachers I have learned from, mentioned in About the Author section, are vastly important. Without them, there would be no content here. Those who pass on the spiritual truths of the Western Mystery tradition are important—both human and spirit teachers. Without teaching and the speaking from mouth to ear in the tradition, there would be no tradition.

I also want to give a shout out to the self-publishing community, especially those at the Self-Publishing Show for their guidance along the way. Also, Dr. Julian Smart, developer of the Jutoh eBook formatting software is thanked for his helpful answers to many questions.

And, most importantly, I acknowledge you, the reader. You have come to this work with interest and a willingness to invest your time and become a part of the lineage of Western Mysteries.

Style Notes

Followers of tarot may notice the lack of capitalization of "tarot" in this book. While many authors of tarot books (Rachel Pollack, Mary Greer, & Angeles Arien) will always capitalize "tarot," there are several who do not (including Lon DuQuette & Chic Cicero). I have chosen to not capitalize it in general so that "tarot" is treated in parallel with "astrology" and "shamanism" that all refer to parallel philosophical or spiritual systems.

The exception is "Tarot Spirit" that refers to a specific spirit entity and the name of tarot decks, like *DruidCraft Tarot*. Spirits is not capitalized when a general reference. Planets and signs of the zodiac are capitalized, as are the mystery references to Major Arcana, Minor Arcana, Qabalah, and Western Mysteries.

The British spelling of "judgement" is used to match the name on tarot key 20 in the *Waite-Smith Tarot*.

About the Author

Reid Hart is the author of *Tarot Spirit Healing: A Shamanic Path to Clear Your Astrological Challenges.* He is a popular teacher and leader in the shamanic community. He has helped hundreds of people in the U.S. and Australia to heal, find gentle practical methods to reconnect to the spirit world, and move more deeply into a mystery connection with the universe.

A healer and spiritual teacher for over 31 years, he has taught hundreds of people to work more deeply with shamanism, Otherworld exploration, and the Western Mysteries. His teaching focus is a fusion of Western Mystery traditions with core shamanic methods. He works with Celtic, Nordic, Druidic, and Faery traditions, as well as the runes, tarot, astrology, and Qabalah.

He counts as his most important teachers: Michael Harner, Sandra Ingerman, Tom Cowan, Claude Poncelet, the Q'ero of Peru, Sarangerel, R.J. Stewart, Orion Foxwood, Demetra George, Edwin Steinbrecher, Caitlin and John Matthews, Chagdud Tulku Rinpoche, and, of course, his own wise and loving spirit allies.

He has also volunteered at White Bird crisis center and studied Hakomi Psychotherapy. He achieved a *Certificate of Competency in Advanced Hellenistic Astrology* from Demetra George in 2024 after a 3-year program of study.

He co-founded Hearth of the Dancing Drum Healing and Drumming Circles in 1991 to foster shamanic healing in his local community and regularly teaches online through BirchGrove Hearth.

www.ingramcontent.com/pod-product-compliance
Lightning Source LLC
Chambersburg PA
CBHW071136130626
46553CB00004B/1399